FINDING
Rose

To my husband, Rick, who believed in
me from the beginning and who continues to provide
constant love and encouragement.

Walnut Springs Press, LLC
110 South 800 West
Brigham City, Utah 84302
http://walnutspringspress.blogspot.com

ISBN: 978-1-935217-77-0

FINDING
Rose

STEPHANIE HUMPHREYS

WALNUT SPRINGS PRESS

1

The letter on the mantle ruined everything, and Rose couldn't help glancing at it as she stirred the coals in the fire. It would be so easy for a draft to catch the edge of the paper and carry it into the flames. She sighed. It wouldn't change anything, but if she kept herself busy, she could almost imagine things would always stay the same.

Turning back to her chores, Rose opened the oven door and smiled as the aroma of apple pie filled the kitchen. She put the pie on the sideboard and admired its golden, flaky crust before she began setting the table for dinner. It was her father's birthday and she wanted the meal to be perfect, since it would probably be the last birthday in the family home. She stole one more look at the letter, then hurried back to the stove to stir the pot of stew.

All her work finally done, Rose went into the parlor and sat in her mother's rocking chair. She gazed out the window and etched the winter scene into her mind. *I should ask Carrie to draw a picture for me so I'll never forget,* she thought.

Movement down the lane caught Rose's eye and she stopped rocking as she watched the person walking toward the house. At first she thought it was her brother, but then she decided the man was too tall. Also, Sean had a certain swagger to his walk that the stranger lacked. In fact, the man on the road almost seemed to be stumbling. Suddenly, he stopped and put down the black bag he carried, then stood with his head bowed. Rose's curiosity grew when she realized he was studying a piece of paper. He shoved it back into his pocket and looked toward the house. After wiping his brow with the back of his arm, he reached down to pick up the bag. He tripped and almost went down in the snow.

Is he ill or drunk? Rose wondered. She had no idea what to do. Her mother and father were visiting with a new family in the ward, Carrie was out with friends, and Sean was off working for Brother Jensen. Rose didn't expect any of them home for a while yet. She stood, went to the narrow window next to the front door, and pulled back the lace curtain a fraction of an inch to get a better view.

The man kept plodding forward, going slower with each step until he finally reached the wide porch that encircled the house. He approached the door and Rose heard his knuckles hit the solid wood. He rested his head on the doorframe and closed his eyes. *If he opens his eyes now, he'll see me,* she thought. Rose stepped back from the window, letting the curtain fall from her fingers. She jumped as the man's bag hit the porch with a thud. He straightened and knocked again, leaving the bag lying on the mat.

Rose watched for a moment. Whoever he was, she couldn't leave him out in the bitter January cold. He didn't know she was there, but she couldn't live with herself if he really was ill. She took a deep breath and opened the door. The man must have heard her coming, because he had picked up the bag again and stepped away from the door.

"I'm sorry to bother you, miss," he said.

"Can I help you?"

He switched the bag to his left hand and Rose noticed the tremor in his shoulders. "I'm looking for the Sterling farm." With his free hand, he pulled the paper she had seen earlier from his pocket and held it out to her.

Rose took the note and opened it. Her brother's handwriting spelled out directions to the farm from the train station in Logan. Whoever he was, Sean had sent him.

"Well, you've found it," she said, still trying to decide what to do with the stranger. It certainly wasn't proper to invite him in when there was no one else home. She wished she could get a better look at him. Her father always said you could tell a man's character by his face, but the snowy scarf and hat hid most of the visitor's features.

"Is Elder Sterling at home?" the man said as he leaned against the doorframe again. "If he's not, I'll just wait here on the porch."

Rose shivered as the outside air worked its way around her ankles. Wondering what her mother would say if she let an ill man sit on the porch until someone else came home, Rose opened the door a little wider. "There's no need for that. Come in and sit by the fire."

The man nodded and stumbled through the door. Rose pointed to the kitchen and followed him as he hobbled toward the back of the house. They entered the kitchen and he stood as if unsure what to do. Rose pulled out a chair and gestured to it. "Let me take your coat." She held out her hands and waited.

He looked like he wanted to argue, but the man finally slid his arms out of the sleeves and handed the coat to her. His woolen cap and scarf followed. As he removed the snow-encrusted outerwear, Rose realized he was much younger than she had first thought.

She caught a glimpse of brown hair as she took the clothing and hung it to dry on the hook next to the stove. When she turned back to him, she caught him studying her. She felt herself blush and busied herself stirring the stew. It would be at least another half hour until her parents came home, and until then, she had to entertain her guest somehow. *I wish Sean would have given us some warning. That's just like him to think a surprise would be fun.*

"May I ask your name?" she said.

"Dr. Miles Crandall." He extended his hand and started to rise, but then he gave up the effort and sank back into the chair. "You must be Rose."

She smoothed her apron and smiled. She'd heard of Dr. Crandall many times. Sean wrote often of the young man who was attending school in the East to train as a doctor. The family had followed his conversion and the growing friendship between the two men for more than a year. Relieved that the man wasn't truly a stranger, Rose took a glass from the cupboard, poured some water from the ceramic pitcher her mother kept on the counter, and handed the glass to him. She could only imagine the things Sean had told his friend about her. Surely they included stories of her following him and his friends everywhere, and all the trouble she used to get into.

"You don't look well, Dr. Crandall."

"Just cold. I don't think I've ever been so cold."

"Papa says there's a blizzard all across the country and he's never heard of such low temperatures." Rose pushed a stray curl away from her forehead.

"Of course I chose to do my traveling during a severe cold snap," Dr. Crandall said with a wry grin. "The man at the station assured me it wasn't a long walk to your place, and I guess in regular weather it's not."

"It's almost two miles!" Rose put her hands on her hips. "Of all the addle-headed . . ." She turned, shaking her head, and put another log on the fire.

Dr. Crandall put the empty glass on the table. "I'm afraid I'm not at my best, but I don't think 'addle-headed' is quite fair."

Rose put her hand to her mouth. "Oh, I'm so sorry. I didn't mean you. I was referring to the station master, and I probably shouldn't even have said that." Her cheeks burned and she sighed. *Now that's the way to make a good impression—talking ill of someone and then blushing every time Dr. Crandall looks at you.*

He seemed unaware of her discomfort. "If you'll let me sit by the fire for a few minutes until I get some feeling back in my feet, I'll make my way back to town and find a room for the night." He stood, swaying slightly. "Just tell your brother I'm in Logan . . ."

"Don't be ridiculous." Rose refilled his glass. "Sit right there and I'll make up a bed for you. The rest of the family should be home for supper soon, and you're welcome to stay and share a meal with us." She studied her guest. His cinnamon-colored hair curled around the collar of his shirt, and his eyes nearly matched his hair. Broad shoulders trembled as his body adjusted to the warm air in the kitchen. She realized how closely her guest was watching her in return, but she couldn't tear her gaze away from his.

Finally, he closed his eyes and leaned back in the chair. "Thank you." The words came as a whisper.

Rose watched him for another moment, then went to the parlor and took her mother's knitted throw from the back of the rocking chair. It wasn't like she'd never seen a handsome man before, but something about this man had captured her interest—probably the result of finally meeting the subject of so many of her brother's stories. It was ridiculous to be so taken in by the good looks of a stranger, so Rose tried to change the direction of her thoughts. Returning to the kitchen, she went to the man in the rocking chair. "Brother Crandall, wrap this around you."

He opened his eyes and reached for the blanket. She handed it to him and helped arrange it around his shoulders, being careful not to let her fingers accidentally brush against his.

"You really should take off your shoes so your feet can warm up properly." Without waiting for a response, she knelt at his feet and began undoing the laces on one of his shoes. He jerked his foot away from her. The sudden motion caused her to lose her balance and she tumbled to the floor, surrounded by a tangle of skirts. He leaned forward, extending his hand, but then quickly withdrew it as she glared at him.

"Sorry," he said quietly. "I can do that." He avoided her eyes as he removed his shoes and wet socks and put them near the fire.

Rose waited for the briefest of moments, wondering if he would offer his hand to her again, but Dr. Crandall simply wrapped the blanket back around his shoulders and stared into the flickering flames. *How rude!* she thought. She picked herself up off the floor, stumbling when the heel of her shoe caught on the hem on her skirt. *Someone ought to teach him some manners.* She felt the heat rising in her cheeks again.

"I'll go make up a room for you," she mumbled, avoiding his eyes. Then she hurried out of the kitchen.

Miles listened to the tapping of Rose's feet as she hurried up the stairs. Her steps were brisk and businesslike, and Miles knew he'd offended her. *She's just as beautiful as Sean said.* Miles didn't often have much to say to the fairer sex, and Rose was no exception. As he had watched her, all sorts of brilliant snippets of conversation had danced just out of reach of his tongue. Instead he'd only managed the briefest of comments and then proceeded to dump her on the floor. Then he couldn't even gather enough composure to help her up. He sighed and propped up his feet by the fire, wincing at the burning sensation as they regained their feeling. At least he was out of the cold. He wrapped the blanket around his shoulders again, then slid the chair a little closer to the warmth. *I hope I make a better impression on the rest of the family,* he thought as he began drifting off to sleep.

"Well, hello," a voice said.

Miles woke to see an older man tilting his head and scrutinizing him. Miles stood quickly, the blanket slipping to the floor.

Rose rushed down the stairs and into the room. "Papa, Mama, this is Sean's friend, Doctor Miles Crandall."

Maggie Sterling clapped her hands together. "Good heavens. What a surprise!"

Miles stepped forward, holding his hand out. "Brother and Sister Sterling. I'm so glad to finally meet you."

Rose propelled herself to action, taking her father's coat and hanging it on the hook by the door. She was grateful her parents had returned home and could entertain their guest. Since she had set the table earlier, there was nothing to do but wait for the others to arrive. She melted back into a corner, hoping to observe without having to be part of the conversation. It gave her the opportunity to watch the young doctor without being too obvious.

"Brother Crandall, today is my husband's birthday. You've arrived just in time for a party." Maggie went to the stove and stirred the stew, smiling at Rose as she did. "It smells delicious, dear."

Peter Sterling pulled a chair close to the fire and motioned for Miles to sit back down. "Sean didn't tell us you were coming."

"He didn't know. It was kind of a last-minute decision." Miles sat and retrieved the blanket from the floor.

"Sean will be pleased you came." Peter patted Miles's shoulder. "I'm glad you're here. We've heard so much about you."

"Once I get back to Montana and take over Doctor McTavish's practice, I won't be getting back to Utah for a long time. I wanted to visit with Sean and meet the family he's told me so much about. I also thought I would take the opportunity to go to the temple while I'm here."

The older man nodded his head. "It's a fine plan and we're glad to have you."

"Of course you will stay here." Maggie put a crock of butter on the table and started slicing a loaf of bread.

"I hate to be an imposition. I had planned on taking a room in town."

Peter laughed. "Good luck with that, young man. My wife would be mighty offended if you turned down her hospitality. Unless I'm mistaken, Rose has already aired out the guest room."

Both men looked at Rose and she nodded.

"We'll pick up your trunk tomorrow," Rose's father said, ending the discussion.

"Thank you." Miles allowed the briefest of smiles to tug at his lips. "I wasn't relishing the idea of another walk in the cold."

The outside door swung open and Carrie blew in, with Sean right on her heels. She stopped short when she saw Miles, and a slow grin spread across her face. Sean gave her a slight push. "Keep going so I can get this door shut."

Carrie giggled and stepped out of her brother's way. Sean stomped his feet, sending snow flying from his boots. He twisted the scarf from his neck and finally looked up.

"Miles!" In three long strides he reached his friend and grabbed him in a bear hug.

Miles stepped back and shook Sean's hand. "Just thought I'd pop in for a visit, Elder Sterling."

"Enough of that. I'm just Sean now. No need for such formality."

Miles intrigued her. He had relaxed a little when Sean arrived, but he still seemed somber and reserved. Occasionally when Sean laughed, Rose caught the smallest glimpse of a grin from Miles. She found herself imagining what his face looked like with a real smile rather than the pained curve of his lips that only briefly changed his expression.

Her brother always had a ready joke on the end of his tongue and saw the world as an adventure, but Miles acted much more serious and even managed to keep a straight face as Sean told the family about ending up on the wrong side of a skittish horse earlier that day. Rose wondered how the two men had ever become such good friends. They were complete opposites.

"Well, I'm hungry and it smells wonderful," Peter said when Sean finished his story. He took his seat at the head of the table and motioned for the rest of the family to join him.

Sean gestured for Miles to sit next to Carrie. Rose groaned inwardly. She would have to sit across from their guest for the entire meal. She tried not to remember her unceremonious dumping on the floor and was grateful he hadn't mentioned it to anyone else. When she smiled at him and took her chair, he gave her a slight nod, then bowed his head to wait for the blessing on the meal. As soon as her father finished the prayer, Miles looked up and turned his attention to Carrie and Sean. Rose rolled her eyes. She could ignore him as well as he could ignore her. For a brief moment, she almost wished she had let him sit out in the cold a while longer.

Her sixteen-year-old sister pulled out all the charm, tossing an auburn braid from her shoulder and beaming at Miles. But even though he was unfailingly polite to Carrie, Rose could see Miles wasn't really interested. It didn't matter. He would only stay for a few days and then return to Montana, and neither she nor Carrie would see him again. In the meantime, she had enough things to keep her busy without wasting her thoughts on her brother's friend.

The meal passed quickly as everyone listened to Sean and Miles share stories of Boston and of their common acquaintances. When everyone's soup bowl was empty, Rose stood to get the pie from the sideboard, but her father waved her back to her seat. Several times throughout the meal, she had noticed him put his spoon down as if he had something to say, then pick it up again and continue picking at his food without a word. It had to be about the letter. *I wish he would save whatever it is he has to say until Miles is gone,* she thought.

"Before we get to the pie, I have news about our plans to go to Canada," Peter finally announced, patting Maggie's hand. She nodded and he continued.

Rose held her breath. Maybe he would finally abandon the idea. She looked at her father and noticed how hollow his cheeks had become since Christmas. He had always been a big man, but lately he seemed to be shrinking in on himself. He tired easily and Rose noticed he hardly ate at all. When Rose had asked her mother if anything was wrong, her concerns were brushed aside with, "He just feels the weight of his calling as bishop." Rose didn't believe her, and even as she watched her father preside over the meal, she knew it was something more than that.

She listened closely as he continued, "Brother Hansen has agreed to buy most of the cattle, and I may have a buyer for the farm. Everything seems to be falling into place for us to leave in the spring."

Rose blinked back the tears and looked again at the letter on the mantle. There would be no turning back once the farm sold. *If we move to Canada, maybe his health will improve.* The silly thought hovered in her head before being banished. *No one goes north for their health.* She sighed.

"Canada?"

Everyone looked at Miles. Rose waited to hear how he would react to the news. Not that it mattered; he had just met the family, and her father had his mind made up.

"That's right." Sean leaned back in his chair. "If you had shown up much later, we wouldn't have been here at all."

Peter Sterling sat a little straighter. "I received a letter from the prophet, calling our family to Canada to help build the irrigation canals. The Church has a contract to fill, and we are going to help do it."

"But you have such a wonderful life for your family here."

Rose could almost like Miles for that statement. At his puzzled look, she remembered he hadn't grown up with stories of pioneers who left everything for religious freedom. But even though Rose believed President Snow was a prophet, she didn't understand the need to leave. Granny, her father's mother, had abandoned Nauvoo with hardly anything as her home burned behind her. *But we're safe and happy here.* Isn't that how the Lord wants us to live? She tipped her head and stared at her lap, willing the subject to change quickly.

"After we received the letter, Maggie and I spent many nights on our knees praying about it. We know it is right for our family—" he paused "—all of our family." He looked at Rose.

She turned from her father's silent lecture and stood to get the pie. *How can he make us give up everything?* she thought as she dished up the pieces. The plate she placed in front of her father landed with more force than she intended, and the fork rattled and fell to the table as she took her hand away. Her mother gave her a withering look.

"Rose doesn't want to go." Carrie glared at her older sister, then turned her charm on Miles. "I think it will be an adventure. We'll have to go right through Montana, won't we?"

"You will," Miles said as he finished a bite of pie. He put down his fork. "Canada's beautiful country. I've driven cattle up there with my pa and brothers."

"Maybe we can stop and visit your family on our way." Carrie lowered her eyes and blushed.

Miles raised his eyebrows and turned back to his pie. The conversation continued, though Rose didn't hear much of it. She tried to be excited about the journey, but she didn't want to leave Utah. *Why have we fought so hard to build such a good life, only to be told we have to start over again?* The letter had explained that there were few towns, only areas marked for towns. She would go from Logan with its beautiful homes and schools to a place where people were still living in tents. All her friends and dreams would remain behind. She looked around at her family. She could only think of one thing that could make it possible for her to stay, but she knew her father would never approve.

Rose's thoughts were interrupted by the sound of plates being stacked, and she looked up to find Miles watching her. "It was a fine meal." As she had guessed, his smile transformed his face and made him breathtakingly handsome. Only now she was the one who couldn't smile back.

2

The next day dawned bright and warm. The steady drip of water tapped a staccato rhythm as the sun melted the icicles along the edge of the roof. Rose grabbed a shawl and went out to the barn to milk the cows. Sean would already be there and would probably tease her for sleeping too long. She looked forward to spending the quiet time with her brother each morning.

She reached for the door, but stopped when she heard voices. It seemed Miles had beaten her to the chores. Rose tried not to resent his help, realizing he couldn't know how much she treasured the morning routine. Putting her hand on the latch, Rose started to open the door, but then stopped and leaned against the aged wood instead. She didn't want to interrupt their conversation and she had to admit to being more than a little curious about Miles. She closed her eyes and listened.

"You have a wonderful family," she heard Miles say.

"I'm just glad someone was home when you got here."

The two men were silent for a few minutes, and the sound of milk hitting the metal pails in perfect rhythm reminded Rose she still had chores to do. She stepped away from the barn, but stopped when Miles spoke again.

"I'm afraid things were rather awkward when I first arrived. I was so cold I could hardly think straight. Rose didn't seem to know what to say, and then when she fell as she was trying to help me, well, let's just say I probably didn't react properly."

"How so?" Sean asked.

"She looked so funny, sprawled on the floor, and then her skirts tripping her up when she tried to stand. It was all I could do not to laugh."

Sean chuckled. "That wouldn't have been well received."

"I thought not. In my effort not to laugh and embarrass her further, I neglected to help her up. I must seem like a clod to her."

So my embarrassment is the one thing that can make you smile! Rose thought as she stomped away from the barn. *Dr. Crandall, you most certainly are a clod.*

Rose could hardly look at Miles as the family ate breakfast. She finished her meal in silence, hoping she could escape the house before her mother assigned her the task of playing hostess to him.

"Carrie, let me walk with you to school," she said as they finished eating.

Maggie took a jug of milk from the icebox. "Brother Crandall, why don't you go with them? Rose could show you the temple and the rest of town."

Rose held her breath. *Please say no.* She wished Sean had been able to stay home today, but Brother Jensen expected him at work, and Miles had insisted he would be fine.

"I would appreciate that," he said. "And please, all of you, call me Miles." He didn't look at Rose, and she scowled as she let out a sigh.

The prospect of being escorted to school by such a fine-looking man must have spurred Carrie on, because she finished getting ready in record time. When she returned to the kitchen, she grabbed her tin lunch bucket and smiled at him. "We can go now."

He took the flirting patiently, but Rose wondered how Carrie could miss the look on his face. He certainly wasn't enjoying the attention.

Rose handed a coat to her sister, then put on her own. She pulled mittens onto her hands and opened the door. "You'll be late if you don't hurry," she scolded. Then the three young people stepped from the warmth of the kitchen, waving as they left.

Rose breathed in the crisp air and wondered how to get rid of Miles for the day. Carrie chatted on and on about how this was her last year at school and how she just didn't know what to do next, all said with coquettish glances at her handsome escort.

"Papa insisted we get a good education," Carrie told Miles. "Some of my friends say a man only wants a woman who can care for his home and family, but Papa says a good woman is smart, too, and any good man will appreciate book learning." Walking backward for a few steps, Carrie turned and looked at Miles. "What do you think?"

Rolling her eyes, Rose quickened her pace until she realized the other two weren't keeping up. She turned. Carrie was doing a funny sideways kind of walk as she waited for Miles to answer her.

"Well, what do you think?" she asked again.

Miles looked at Rose. "I'm sure you're father is right."

The bell rang and Carrie waved. "I'll see you at dinner tonight," she said as she skipped up the stairs to the school, leaving Rose alone with Miles.

Miles watched the teenager enter the building. *She sure is energetic,* he thought. Carrie was easy to figure out—all smiles and dimples and a casual touch on the arm. He had met many women in the East who had shown the same kind of interest, but he had never responded. It was something Sean always teased him about. If Carrie weren't so much younger than he, he could almost be interested. *Almost.*

It was Rose who had caught his eye from the first moment they'd met. Through Sean's stories, Miles almost felt like he knew her. He remembered the photo Sean always carried in his pocket, but the image hadn't done Rose justice. Her hair hung in black, shiny curls almost to her waist. From the lightness in the sepia photo, Miles had expected her eyes to be blue, but in person, they shifted from the deepest gray to the most becoming green. Green eyes that flashed annoyance at him. He cleared his throat and gathered his thoughts.

"Shall we continue?" Rose asked, and he realized it probably wasn't the first time. She shook her head and turned, and he caught up to her in two long strides.

She must think I'm some sort of idiot. She seemed determined to play the hostess, but from the stiff set in her shoulders and the tight expression on her face, he could tell her heart wasn't in it. He began to wonder if she might have other plans for the day that her mother wasn't aware of, and if he was intruding.

"If you'll just show me where the temple is," he said, matching his step to hers, "I think I'd like to spend some time there." He hoped she would argue and offer to stay with him, but her shoulders relaxed and she nodded. He tried not to show his disappointment as he walked silently at her side for several blocks.

Sean had told Miles that Rose was a bit reserved, though once she got to know him she would talk his head off. But this morning Miles could see more than shyness at work. *If I didn't know better, I'd think she was angry with me,* he thought, shaking his head.

Rose walked just ahead of him, and he wondered how she was managing to keep up the ridiculous pace. She took two steps for every one of his. When he finally reached forward and touched her shoulder, she stopped and faced him.

"I'm not in that much of a hurry, but if you have somewhere else to be, I think I can find the temple on my own," Miles said as he saw the imposing building about a block ahead of them.

She looked at him and graced him with the barest of smiles.

"I'm sorry your mother insisted you let me come along on your walk. I don't mean to be trouble."

"Stop apologizing," Rose said, starting forward again. "You can see the temple from here. Will you need help finding the farm again or shall I just assume I'll see you at dinner tonight?"

Miles shook his head. She couldn't possibly be this rude because of the incident the previous day. "I don't know how I offended you, but I really am sorry."

"Next time you have a good laugh at my expense, you'll have your answer. Enjoy your day, Brother Crandall." She smiled sweetly at him and then abruptly turned and walked back toward the school.

Rose blushed as she hurried away from her brother's friend. An apology sat on the tip of her tongue. She had never spoken to anyone so rudely before, but she just couldn't make herself turn around. It would just be one more thing for him to talk about with Sean. Well, she wouldn't give him the satisfaction of having her grovel for forgiveness. He would leave for Montana soon, and she'd likely never see him again. As she turned a corner she sneaked a glance behind her, but he had gone, and he grew smaller as he walked away from her. *That's fine. At least he didn't see me look back.*

Once Rose knew Miles wasn't watching her, she changed direction again. The short walk to the Andersen farm gave her a little time to gather her thoughts. She adjusted her bonnet and walked up to the small house. As she rapped lightly on the door, she noticed how badly it needed a coat of paint. She steeled herself when she heard footsteps. With any luck, Mr. Andersen would be working in one of the dilapidated outbuildings.

Sister Andersen opened the door and smiled at Rose.

"Hello." She paused and realized she hadn't given any thought to just showing up. Then she remembered her mother talking about Sister Andersen's bad back and failing eyesight. "Mama sent me over to see if you could use any help today." A little lie, but surely she would be forgiven if she did a little service to go with it. She cringed at her faulty reasoning and just about backed away until she saw the other woman's eyes light up.

"Please come in." Sister Andersen stepped back from the door and motioned Rose into the house.

Rose had never visited the Andersens' home before and was surprised at the immaculate room. "You have a very nice home."

Sister Andersen led her into the kitchen and motioned for her to pull out a chair. "Your mother always seems to know when

I need a helping hand, and I've heard her talk about how fine your stitching is." She reached into the corner and took a sewing basket from a shelf. "My mending seems to be stacking up a bit, and it takes me so much longer than it used to." Putting the basket on the table, she opened it and handed Rose a needle and some thread.

Rose threaded the needle as Sister Andersen reached for another basket of clothing. She gave Rose a pair of pants that needed a knee patch, then sat back in her chair. Scooting closer to the window to take advantage of the morning light, Rose bent to her task. The mending in the basket wouldn't take long, and she knew she could only prolong the visit for a little while. If only Karl would come in soon, she could talk to him and then be on her way.

"Is your father still taking the family to Canada when the weather is better?"

Rose cut another length of thread. "That seems to be the plan."

"You don't sound too happy about it."

"It's hard to think of leaving everything behind, but we'll be fine I suppose."

"I wish I could go with you. It would be such an adventure."

Rose looked up at Sister Andersen. The woman sitting across from her was world-weary and worn. Gray liberally streaked her dark hair, and wrinkles fanned themselves away from her eyes. Though she sat straight as a post in her chair, Rose couldn't imagine how she would find the energy to make the journey. *Mama talks about school days with Sister Anderson,* Rose thought, *but I can't even believe they are the same age.*

"If you'd like, I'm sure Mother will write to you and share all sorts of details about Canada."

Sister Andersen nodded. "I would like that very much."

The short conversation ended and the room fell silent. The squeak of Sister Andersen's rocking chair was the only sound, and Rose tried to think of something else to talk about. Sister Andersen seemed content to stare out the window at the piles of snow as she rocked slowly in her chair.

A scraping sound outside the door caused Rose's hostess to stiffen. Rose looked toward the entrance and straightened her shoulders. She knew Karl worked at home with his father. They needed the money a second income would bring, but Mr. Andersen insisted he couldn't run the farm without Karl's full-time help. Rose's father always said the only reason Lars Andersen needed full-time help was because he spent half the time passed out with drink. She had wondered what possessed Laura Andersen to marry outside the Mormon Church, but when Rose had asked her mother the question, she was told to put it out of her mind and stop gossiping.

Jumping from her chair, Sister Andersen went to the icebox and took out a plate of sandwiches. She placed them on the table, then took the mending pile and placed it out of the way. Rose took the sewing basket and put it on the floor by her feet. Before the door could open, she ducked her head and continued to make tiny stitches in the pair of pants.

Mr. Andersen entered the room, followed by Karl. "Good. Lunch is ready. I'm starved."

Sister Andersen didn't say anything but began bustling around, putting tin cups on the table and filling them with milk from the icebox. Mr. Andersen threw his coat across the back of a chair without ever directly acknowledging his wife.

Rose stole a glance at Karl and caught him watching her. She grinned and looked back down at her work.

"Who do we have here?" Mr. Andersen sat across from her and grabbed a sandwich from the plate before sliding it over to

Karl. "Well, girl, speak up." He took a bite from the sandwich and continued before Rose could answer. "Glad to see the mending getting done, but I hope you weren't planning on paying her."

Rose waited a moment for an answer, but the woman only shook her head.

"I just stopped by to say hello and offered to help out a bit." Rose tied a knot in the thread and reached for another pair of pants. The sandwiches looked good, but she knew Mr. Andersen wouldn't invite her to eat with them.

"It's about time your church did a little more for us. Aren't they supposed to help their members? Seems like most of the time they just leave my poor wife here to fend for herself and come bother me with their preaching." He glared at Rose.

She bit her tongue. "Well, I'm here now." She stole another look at Karl, and this time when she caught him watching her, he blushed.

Mr. Andersen took another sandwich from the plate and continued to eat. He didn't say another word throughout the entire meal.

"Glad to see you, Rose," Karl spoke up.

The young man turned an even deeper red as he said it, and Rose wished she had been nicer to him through the years. His scarlet face made his white-blond hair seem even lighter. He had always liked her and had even promised to marry her when they were only nine years old, but she had never felt anything but friendship for him. And even though his pursuit had been ardent, she just hadn't been interested until now. If he still felt the same way, maybe he could be her ticket to staying in Utah. *Mama always tells how she knew she was supposed to marry Papa, even though they weren't in love. But look at them now.*

Rose smiled sweetly at Karl. "I just came by to see if your mother could use a hand, but I'm done." Rose folded the last pair of mended pants. She stood and placed the sewing basket back on the shelf, lowering her eyes as she glanced at Karl. "I really should be getting home."

Karl finished off his sandwich in a huge bite, then pushed his chair from the table. "Let me walk you out," he said, still chewing.

Sister Andersen stood and retrieved Rose's coat from the hook. Karl extended his hand for the coat and his mother relinquished it to him. He held it out so Rose could slip her arms into the sleeves, then led her to the front door. She thanked him and nodded briefly as she walked out. She thought he would go back inside and finish his lunch, but he followed her onto the tiny porch.

"I really appreciate you helping Ma this morning." He held her elbow as she walked down the icy steps.

Remembering the reason she had come in the first place, Rose leaned toward him and looked up, trying to imitate the fluttery eyes Carrie managed so well. "I was pleased to do it." Rose wondered how much flirting she would have to do to really recapture his interest. *I probably look stupid,* she thought, until a slow grin spread across Karl's face.

"If you'll wait just a moment, I'll get my coat and walk with you a little way." Karl released her elbow and sprinted into the house.

Do I really want to do this? Rose thought. But then she remembered Canada and squared her shoulders. When Karl came back out of the house, she beamed up at him and took his arm. "This is wonderful. With all the ice, I never know when I'll slip."

She cringed at her own words and hoped Karl wouldn't hear the false brightness in her voice. Karl wasn't one of the popular boys, and she felt a little bad about using him for her own agenda.

As they walked to the road and then headed south toward the Sterling farm, Rose kept a tight grip on Karl's arm. With a little encouragement, he shared the smallest details of his life.

Though her parents always insisted she was beautiful, Rose had never been popular with the boys. She could never figure out why Karl pursued her when all the others treated her like she didn't exist, or at best, as just a friend. Maybe she should have given him more of a chance when they were still teenagers. She wished she could attract young men like Carrie, or act weak and needy like some of her friends. It didn't matter now. Karl wasn't so bad, and she just needed one marriage proposal to be able to stay in Logan. She looked up at him and realized he was saying something about the social at the end of the week.

"Maybe you'd let me escort you there."

Rose nodded and tried to flutter her eyelashes. Karl blushed and Rose wondered if it'd had the effect she wanted or if he was just embarrassed for her sake. They were approaching the farm and Rose needed to extricate herself from his company before they got too close to the house. A door shut and at the sound, she pulled her hand from Karl's arm.

"I really should get home. Tell your mother how much I enjoyed helping her. I'll try to stop in later this week." She wiggled her fingers at him and then hurried into the yard. She came around the corner of the barn and ran into her father. "You scared me!" she cried as the big man let out a laugh.

"Sorry." He placed a hand on her shoulder.

Rose knew he had seen her with Karl, and she braced herself for a lecture.

"I didn't know you were out with the Andersen boy."

"He offered to escort me home and I accepted because of the ice." Her cheeks warmed and she ducked her head so her father wouldn't see her blush.

Peter raised his eyebrows but didn't question the statement. "Go inside and help your mother," he said before entering the barn.

3

A month passed quickly and Miles began to seem like one of the family. Rose's father especially enjoyed the young doctor's company, and the two men spent hours talking. When Peter introduced Miles to the family doctor, Dr. Williams, the two men started doing rounds together. Miles called it training, but Rose thought it sounded like an excuse and wondered if he would ever leave. She made a point of dropping hints about how he must miss his parents and siblings, but he didn't pay her any notice.

"Let it be, Rose," her mother said. "He is a pleasant young man, and he needs this time to see how the Saints live before he returns to Montana. He won't have the support there that we take for granted here in Utah. Besides, maybe we need him as much as he needs us."

The cryptic comment left Rose watching Miles more closely than ever, but she only succeeded in getting strange looks from him and teasing stares from her brother. Finally, she decided to ignore Miles completely; she had no time to figure him out anyway. The anticipated lecture about Karl never came, and Rose found herself spending more and more time with him. Karl's courtship of Rose proceeded in earnest. Most days he would call sometime in the early afternoon and they would walk for a little while before Rose had to return home to help with the evening meal. She had forgotten how much fun Karl could be, and she truly enjoyed his company as they spent their walks talking and laughing.

Often Karl would take Rose to visit his mother, and the three would talk while Rose helped with the mending or other little chores Sister Andersen thought up for her. Sometimes she wondered if Sister Andersen enjoyed her coming around or if she just wanted the free help. In the end, it didn't matter, she decided. Still, she wished her family would support her growing relationship with Karl. As much as she needed Karl's proposal to stay in Utah, she wanted her father's blessing even more. No one said a word to discourage her, but she caught the occasional look between her parents when his name was brought up.

"I can't believe you let Karl call on you," Carrie said as the two sisters worked on a quilt one afternoon.

"What do you have against him?"

"Well, he's certainly good looking, but you know his father is a drunk."

"Carrie! You shouldn't gossip and you know it. What would Mama say?" Rose snipped a thread and glared at her sister. "Besides, Karl is fun to be with, and he isn't his father."

"Well, it's true. Patience Johnson said she saw Karl with the Branson brothers, and you know they are no good." Carrie slid her chair to the side so she could reach a new section of the quilt. "If Papa knew how much time you were spending at the Andersen home, he'd probably put a stop to it right away."

"Sister Andersen appreciates my help and we've become good friends." Rose ducked her head a little and hoped her sister wouldn't read the uncertainty in her face. Even though Rose spent considerable time helping Sister Andersen, "good friends" definitely exaggerated the situation. She never could quite break through the older woman's silence. *How she manages around her domineering husband I'll never guess,* Rose thought.

She paused, her quilting needle poised in midair. She was becoming quite taken with Karl. Could she be falling in love with him? She had done such a thorough job convincing herself he would be the ticket to staying in Utah that she hadn't taken the time to closely examine her feelings. Her parents loved each other, but they never talked about their relationship. Rose had always been convinced she would just *know* whether or not she should marry a certain young man, but now she wasn't so sure.

It shamed Rose to think about her first flirtations with Karl, which had been self-serving at best. Now she found herself looking forward to spending time with him, despite the unease it caused her parents. She loved the attention and loved the feeling of falling in love. But she had to admit that though they had fun together, she often felt a little uneasy herself. She attributed it to nervousness about the family's scheduled departure for Canada, the date of which fast approached. Somehow, Rose knew, she had to pull it all together and get Karl to propose before she had to step on the train and leave her home and Utah behind. She wouldn't push it too much, though. It was bad enough that she had practically thrown herself at him. He had to be the one to bring up marriage.

Carrie flashed a knowing look at Rose, whose thoughts rushed back to the present. Rose blushed and pushed herself away from the quilt. "I'm going outside for a little while." She took the thimble off and placed it on the pieced fabric.

She went into the kitchen and took her shawl off the hook, then opened the back door and walked outside. She took a deep breath of the cool air and pulled her shawl tighter around her shoulders.

"Come help me, my Rose." The deep voice carried across the yard.

Rose smiled at her father as he walked past her, carrying an armful of wood. Some of her favorite memories involved helping him in the barn. Even though she had mastered many of the household skills her mother had spent years teaching her, Rose would still rather be with her father outside. She crossed the yard and followed him, hoping he wouldn't bring up her courting habits.

As she entered the barn, fine sawdust particles floated in the air, illuminated by the sunlight streaming through the window.

In the stall to Rose's left, a horse whinnied and nudged her with his muzzle. "Hey, Chester," she said quietly, petting her favorite horse on the neck. She watched her father put his load of lumber in a pile under the window. As he stood, he rubbed his abdomen with a large hand, a painful grimace crossing his gentle face. Rolling his shoulders, he stretched, then picked up one of the spindles for the kitchen chair he was building. He was nearly finished making a new set of chairs for his mother. Besides farming, Rose's father had a gift for turning wood into beautiful objects, and all of the family's furniture had been made by his loving hands.

Rose gave the horse another pat and walked to where her father sat with the chair and spindle. "These are wonderful, Papa. Granny will love them."

"I hope so. I'd hate to have her toss them in the stove because they aren't quite right."

"You know she'd never do that," Rose said. "She loves everything you make, and you can't do anything wrong in her eyes."

He laughed. "You should've seen some of the trouble I got into as a boy."

"Like what?"

With a shake of his head, Rose's father grabbed another spindle and began putting it in place. "Another time. Wouldn't want to give you any ideas," he said with a wink. The chair continued to take shape under his skilled hands. "Tell me about the Andersen boy."

Rose pushed a stray hair back behind her ear and focused on the floating sawdust again. "What do you want to know?"

"How serious are you? He hasn't even asked my permission to court you."

"Well, we didn't start out courting. You know we've been friends forever, and I was just spending time with a friend." The half-truth slipped too easily from her tongue and Rose felt a pang deep in her heart. She had never lied to her father before. "I guess I realized how much I'll miss my friends when we leave."

"Friends are a good thing, but be careful that your intentions toward this young man are clear." Peter reached toward the ceiling and stretched. "And if he wants to court you, he needs to come talk to me."

"I'll tell him, Papa." Rose ran her hand along the back of a finished chair. The satiny-smooth surface testified of the many hours spent sanding away the roughness. Rose's father could always sooth away her hurts and worries as easily as he could smooth away the splinters on a piece of wood. "I'll miss this barn when we leave. I like spending time out here helping you."

Her father nodded and continued working. She knew he wasn't ignoring her, but collecting his thoughts. Finally he put down the tools he was using and sat down on one of the chairs. "This is just a place. You know that, right?"

With a sigh, Rose sat in the chair next to her father.

"Wherever we live, as long as we have family, we'll be fine."

This discussion wasn't a new one, and Rose wondered what her father would think if Karl did propose. Would he be willing to leave his daughter behind? It would split up the family, but with the railway, visiting Utah would only get easier. So many of the stories Granny told were of hardship and suffering, even after the Saints reached the Salt Lake Valley. *I don't want to start again.* Rose sat up a little straighter and stuck her chin out. Before she could say anything, her father put his hand on her shoulder.

"I see that stubborn look in your eyes. You don't want to go. I understand that, but I feel you've never even given the idea a chance." He gave her shoulder a light squeeze then stood up. "I believe the prophet called this family for a reason, and I don't feel that leaving you behind is part of the plan." He picked up another spindle and turned it in his hands. "Have you prayed about it?"

Rose lowered her eyes and fiddled with her skirt. "No."

"Are you afraid of the answer?"

The silence of the afternoon settled around them as he waited for her response. Rose closed her eyes. How did her father do that? It was like he could see into her deepest fears. She looked up to find him watching her intently.

"At least consider it, my Rose. That's what faith is all about— relying on Heavenly Father to lighten our burdens."

"I'll try, Papa." Rose stood and wrapped her arms around her father. He pulled her into a comforting hug, then gently propelled her toward the door.

"Go help your mother get dinner on the table. I'm mighty hungry." He turned from her and began working on the chair again.

Rose's suspicions grew as she watched him work. She'd pestered her mother about his health, and the hug only confirmed what she already believed. He had lost weight and didn't stand as tall as he used to; it was almost like he hunched over with some inner pain. As she walked from the barn to the house, she decided to keep a closer eye on him. Even though her parents were determined to keep the truth from her, she would figure it out somehow.

4

Rose watched her father over the next few days and became more and more convinced something wasn't right. Despite all her prodding, however, her mother wouldn't tell her anything. She tried asking Sean, but he just patted her shoulder and told her to stop worrying. On the third day, she finally decided to corner Miles. She stood at the back door waiting for him to arrive home from helping Dr. Williams all day. As she saw him coming up the lane, she grabbed her coat and ran out to meet him. She knew her mother would consider her forward, but she couldn't think of anything else to do.

"Will you walk with me for a bit?" Rose said as she approached him. She pulled her coat closed and fastened the buttons. Snow still made the ground uneven and icy, even though it had warmed up some.

He stopped and raised his eyebrows in surprise. Offering his arm to her, he turned and they began walking toward the pasture. Rose wondered how to bring up the forbidden subject of her father's health.

"Was there something you needed?" Miles asked, his voice cool and stiff.

Even though he had been a guest in their home for over a month, Rose hadn't warmed up to him the way the others had. He wasn't a bad person or anything; she just didn't want to share her family with anyone. The changes ahead scared her, and she wanted to keep things the same for as long as possible. Miles just wasn't part of the picture. Even though she hadn't meant to be rude, she knew she had been.

She put on a friendly face. "I need to apologize. I haven't treated you the way a guest and friend should be treated."

Miles nodded. "Apology accepted. I know I'm intruding, but you have no idea how much I love being here among the Saints and attending the temple."

"You do spend a lot of time there."

Rose slipped on a patch of ice and caught her breath as she struggled for her balance, but Miles tightened his grip on her arm and kept her upright.

He started walking back to the house. "We should go inside. I don't want you to fall and hurt yourself."

She stood her ground. "I'll be fine. There's something I wanted to ask you before we go back."

Miles tucked his chin deeper into his scarf, then looked down at her and waited.

Rose stuffed her hands into her pockets. When she looked up at him, she felt the world go still. Something about the way he looked at her left her knees weak. *You are falling in love with Karl,* she reminded herself, tearing her gaze from Miles's rich brown eyes. He was her brother's friend and part of the family.

"I'm worried about Papa," she blurted out. "There's something wrong with him, but Mama won't see it, or she just won't tell me what's going on."

Miles glanced toward the house.

"You know something, don't you?" Rose stepped closer to him and put her hand back on his arm. "Please tell me."

"I can't."

"You're not really here because you aren't ready to go home, are you? They asked you to stay longer because Papa is sick!"

She could see the conflicting emotions in Miles's eyes as he looked down at her. He put his hand over hers and sighed. "I can't say anything. You'll have to talk to your parents." He took her hand and tucked it back into the crook of his elbow. "Let's go inside. I'm getting cold."

Pulling her hand away, Rose stomped her foot. "Don't brush me off like that. I'm an adult too, and they still treat me as if I'm a flighty teenager like Carrie."

Miles leaned against the fence that circled the pasture and put his hands in the pockets of his coat. "I'm not choosing to treat you like a child, but it isn't my place to share my patient's problems with you. Things are told to me in confidence. Would you really want me to betray your parents' trust?"

"No. But you admit he's a patient? At least that's something." Rose put her hands under her arms and hunched her shoulders against the cold. "Why would they need you when Dr. Williams has always taken care of us?"

Miles ignored her question. "Come inside, Rose. It isn't doing any of us any good standing here in the cold." He held his hand out to her and grasped her cold fingers as she put her hand in his. They walked quickly back to the house and hurried into the warm kitchen.

When she realized she had let him hold her hand all the way to the house, Rose blushed and snatched it away from him. She busied herself undoing her coat, but he didn't seem to notice how flustered she was as he took it from her and hung it on the hook. Her parents sat at the table, peeling potatoes and laughing together. Rose studied them for a moment and then turned to the stairs, but Miles grabbed her elbow.

"Brother and Sister Sterling, could we talk about something?" He approached the table, pulling Rose with him.

Rose's mother halted her work, a question in her eyes.

"You need to tell her," Miles said in a quiet voice.

As Rose's father looked at her mother, pain filled their faces. He pulled out the chair next to him and motioned for Rose to sit. Miles stepped back. Silence filled the room and Rose noticed tears in her mother's eyes. She watched her father try to gather his thoughts until he finally motioned with his hand.

Miles nodded. "Rose, your father has cancer of the stomach."

The room spun and Rose shook her head. Pushing her chair away from the table, she tried to stand, but her father put a hand on her arm.

"Let us explain," he said.

"What does that mean? Why isn't Dr. Williams taking care of him?" she asked, ignoring her father and directing the questions at Miles.

"Dr. Williams is the one who suggested we consult with Miles," Rose's mother said, putting a half-peeled potato back in the bowl. "We were hoping he might have new information about the disease, since he just graduated from medical school and has learned all the latest techniques."

"And does he?"

"New things are being discovered all the time, but stomach cancer is almost impossible to cure." Miles sat next to Rose's mother and let out a deep sigh. "Especially when it is this far along."

"I'm dying, my Rose," Peter said.

"Did you think I wouldn't notice?" Rose stood quickly, the chair crashing to the floor behind her. "Why wouldn't you tell me?" She tried holding them back, but tears streamed down her face. She brushed at her cheeks and then wiped her wet hand on her apron.

Her father got up and put his arms around her. She sobbed into his shoulder until she felt her mother's arms wrap around both of them. They stood like that until Rose finally stopped crying.

She swallowed hard, then looked up at her parents. "Why didn't you tell me?"

"We wanted life to be normal for as long as possible," her mother said. "There is nothing we can do about it now, so we just have to press forward the best we can."

We can't go to Canada without Papa, Rose thought. "Why are you trying to sell the farm then?" she asked her father as she rested her head on his shoulder.

He sighed deeply. "We started working on that before the cancer was diagnosed. I believed whatever illness I had would go away, since this call from the prophet needed to be filled. Don't worry about it right now, Rose. Your mother and I will figure it all out." Her father patted her back, then sat in his chair again. "Now if we are going to get any dinner tonight, we need to get these potatoes peeled." Rose's mother took her place next to him and left Rose standing by herself.

Obviously, the discussion was over. Her parents began talking quietly with Miles. Rose shrunk back from them, then whirled around and rushed up the stairs. *How can they be so calm about this? Papa is dying and they sit there peeling potatoes as if nothing is wrong at all.* She shut the door to her bedroom and threw herself onto the bed.

As she lay there, the shadows began to slip across the ceiling, and she pulled a quilt around her shoulders to keep the evening chill away. Below her a door shut and she could hear Carrie's cheerful voice. Then silence. Rose pictured them sitting around the table as they told Carrie the horrible news. She waited for her sister to rush up the stairs and slam her bedroom door, but nothing happened. *Apparently she took it better than I did. Maybe I'm not as grown up as I thought I was.*

The evening shadows deepened and Rose's eyes grew heavy. She awoke a short time later when a soft knock sounded on her door. "Come in," she said as she sat up and stretched. The door opened and her mother entered the room.

"Are you coming down for dinner, dear?"

"Yes, Mama." Rose stood and folded the quilt. She turned to see her mother still standing there.

"Please don't be too upset with us. This is extremely difficult for both your father and me."

"Mama, it just hurts that you didn't trust me enough to tell me." Rose sat on the bed and rested her chin on her hands.

"It's not about trust. Your father and I have been struggling with how to tell you, and we've been trying to figure out what this means for our future." Maggie sat next to her daughter and pulled her close. "We wanted to give you the whole picture so we wouldn't leave you with any worries."

"How can I not worry? Papa is dying and thinks he is still going on some grand adventure to Canada. How are we going to survive without him?"

"We can't solve every problem all at once. The Lord has a plan for us and we don't always need to understand it. Right now we need to be together as a family. We just need to have faith."

"I know." Rose kissed her mother's cheek. "We should go downstairs. Everyone must be waiting for us."

Maggie Sterling nodded and the two women went to join the rest of the family for dinner. Rose tried to leave her worry tucked in the safety of her bedroom, but it followed and haunted her for the rest of the evening.

5

Rose looked at the clock on the mantel again. The afternoon had slipped away from her; dinner dishes still filled the washbasin, and supper needed to be started. She immersed her hands in the warm, soapy water and wondered again how her mother kept up with everything. Voices outside distracted Rose and she pushed aside a flicker of irritation as she dried her hands on the dishtowel she had tucked into the waistband of her apron.

A giggle told her that one of the offending voices was Carrie, and she wondered how long her sister had been home from school. Glancing out the kitchen window, Rose stomped her foot as she saw Sean and Miles talking, with Carrie hanging around them like a puppy waiting for a scrap. She sighed. How could she fault Carrie for wanting to spend every waking moment with Sean and Miles? Sean's three-year mission had felt like a lifetime, and Miles had caught Carrie's attention the first time she saw him.

Rose realized she hadn't had a chance to spend much time with Sean. Only days after Miles told her about the cancer, her father had collapsed, and he'd hardly left his bed since. The household responsibilities had fallen on Rose's shoulders while her mother took care of her ailing husband. It left little time for Rose to spend socializing, though Karl still called daily and she took every opportunity to walk with him. She wondered if he would come to the door with Miles and Sean sitting on the step. Sean didn't like Karl, and the two avoided each other whenever possible. The one time Rose had invited Karl to dinner, the entire meal had been spent in awkward conversation. Sean and Miles seemed determined to make Karl stumble over something— anything to prove to Rose he wasn't good enough for the family.

Rose had dragged her brother from the kitchen as soon as Karl left. "How dare you treat my guest so rudely?"

Sean laughed at her. "You aren't really serious about him."

"And why shouldn't I be?" In truth, Karl had her sympathy throughout the entire meal. The conversation kept returning to discussion of the gospel, which always make Karl uncomfortable. "You kept trying to trap him by asking questions he knew nothing about. Can he help it if his father won't let the scriptures into his home?"

Sean grasped her shoulder and his face became serious. "Do you want to end up like Sister Anderson?"

"That's not fair. Karl is better than his father."

"Why do you think he always calls on you in the afternoon? Most young men court in the evening."

"You know Papa wouldn't let me walk with Karl after dark, and you have all made him so unwelcome here." Rose brushed Sean's hand away.

Folding his arms, Sean leaned against the wall. "He spends the evening with his friends, drinking and gambling. He's not as innocent as he would have you believe."

Rose shook her head. "He needs me, Sean. No other girl in town has ever looked twice at him. He loves me."

"You know, I think I've finally figured it out," Sean said. "You hoped to marry him so you could stay behind. But now we might not go anywhere, and you don't have to settle for someone who won't give you everything you deserve. He can't even marry you in the temple."

"Just be quiet," Rose yelled. "You know nothing about this." She fingered the gold ring in her pocket. Karl had given it to her just that afternoon as he walked her home from church. The little chip of a diamond sparkled in the sunlight, and it didn't seem fair that she had to hide it. How could she tell her family she finally had Karl's promise if they were so against him?

"I know there are better men out there that would love you even more than Karl says he does," Sean had said. "Men like Miles who take their commitments and religion seriously."

The cool water in the washbasin brought Rose's thoughts back to the present. *If only Sean hadn't brought Miles home with him.*

She took a moment and studied her brother's friend through the window. His good looks couldn't be denied, but Rose couldn't get past his serious demeanor. At least Karl knew how to have fun. She fingered the ring again. Karl still needed to talk to her father, something he kept putting off.

With a shake of her head, she turned back to the table to begin making biscuits for dinner. Footsteps sounded on the porch. She straightened her shoulders and pasted a smile on her face as the outside door opened and Sean and Carrie entered the inviting warmth of the kitchen.

"Is Mama upstairs?" Sean asked. "I need to talk to everyone."

"Of course," Rose said as she handed him a plate of cookies. "Where's Miles?"

Sean took a bite of a molasses cookie and mumbled through his full mouth, "He's gone over to Sister Browning's. One of the kids came running over, saying the youngest fell down and tore his leg open."

Rose took a few cookies from the plate and put them aside. "I suppose if I don't save a few, you'll eat all those before he gets back."

Carrie ran out of the room and returned a few minutes later with her mother, who smiled at Sean. "Carrie says you wanted to talk to us."

Sean drew a sheet of paper from his back pocket, then unfolded it and put it on the table.

"I want to go to Canada," he said, then stepped back and waited for a reaction.

Rose and her mother quickly scanned the advertisement.

"Isn't it exciting?" Carried said as she took a cookie from the plate.

Rose looked again at the paper on the table. "Sean, we need you here. We decided that since Papa got sick we shouldn't go after all."

"You decided that, but this is such a great opportunity. I have to start my own life somewhere, so I might as well do it up north. Brother Card held a meeting last night and I've been thinking about this all day." Sean picked up the notice again and read part of it out loud.

> *Two hundred men with teams wanted who will become actual settlers in southern Alberta, Canada. To the Latter-day Saints who desire Good places to make Comfortable homes, we offer a grand opportunity to accumulate means to pay for them without incurring the bondage of debt. We have about fifty miles of the Alberta Irrigation Company's canal to construct, for*

*which half will be paid in cash and the balance
in excellent prairie land, at $3 an acre, with free
water for two years to the first settlers on these
lands.*

Sean set the paper on the table. "They won't be starting the canals until later in the spring, but if I leave now, I can find some good land and work for President Card for a few months. I've already talked to him about it, and we've struck up an agreement."

"Miles put you up to this, didn't he? Why can't he mind his own business?" Rose pushed her chair back and stood. "With Father so ill, how can you even think of leaving?"

Her mother's stern gaze stopped her rant. "Sit down, Rose. I'll not have you insulting our guest, especially when he isn't here to defend himself. Sean is a man and can make his own decisions. And, actually, this is the way our family can heed the prophet's call, especially since your father can't answer it now."

"I think it's exciting," Carrie said, a dreamy look in her eyes.

Rose hissed. "It's not like you're going too. He's just leaving again."

"I'm not going anywhere until . . ."

"Don't say it, Sean. I know it's inevitable, but just don't say it." Rose could hear the tears in her mother's voice.

How unfair! Rose thought. She missed her old friendship with Sean, who had only been home for a few months and spent most of his time with their father and Miles. She had to admit that having Miles live in their home had been a blessing when it came to her father. A doctor right in the house who wasn't asking for pay and could tend to her father whenever the need arose was undeniably convenient.

Still, Rose resented Miles. His serious nature rubbed her the wrong way, and every time she wanted to be alone, he seemed to be there. Just the day before, she had sat in front of the glowing fire in the front room, hoping for a few quiet moments before she went up the stairs to her chilly bedroom. She only got two minutes before Miles came in and sat in a chair across the room. He greeted her politely and then opened the book he was reading. She noticed it was a medical text and wondered how he could possibly find it interesting enough to keep him awake.

Even more than that, Rose resented the way everyone else had accepted him with open arms. The moment her father had met Miles and listened to Sean's glowing recommendations, Peter had gotten a gleam in his eye and Rose knew he had matchmaking on his mind. As soon as she'd figured that out, her dislike of Miles increased tenfold.

She knew she was being unfair, but she didn't need her father to arrange her life for her, especially if he wanted her to settle for someone as dull as Miles. She remembered how he had held her hand as he helped her over the ice the night she found out about the cancer. Just the thought made her blush, and she wondered if Miles knew about the matchmaking going on in the house. She wished he would just pack up and go home to his family in Montana. She just wanted her family back the way they were.

As if her thoughts summoned him, Miles came in from the cold. He greeted Maggie warmly and winked at Carrie.

"Don't encourage her," Sean said with a smile. "She's much too young for you anyway."

Carrie stuck her tongue out at him and beamed up at Miles.

Rose huffed and pushed herself away from the table. "I'm going to see how Papa is doing."

She left the kitchen in a swirl of skirts. Rustling up the narrow stairs, she stopped outside her father's room and smoothed her hair. It wouldn't do for her father to see her so upset.

She pushed the door open and stepped softly inside. "How are you?" Rose smiled as she said the words and she hoped the smile reached her eyes.

The once large man had become nothing more than a shadow of his former self. He chuckled at her and his green eyes flashed. "Do you think I can't hear you giving your brother the what-for?"

Rose ducked her head. She sometimes forgot how well sound traveled in the house.

"Sean is his own man and he has to choose his own path. He won't thank a meddling sister for trying to hold him back."

"Why does his path have to take him so far from home?" Rose sat on the edge of the bed and took her father's hand. "Doesn't he know we need him?"

"We managed just fine when he was serving a mission and we'll manage just fine if he goes to Canada. Besides, he isn't leaving tomorrow."

"Carrie thinks we all should go," Rose said in a low voice.

He let go of her hand and tried to push himself up in the bed. The pain in his face pierced her soul. She reached forward to help him but withdrew her hands before he noticed. Maggie kept reminding the children to let him have his independence for as long as possible.

"If I could get out of this bed, I'd still go too." He grimaced as he tried once more to sit up. "I guess if the prophet believes it's a good place to send families, then we can let Sean go."

"I think Sean just sees an opportunity to make some money," Rose said.

"This is nothing new. You know people have been sent to Arizona and Mexico. Why not Canada?" Peter Sterling leaned back and closed his eyes. "Sean needs to find his way in the world, and someday he'll have his own family to support."

Rose watched her father as he slept. *Why not Canada?* Even as she wanted to argue that her brother should stay in Utah, she knew it was an argument she was bound to lose.

6

Miles left the temple. He couldn't seem to get his fill of the magnificent building, and he wished he didn't have to return to Montana soon. He wanted to start his medical practice before the winter snows fell again, and that would require building a clinic in Spring Creek. Old Doctor McTavish had always practiced medicine out of his own home, but Miles knew his parents' ranch was too far from town to be accessible to most of his future patients. He hoped the community would accept him without complaint, but it was hard to imagine caring for people who had known him since he first toddled around after his father.

The walk back to the Sterling farm was a pleasant one now that the blustery winter winds had given way to spring breezes. A wet snow had fallen the day before, but it was already beginning to melt. Miles's two months in Utah had passed quickly, and he would miss the Sterling family. It saddened him doubly to think of leaving, since he knew his departure wouldn't happen until Peter succumbed to his illness.

Taking a breath of fresh air, Miles thought about his patient. Peter assured him daily that this was how things had to be and that everyone would learn to function without him, but Miles wasn't sure how.

Miles remembered the loss in his own life and understood why Rose had been so touchy lately. He'd never met a woman as deep as Rose. She tried to hide it, but he could see it in the way she interacted with the rest of the family. She hardly spoke to him other than to call him to meals. The silence from her wasn't uncomfortable, though, because she seemed to simply pretend he wasn't there. Miles tried not to feel hurt, but he wished she would at least give him an occasional smile.

He turned a corner and continued on, lost in thought. Not watching where he was going, he crashed headlong into another man. He looked up to find himself face to face with Karl Andersen.

"Brother Andersen." Miles reached out his hand. "I'm so sorry to run into you like that. I must have been woolgathering."

Karl nodded at Miles. "No harm."

As he'd watched Karl court Rose, Miles had sensed the concern from her parents. They never said a word to him, he assumed because they made it a practice not to gossip, but he'd been in Logan long enough to hear the rumors from other sources. Just the previous week, Miles and Sean had attended a meeting held by Charles Ora Card, the main promoter of the Canadian experience. Card and his family had lived in Canada for ten years, and he had helped secure the irrigation contract for the Church. At the meeting, Miles could see the potential for the families that chose to go. He could also see Karl sitting across the room with some of his rowdy friends, with his arm wrapped around a girl who was definitely not Rose. It was no secret to any who witnessed the display that Karl was drunk.

Miles nodded at the other man and stepped around him. Before he could move on, Karl placed a hand on his arm.

"Can I ask you something?" Karl dropped his hand. "Did you say something to the Sterlings about me?"

"Why do you ask?"

"Sean just came by the house and gave me a note from his father. Apparently I'm not good enough for his daughter." Karl's voice was bitter.

"I'm sorry to hear that." A surge of sympathy washed over Miles. It couldn't be easy being raised in a Mormon community with a father like Lars Andersen, and Sean had told him how ostracized Karl had been as a child. Even though Church members taught their children the Golden Rule, they didn't want them anywhere near Mr. Andersen or his family. Miles wondered if it wouldn't have been easier for Karl to grow up in Spring Creek, where the expectations were different.

"So what did you say to them? I know you came to the house with Dr. Williams the other night after Ma fell."

"Brother Andersen, we both know your mother didn't fall, but I didn't say a word about it to anyone. When I treat a patient, the information I am privileged to hear stays with me."

Karl looked at him skeptically. "It just seems suspicious to me that I got warned away from Rose about the same time."

"Sean and I were at the meeting when Brother Card spoke. We both saw you, your drunken friends, and the girl who was clinging to you. In fact, half the community saw you. Rose came home in tears when her friends began gossiping about the spectacle you created. I'm surprised she is still willing to have you call on her. Really, though, this is none of my business." Miles tipped his hat at Karl. "I'll just be on my way."

"Rose understands me. She's seen how hard it is to be Lars Andersen's son."

Miles raised an eyebrow. "Does she know how hard it will be to be Karl Andersen's wife?" The words slipped out and Miles knew he had crossed a line when he saw Karl's fist coming at his face. He ducked to the right and the punch grazed his left cheek.

"You stay away from Rose," Karl said with a low growl. "She says her father keeps begging her to stop seeing me, but I can see what is really happening. Sean and the good bishop are playing their own game of matchmaking. Well, you can't have her." He swung again, but this time Miles caught his arm.

"That's enough. I won't fight with you." Miles pushed him away.

"Scared?" Karl swore at him, clearly determined to fight.

Years of living with two brothers kicked in, and Miles stopped Karl's next punch with one of his own, grimacing as his fist connected with Karl's nose.

Karl put a hand to his face and pulled it away covered in blood. "I didn't think doctors went around injuring people."

"I may be a doctor now, but I'm a man and a Montanan first. I know how to take care of myself if someone is going to lose his temper and take it out on me." Miles adjusted his hat. "Can you promise you will never use the same method of dealing with anger on Rose? Maybe Bishop Sterling has a right to be concerned." He nodded at Karl and continued down the street.

Rose shut the kitchen door softly. The days were passing too quickly, and she hated watching her father's decline. Having Miles in the house was just a further insult to her—a live-in doctor who couldn't do anything to save her beloved father.

She tiptoed down the porch stairs and then skirted a mud puddle in her path. The snow had almost disappeared, and it wouldn't be long before the first green shoots began to push their way up through the damp earth. She reached the street and crossed it to wait by the creek where she expected Karl to meet her. As she neared the old oak tree, she saw Karl kneeling next to a small pile of snow, grabbing handfuls of the cold, wet stuff and washing his face.

"Karl, what happened?" Rose took her handkerchief from her pocket and wet it in the creek. Then she began dabbing at the blood on his face. "Are you okay? Do you need a doctor?"

He snatched the flimsy piece of cloth from her hand and pushed her away. "A doctor did this to me," he said flatly. "Seems I'm not good enough for you."

"Miles?"

Karl didn't answer but grabbed another handful of snow to hold against his nose.

"Why would you care what Miles thinks? He is just Sean's friend. Once he leaves we'll never see him again." Rose leaned against the tree. She wanted to help Karl but could tell he would push her away again. She'd seen this mood in him before, but it was usually after he'd had a run-in with his father.

"It isn't just Miles. It's Sean, too. He brought a letter to the house asking me to stay away from you."

"From Papa?"

"Of course. Who else would order me away?"

"So what do we do now?" Rose reached for Karl's hand. He slowly uncurled his fist and wrapped his fingers around hers. She squeezed and tried to give him a reassuring smile. Over the past several weeks, her thoughts had become a jumble of emotions. She hadn't admitted the truth to anyone, but even though she thought she might be falling in love with Karl, his dark moods scared her. Every time she saw him like this, Sister Andersen's world-weary face flashed before her eyes. She didn't want to end up like that. But Karl needed someone, and she was developing feelings for him . . . wasn't she?

Karl looked at her and she realized he was searching for the answer in her face. She smiled at him, trying to chase away the uncertainty.

"I guess we'll just have to meet quietly until I can find the right moment to ask your father for your hand." He leaned forward and kissed her on the forehead. "Until then, can you be patient with me?"

Rose nodded. She wasn't sure how Karl would pull it off, but for now she could wait. She reached up and held up the ring he'd given her. She wasn't ready to announce her intentions to the world, and waiting for him to speak to her father bought her a little time to get used to the idea of being Mrs. Karl Andersen.

Most of the family had turned in for the night, but Rose couldn't sleep. She sat by the fire in the parlor with a shawl wrapped around her shoulders. Her Book of Mormon lay open in her lap, but she'd stopped reading and just stared into the flames. When she'd come home, her mother had been waiting for her. Miles had told her what had happened between him and Karl, but after hearing Karl's version of the incident, Rose was in no mood to hear Miles's spin on the story. It didn't matter anyway. With tales of Karl's rowdy behavior circulating through the town, the blows exchanged that afternoon were the final test of her mother's patience.

"I don't want to worry your father with this, so you listen to me, young lady. You won't be seeing Karl Andersen again," her mother had said in her sternest voice, the one she only used when she didn't mean to be crossed.

Rose lowered her eyes. As she listened to all of her mother's reasons to end the friendship, she argued each one of them in her head. With her father dying and Sean leaving for Canada, marrying Karl seemed more important than ever. It would make one less mouth for her mother to try to feed.

Now she sat in her mother's rocking chair, staring at the flames in the fireplace and trying to piece together her feelings. She didn't want to hurt her parents, but even as a child she had been encouraged to make her own decisions. *Mama is only upset over Papa's illness.* Rose absently turned a page in her book. *Certainly she wouldn't tell me to turn Karl away, not after all those years of teaching me that everyone has some worth.*

The stairs creaked and Rose looked up to see Sean enter the room.

"What are you doing up?"

"I could ask you the same thing." He sat across from her in his father's chair.

They sat in silence a while, watching the firelight reflect off the ceiling.

"Papa won't make it through the week," Sean said quietly. "Miles thinks he is nearing the end."

"I wish Dr. Williams would come by more often." Rose leaned her head back and rested it on the smooth wood of the old rocking chair.

"Miles is quite capable of taking care of Papa." Sean watched Rose for a moment. "What do you have against him, anyway?"

"Nothing."

"I think you like him." Sean grinned, clearly waiting for her reaction.

He wasn't going to get one, because Rose had already thought it all through. Miles was undeniably attractive, but liking him and thinking he was attractive were two completely different things.

"Even if Miles was the most handsome man on earth, he's still practically a stranger to me. How do we know the marvelous Dr. Crandall doesn't come from something worse than Karl?" Rose closed her scriptures and placed them on the small, round table next to the rocking chair. "At least I know Karl's background. It may not be perfect, but I can help him."

"You don't marry someone to help him. You marry someone who is equally matched to you."

"So you all think Miles is equally matched to me?" Rose laughed. "We don't know what Miles is like around his family. He could be another Karl, but we are only seeing the best side of him."

Sean shrugged. "I guess we don't know. We'll have to trust he is who he says he is."

Rose pulled the shawl closer around her. "Even if I did want him to love me, he'll be leaving soon and I'll never see him again."

7

"Where have you been, Rose?" Carrie took her sister's shawl and hung it on the peg by the door. "Papa's not doing well at all. Mama's been trying to find you for the last hour."

Rose stomped the late spring snow off her shoes and looked longingly out the window. She could just see Karl's back retreating down the road. If her mother knew she had been walking with him, she would be in trouble for sure. "Did she send for Sean?" she asked Carrie.

"She sent Miles a few minutes ago." Carrie turned to walk up the stairs, and Rose barely heard her say, "I'm scared. What will we do without Papa?"

When they reached the landing, Rose took her sister's hand and led her into the room where their father lay. She could hear a rattle in the breath of her beloved father and knew from her mother's tears that he wouldn't be long for this world. She saw new lines in her mother's face. The beautiful auburn hair Rose had always loved shimmered with the gray that had come quickly these last few months.

"Rose, come sit with your father. He's been asking for you." Maggie motioned for Carrie to follow her out of the room, leaving Rose alone with him.

Tears touched her eyes as she sat next to the bed of her wasted father. The cancer in his body had consumed all his life force and energy. When he opened his green eyes to look at her, Rose saw herself in their depths.

"Papa, it's Rose."

"Hello, my Rose. Did you have a nice walk?"

"Yes, Papa. The wind is brisk, but the snow is beautiful."

"Were you by yourself?" the frail man asked, his words not more than a whisper.

Placing her hand on her father's arm, Rose shook her head. She had never been able to conceal the truth from him.

"Please promise me you will not see Karl anymore. You can't be serious about him, and it isn't fair to either of you. Please promise me this one last thing." There was an urgency in his voice she had never heard before. He tried to sit up in the bed.

Rose pushed him gently back against the pillows, then pulled the quilt up around his shoulders. "You don't understand, Papa." She could feel the tears on her cheeks and she wiped them away angrily. "How can you ask me to do this? He loves me. He has asked me to marry him, but I told him I needed your blessing first."

With a weak hand, her father brushed the hair off his forehead. "Oh, my darling daughter. Don't sell yourself short. Marry someone you really love."

"Maybe I do love him."

"He has been walking out with you for months now and has done nothing to advance his own prospects. Are you sure he really loves you, or is he just interested because you are his ticket away from an alcoholic father and a barren piece of land? Does he somehow think you will pull him into respectability?"

Rose stood and dropped her father's hand. "You're tired, Papa." She pulled the quilt over his thin shoulders and kissed him on the cheek. "I hear Sean. He will come up and see you in a minute."

"Think about what I said." He gently squeezed her hand. "I wish you would consider giving Miles a chance."

"Miles! I wish Sean had never brought him here. He's so serious. In all the time he's been here, he's hardly ever smiled." Then she raised her voice, hoping a little anger would hide the confusing emotions that always arose in her when she thought of Miles. "He annoys me and I wish he would go home." Still, Rose couldn't help but think of his gentleness when he cared for her father.

She tried to pull her hand away from her father's, but he grasped her fingers with surprising strength and sighed. "You are too old to display your temper like that, my Rose. Miles is a nice young man. He has a good career ahead of him and will take care of his family well. Can you say the same about Karl? You are almost twenty-one years old. You need to start thinking more about a future and less about having fun."

Rose gently eased her hand away. "I know, Papa," she whispered. "Now get some rest." She turned and walked slowly from the room.

Her father closed his eyes and his breathing deepened. "Daughter, I love you," he said just before he relaxed into a deep sleep.

"I love you too, Papa," Rose said as she quietly closed the bedroom door.

The deepest part of the night was silent, and Rose could hear every creak of the house as it settled. She knew the time had come. She slipped from her bed carefully so as not to wake her sister and made her way down the dark hallway. The door to her parents' room was open and she could see her mother resting her head on her father's shoulder. The love in the room was tangible, and the scene burned itself into Rose's mind.

"Come in, Rose." Her father's voice was barely audible.

"Mama," Rose whispered, "you should go get some rest."

Her mother looked up as if she was surprised to see another human being. "I can't leave now. I can't leave until it is done."

Rose put her hand over her mouth to stifle the sob that tried to escape.

"Go get your brother and sister. They need to say goodbye too."

Panic welled up in Rose as she fled the room. "Sean! Sean!" She knocked softly on his door. "Sean, wake up!"

"Is it Papa?" he asked as he opened the door.

Rose nodded and went into the bedroom she and Carrie shared. Her little sister was already getting out of bed. Rose took her hand and they hurried to their parents' room.

Sean stood with an arm around his mother and held out his hand to Rose. She took it and the four of them stood around her father as if to protect him from death's grasp.

"My family." Peter gasped. "You do a father proud."

Mama held his hand. "Hush, Peter, save your strength."

"My strength is gone." His voice grew softer. "I couldn't have asked for a better wife. I love you, Maggie." It was a whisper, but the words held so much love, and Rose suddenly knew she couldn't settle for less.

She felt like running to avoid the moment, but the time had come.

"Peter . . ."

Maggie's voice echoed through the room, but it was too late to reach the ears of the man on the bed. Rose could almost feel the air grow colder as her father's life ran out. She had never felt so lost, and she looked at her mother for a cue about what to do next. Memories flooded her mind, but she tried to push them back, emotion already threatening to overwhelm her.

Maggie whispered her husband's name one more time as Sean wrapped his arms around her.

Carrie held tightly to Rose's hand. With her other hand, Rose reached out to smooth the coverlet over her father's still body. The movement seemed to draw her mother out of Sean's protective embrace. As Rose watched, her mother stood taller, a new determination in her expression.

"Children, we have things that must be done."

Rose stood stiffly. "Mother, what are we going to do without Papa?" Everyone turned to look at her. "What are we going to do?"

She threw her hands over her face and sobbed. Her mother's arms came around her.

"We are strong people, Rose. Your Papa taught each of you to stand on your own, and he knew that you would be okay. It's time for him to go."

Sean and Carrie joined in the hug, and they all stood for a few quiet moments and let the tears fall.

Then Maggie held her children out at arm's length. "I love each of you. Now let's be the kind of people your father expects us to be. Sean, run to Brother Hansen's house and let him know that your father has returned to his eternal home."

"I'll go." Miles stepped into the room, and Rose realized he had probably been standing outside the door the whole time. A wave of gratitude rushed over her. He had allowed the family their final moments without intruding. She smiled at him through her tears.

"Thank you, Miles," Maggie said.

Rose heard him run down the steps and then shut the kitchen door as he left. She turned to look at her father.

Maggie smoothed the hair off her husband's forehead. "We will be okay, children. We don't have a choice."

Watching her mother's calm acceptance of Papa's death didn't help Rose feel any better. She turned from a scene she would never forget, then fled down the stairs and into the dark night.

Rose felt lost among all the neighbors in her home. Everyone her father had influenced as a bishop and neighbor had come to express his or her condolences. Rose was grateful winter had finally given way to spring so the doors and windows could be left open, allowing the air to circulate.

She sat next to Granny Sterling and listened to the story about how Granny and Grandpa crossed the endless miles to enter the Salt Lake Valley, bringing their two children with them. Granny told anyone who would listen how tragic it was to outlive your only son. Aunt Mary winked at Rose as Granny proceeded to tell everyone how hard she had it living with her spinster daughter.

Rose hid a grin and walked into the kitchen to look out the open window. Melting snow dripped from the roof, and she could see some life starting to poke out of the earth. Trees were starting to turn green, and buds were forming on the lilac bush. Rose breathed deeply of the warm spring air.

Movement by the barn caught her eye, and Rose knew Karl was hiding in the yard. He would never come in to see her mother, and Rose didn't blame him. *If only he would try harder to make my family like him,* she thought. After she grabbed her shawl off the hook, Rose slipped out the back door and walked towards the creek that ran through her father's property.

As she turned her face toward the rays of the early spring sun, Rose felt a freshness in the air. The two days since her father's death had been awful, and she felt herself wanting to cry at the oddest moments. Little things, like eating Papa's favorite biscuits for breakfast or putting on the brooch he brought back from Salt Lake for her last year, made her eyes water and her nose tingle.

Maggie said with time things would get better, and the spring weather was a testament to that. With their combined labors, the farm would continue to produce. Someday, Sean, Rose, and Carrie would each get married and raise another generation to love the land. Rose felt sure her father was watching them and encouraging them.

She picked her way across the muddy yard. The creek was running high and fast from all the melting snow. Rose could see her tree and knew Karl would be waiting for her behind the wide, old trunk. His whistle pierced the air and she whistled back. With a giggle, she stepped around the tree. Her mother would be horrified if she heard her whistling, even if she wasn't very good at it.

Karl grabbed her in a tight embrace. "I've missed you."

Putting her hand on his cheek, Rose smiled. "You better let me go. There are too many people at the house right now and I would hate to get caught. My brother would be furious with me."

"I'm sorry I didn't attend the funeral." Karl sat on a tree stump. "I didn't want to upset anyone."

"I saw you in the trees. I know you were there for me even if nobody else does." Rose sighed. "This is so hard. Losing Papa is bad enough, but we can't even be together in public."

"I talked to your father like I said I would." Karl stood and took Rose's hand. "He gave me his blessing, so we can go ahead and get married now."

Rose frowned. "I talked to him the day he died and he was still begging me to stop seeing you. If he had given you his blessing, he would have said something."

"Your father must have been confused in his last days," Karl insisted.

"Papa was never confused, even at the end. His body gave up, but his mind remained as sharp as it ever was." Rose felt the tears slip down her cheeks and wondered how she could even have tears left. "Why are you lying to me, Karl?"

The silence stood between them as tangible as the oak tree they hid behind. Birds sang in the background as Rose looked at her first love and felt something fresh and daring turn into something stale. Karl looked at her in stony silence.

"Please, Karl. Tell me you loved me and I wasn't just a way to get into a prominent family," Rose pled. But even as she said the words, she heard the lack of conviction in her own voice. Guilt washed over her as she thought about her own motives in pursuing Karl.

"Are you insulting my family now?" His white-blond hair stood out against his red, angry face. "Just because my father is a good-for-nothing drunk, doesn't make your family any better than mine. Who do you think you are, anyway?"

Rose gasped. "Karl, I am just repeating what you've said many times to me."

"I will speak of my family any way I want, but you have no right." Karl pushed Rose's hands away as she reached for him. "If I am not good enough for you, maybe I should just leave."

"Karl, you're twisting my words. I think you're just right the way you are." But as she said the words, she didn't believe them herself anymore. She had seen too many of his volatile moods. Still, she didn't want it to end like this.

"Stop, Rose. Just stop." His face twisted in hurt and anger. "You never did love me. I don't know why I didn't see it before." Then, Karl turned and stalked away through the woods.

Rose stood in stunned silence. All the excitement of trying to win Karl's love had drained away and left her empty. His words hit hard because they were true. She had thought she could learn to love him, but now she realized she didn't even *like* him. She folded her arms, then walked around the tree and looked back at her home. The sun was beginning to set, and the sky glowed with soft shades that reminded her of her sister's watercolors.

People were climbing into their wagons and leaving the house. The front door stood open and Rose could see her mother silhouetted in the doorway. The house framed her and Rose knew that the house was just that—a frame. The people inside made it a home, and even without her father, they would still love and take care of each other.

Suddenly Karl didn't seem so important. "I don't need him," she said out loud.

"That's good to know." The familiar voice stopped Rose's progress toward the house.

"Miles." Rose tried to be angry at him, but she couldn't find a reason. "How long have you been watching me?"

"Long enough to know you were with Karl again." Miles took Rose by the arm and turned her to face him. "Are you trying to break your mother's heart for the second time in a week?"

"Of course not." Rose shook her arm free. "What gives you the right to challenge me? You aren't even family."

Miles winced. "Maybe not, but I think I have a pretty good idea of how Sean and your mother will react when they hear about this latest meeting."

"Please don't tell them." She looked back toward the house. Her mother still stood in the doorway. "I won't see him again, I promise."

Miles studied her eyes. "I believe you this time, because I heard what he said."

Mortified, Rose turned so Miles couldn't see her face. He patted her on the shoulder as if she were a small child and walked away, leaving her alone.

8

"Where have you been?" Maggie frowned as Rose approached the house. All the guests had gone and the house was quiet. "Surely I have taught you better than to run around the countryside like a boy, especially on the day of your father's funeral."

"I guess that's my fault, Mama," Sean said. He came out of the house and put his arm around the two women. "You shouldn't have let her tag along with me so much when she was younger. I guess we'll never see her grow out of those unladylike ways, will we?"

Maggie smiled wearily. "I'm glad to see a little spirit back in the two of you." She closed the door and took Rose's hand. "Sean, would you please find Carrie and tell her I want to speak to all of you in the parlor? We need to talk about the future."

The future. Rose grimaced. She had hoped for a few days to just pretend nothing else would change. Rose drew the drapes in the window and sat in a chair close to the fire. She loved the parlor. Her mother's embroidery hung on the walls. The fireplace was flanked by two armchairs, but Maggie sat in the rocker that stood between them, in the warmest spot. Peter had placed it there as a place of honor so Maggie could keep cozy as she did her needlework. Rose looked at the chair across from her and could picture her father as he sat every evening reading his scriptures or a newspaper.

The sound of her siblings entering the room broke her reverie. Carrie looked glum, and Sean was teasing her in his best effort to coax a smile from his baby sister. "Come on. If you don't smile, there won't be a boy within a hundred miles that will be interested in courting you."

With a grin, Rose joined in the teasing. "Sean, stop picking on Carrie. She is still a child and has many years before the suitors will come calling."

"Oh, stop it, Rose. Karl was chasing you when you were younger than I am," Carrie said.

Rose frowned at the mention of her former suitor. She hadn't told her mother yet about this afternoon's conversation with Karl.

"Children, please sit so we can talk." Maggie looked up as the front door closed, and Rose knew her mother had seen Miles trying to slip up the stairs without being noticed. "Miles, please join us."

He stood for a moment as if trying to find his place in the family, then sat near the door, declining the invitation to sit closer. He observed them with his arms folded across his chest, and Rose flinched at the sadness in his eyes. She watched him out of the corner of her eye, wondering why he needed to sit in on a family discussion anyway.

Sean took his father's armchair and Carrie sat on the floor so she could lean her head on her mother's lap.

"Sean, your father was so proud of you," Maggie began. "Seeing you home from a successful mission gave him so much energy these last few months." She patted Sean's arm. "Carrie and Rose, you are beautiful, accomplished young women. Your father adored both of you and would have done anything to see you happy."

Rose felt uneasy as she sensed something big coming— something that would change their lives far more than even the death of her beloved father.

"Children, you know we received a letter from President Lorenzo Snow several months ago, asking us to go to Canada and settle in the District of Alberta. We hoped that with time, your father's health would improve. I still feel as if we should still do as the prophet asked."

Rose's jaw dropped. "How can we leave our beautiful home without father to help us?"

"Your father and I talked about this at length before he died." Maggie paused and looked at each of her children. "We've already sold the farm. It is too late in the season to get everything together and leave now, but I hope we can go north next spring."

Rose jumped from her seat. "No, Mama. This is our home, and Papa loved this land."

"Sit down." Maggie's voice was stern. She got up from her seat and stood in front of the fireplace. "You know Sean had already decided to go. He will gather a few things and go at the end of the month. Without him, we can't keep up a farm the way your father would have liked."

"Then Sean should stay in Utah. He should think about the family first." Rose stood with her fists clenched.

"Rose, sit down," her mother repeated.

Rose took a deep breath and slowly sank into her chair.

"It's already done. The farm is no longer ours. Sean is going to Canada, and in a year's time, we will join him there. Your father wanted us to obey the call of the prophet even if he couldn't."

Carrie started to cry. "Mama, what will we do until then?"

"The money from the sale of the farm will help us get supplies together. There should be enough left so if we are very careful we will get by until it is time to go."

"Where will we live, if we can't live in our home?" Rose wondered.

"Aunt Jane has invited us to stay with her and Granny Sterling. She could use a little help with your grandmother, and it will be cheaper for us to live with her and contribute what we can, than to find another house."

Aunt Jane's home was small, and Rose knew that moving three extra bodies in would be trying for all of them.

Maggie turned to look at Rose. "I received a telegram from your Uncle Daniel a few days ago. He would like you to come up and help out on his farm in Montana. I think it's the best thing right now." A tear rolled down her mother's cheek.

The blood drained from Rose's face. "No, Mama. I can't leave."

"Why do they want Rose?" Sean asked.

"Uncle Daniel's wife, Abbie, is expecting a child. She has a difficult time when she is pregnant and they could use some help."

"Mama, we've never even met Uncle Daniel or his wife," Carrie said.

"They settled in Montana when you were still very young, but Daniel is a good man and I think it could be at least a temporary solution to our problem. They live near Miles's family, so you would know someone." Maggie stood and put her hand on Rose's shoulder.

Rose glared at Miles, who seemed unsurprised at the announcement. She felt her world fall away beneath her feet. "I can't believe you would send me away." She took her mother's hand and pleaded, "Mama, if this is about Karl, I don't love him and I won't see him again. I promise I'll behave better."

"Oh, Rose," Maggie said, "this isn't about your behavior. It isn't even about Karl."

"I'm glad I won't have to teach him a lesson, though," Sean said under his breath.

"Sean, please." His mother motioned for him to leave the room.

"Come on, Carrie," he said. "Let's go make some hot cocoa."

Carrie stood and looked back at Rose, but Sean took Carrie's hand. "Let them talk it out."

"Mama, why me?" Rose asked. "Carrie would love the adventure."

"She's younger and still needs my instruction and guidance. You are a very capable young woman. You'll be fine, and it won't be forever."

"I can't do it." Rose started to cry.

Her mother answered with tears of her own. She took her daughter in her arms and held her as she sobbed.

"Don't cry, dearest Rose. I know this is hard, but don't cry. I just can't bear it." Maggie sighed. "Truth is, you are old enough to make your own decisions. Your father hoped you would find a nice young man to marry before he died, but he was still very proud of your desire to get an education. You could stay here and find a teaching job, but Uncle Daniel really needs the help, and we have always taught you children that family comes first."

Even as she fought against the decision, Rose knew she would do whatever was best for the family. "When do I leave?"

"At the end of the month. I'll send a telegram so they will know when to expect you." Maggie held Rose's shoulders and leaned back to look in her eyes. "Everything will work out."

Miles unfolded himself from the chair and approached the women. "Mrs. Sterling, Sean and Rose can travel with me as far as Great Falls. Then Sean will have to continue on to Alberta on his own. It would be my pleasure to accompany Rose the rest of the way to Spring Creek. I was getting ready to return home anyway. She shouldn't travel by herself in such rough country."

"She shouldn't travel unaccompanied with only a young man to watch over her, either," Maggie said. "I really see no other option, though."

"It will be like traveling with my little sister." Miles looked at Rose. "My very annoying little sister."

9

Rose decided the wagon could have been a rickety, old donkey cart for all the comfort it provided. The conveyance bounced and swayed over every bump on the well-worn trail. Besides the grizzled old driver, she and Miles were the only passengers, and since there wasn't anyone she wanted to talk to, she simply closed her eyes and shut out everything around her. The train ride to Great Falls hadn't been too bad, but the last leg of the journey to Spring Creek promised to give her a shaking she wouldn't soon forget.

She could still picture her mother standing in the doorway of the family home on the day of the funeral. Her mind embellished the simple spring day, and her memory now held a vision of spring lilacs and summer roses. Sometimes she could even imagine her father, with his arms around his wife. But the house was no longer theirs, and Carrie and her mother were settled in with Aunt Jane and Granny. Rose already missed Sean, even though they had parted only hours before. Life was moving forward, and Rose would need to keep up.

The last week at home had been a busy one. Everything was given away or packed, and Rose's mother insisted that the house be left spotless. She didn't want the new owner thinking she was a slovenly housewife. Carrie had become ill partway through the week, so her help was minimal at best. Rose sighed.

Saying good-bye to her family had been hard enough without mentioning she was getting ill herself. It would never do to give her mother something new to worry about as she sent her oldest daughter to live with people who were almost strangers. When she had awoke that morning, Rose's head had pounded and her throat ached. Now the warm air was dry and Rose wished for a glass of cool water to sooth the irritation.

Looking out over the land, Rose saw a wide expanse of prairie, the grasses dotted with wildflowers that reminded her of her mother's garden at home. The mountains on the horizon shone purple in the morning light, and a line of trees and greenery marked out the path of a river. As Rose pictured the creek that ran through the farm, she remembered playing in the fast-moving water with her brother and sister. She already missed the mountains in Utah.

"Are you all right, Rose?" Miles asked.

"I'm just tired." She watched him as he turned his attention back to the wagon driver. Miles called the man "Beans" and appeared to be enjoying their conversation. Rose listened as the two men caught up on all the local news, but she found it hard to follow discussions about people she didn't know. She tried her best to be pleasant company, but her father's last request that she consider Miles as a suitor made it hard to focus on casual conversation.

She found him attractive but knew a relationship couldn't be built entirely on physical attraction. Yet whenever he looked at her, he seemed to see beneath the lighthearted façade she put on.

The sympathy in his look led her to believe he understood her somehow.

Tears that always hovered near the surface threatened to spill again, and it took all of Rose's strength to hold them back. She didn't want Miles to know her worries and fears, and she especially didn't want him to know how poorly she had treated Karl. She deserved the harsh way Karl had treated her the day of the funeral. Her father had been right, but she would never be able to tell him that. She had used Karl, and she'd hurt him and her family in the process.

Holding tighter to the bag Aunt Jane had made for her, Rose pictured the contents again—a small watercolor of her mother's treasured lilacs that Carrie had painted for her, a packet of hard candy from Sean, a new crocheted collar from her mother to liven up some of her dresses, and most importantly, a letter from her father written just before he died. The mere presence of the items comforted Rose.

Dust from the trail made a fine layer on her skin, and she attempted to brush it off with her gloved hand. She swallowed and found her throat still hurt. An invisible weight pressed on her chest, forcing her against the hard wooden seat of the wagon, and she hugged her jacket tighter to herself to try to ward off the chills. The land outside slowly passed by, and as hard as she tried to stay awake, she couldn't keep her heavy eyelids from closing.

"I'm so tired," she said as she awoke several hours later. She straightened quickly when she realized she had been sleeping with her head on Miles's shoulder. "This is an awful way to travel. My teeth feel like they are going to fall out of my head all at once. I wonder what Uncle Daniel will think when he meets his toothless niece for the first time."

Miles didn't even grin. "Your Uncle Daniel will find you quite presentable, and you are very capable around the house."

"Lots o' young men will find her more than presentable," Beans said with a chuckle.

Rose raised her eyebrows and shifted a little closer to Miles.

"Take it easy," Miles said. "She's hasn't come to Spring Creek to find a husband."

Beans chuckled. "She don't have to be lookin'. There'll be a few lookin' at her, though. Maybe I might if I weren't so old and had a few of my own teeth left."

Rose smiled at the crusty old man.

"Guess I'll grab a few minutes o' rest myself. Still a ways to go." He winked at her. Then he handed the reins to Miles and pulled his hat over his eyes.

As Beans snored softly, Rose wondered if she should tell Miles how awful she felt. *After all, he is a doctor,* she mused. But the idea left her head almost as quickly as it had appeared. After all, what could he do to help her, out here in the middle of nowhere? She forced herself to think of something else. "Well, I hope being in such uncivilized country doesn't mean there are no social gatherings. I hate the thought of being a slave to my uncle without any diversions."

"Daniel is the last person to treat someone as a slave, and I don't think you should judge our way of life without giving it a chance. We are building a country out here. There is plenty to keep us busy without the social refinement you seem to think so necessary, but we still have time for dances and picnics." Miles motioned with his hand. "You see all that land out there? Once you set foot on it you will learn to love it, and it will have a hold on you."

The softness of Miles's voice surprised Rose. She looked up at him and watched his eyes focus on something in the distance as he continued to tell her how the beauty and wildness of the place outweighed the hardships. She almost liked him when he talked that way.

"This really is where you belong, isn't it?" she asked. "Why did you become a doctor rather than work your family's land?"

"Dr. McTavish got too old. We advertised but could find no one who wanted to move to this untamed land. Learning comes easy to me, and I love people and want to help, so it made sense for me to be the one to go back east and get an education."

"Didn't Boston lure you in with its refinements and entertainments?"

"I didn't go to have fun—I went to become a doctor." A faraway look settled in Miles's eyes. "Your Uncle Daniel has always been a good friend to me. He never attends the Church meetings in town, but he is the most Christlike person I know. When Daniel found out I was going to Boston, he told me he had a nephew serving a mission for his church there and suggested I look him up. When I met your brother, I ended up coming home with far more education than I went for."

"Why did you stay in Logan so long if you love your home so much?"

Miles's brow furrowed. "I don't know. I wanted to meet Sean's family." He leaned forward, resting his elbows on his knees. "I just felt that I had to be in Utah. Maybe your father needed me, or maybe I needed to be around the Saints for a little while before I returned to Spring Creek, where the Weavers are the only other members of the Church. Whatever the reason, it feels like the right time to return home now. I just hope I can help my family see the light of the gospel."

Rose shut her eyes. "Well, I wish you luck."

"Are you all right?" Miles asked again.

She hadn't mentioned how terrible she felt, and she wasn't about to beg his sympathy now. "I'm just tired."

Soon, she fell into a deep sleep. She dreamed she couldn't wake up and that someone kept tugging on her, trying to rouse her.

Now the jostling was no longer a part of her dreams, and the insistent voice continued. "Miss, you must wake up." She tried to open her eyes, but she was so tired. "Miss?"

"She's burning up," another voice said.

"Help me get her trunk down and we'll take her into the station."

Rose felt strong arms lift her. Then the blackness closed in again.

Miles lifted the young woman out of the wagon and noticed how slight her body was in his arms. Her trunk was unceremoniously dumped in the dust, and Beans saluted Miles as he drove away. After shifting Rose in his arms, Miles walked toward the small wooden building that had once served as a stopping point for the stage line, which no longer ran. The afternoon sun warmed Miles's back as he looked down the main street of Spring Creek. With several new buildings, the town had grown in his absence, but it still held the welcoming feel of home.

Miles heard footsteps behind him and turned to see a gold badge flashing in the afternoon sun. "Hello, Sheriff."

"What have we here? Looks like you may need a little help." The sheriff took a long look at Rose's still body, and Miles could see the desire in the man's eyes. "So who might you be?" the sheriff asked, glancing up to meet Miles's eyes.

"Miles Crandall. I've been attending school in Boston."

"Ah, yes. The whole town has been looking forward to your arrival." The sheriff put a hand to his badge and absently polished the metal with his thumb. "So you arrive carrying your first patient. Are you afraid people will be reluctant to see a young doctor?" He smiled at his own joke.

"She's a friend of the family and is Daniel Weaver's niece. Old Beans' driving was a little much for her." Miles held Rose a little closer, hoping to shield her from the sheriff's lustful stare.

"Miles Crandall. What are you doing, young man?"

He looked over the sheriff's shoulder to see Rose's uncle approaching. "Hello," Miles said with relief, adjusting the girl in his arms.

Daniel stepped around the sheriff and stopped. "Why, that's got to be Rose. What's going on here?"

"She seemed tired most of the way and slept through the rough wagon ride. We couldn't wake her up when we stopped, and you know old Beans—he wasn't going to hold up his run even for a sick girl."

"Well, now, since you don't have a clinic yet, I think we could find a room at the hotel, and one of the girls could take care of her until she is on her feet again." The sheriff picked up Rose's bags. "Just follow me and we'll get her settled."

Daniel ignored the sheriff and put his hand on Rose's forehead. "What am I going to do with her now? If I take her home like this, Abbie will have a royal fit."

"Well, we won't be taking her to any hotel, that's for sure." Miles laid Rose's still form in the bed of Daniel's wagon.

Daniel retrieved the bags from the sheriff. "You're the doctor, Miles. What do you suggest?"

"Yes, Mr. Crandall, what do you suggest?" The sheriff rubbed his thumb across his badge as if to draw attention to his authority.

"I just got back and I had thought to get a clinic built first."

"Well, you're the only doctor we've got. If you can assure me she won't get all of us sick, I guess I could risk upsetting Abbie." Daniel took off his hat and rubbed his balding head. "She isn't going to like this one bit."

"I don't know what's wrong with Rose. I've spent hours with her this week and didn't suspect anything more than a little tiredness. Carrie did come down with a cold before we left, and Rose may have caught that." Miles pulled a pieced quilt out of one of his bags and wrapped it around Rose. "I don't even have an office in town yet. Pa and the boys were going to help me build something this summer."

"How were you getting home today?" Daniel asked. "I don't see anyone here to meet you."

Miles looked sheepish. "I couldn't wait to get out of the city and get back to the wide open spaces of home. My train wasn't supposed to leave until next week, but I changed my ticket as a favor to your sister Maggie and came early." Daniel and Miles loaded Rose's trunks into the wagon. "I hoped I could catch a ride with you."

"Get your stuff in here and I'll drop you at your place," Daniel said with a smile.

Miles carefully arranged his trunks in the wagon next to Rose, hoping they would help steady her during the short trip. He checked her once more, but she was still unconscious. Her breathing was steady but he was worried about her. Daniel and Miles quickly climbed onto the wagon, and the horses started to carry them home. The sheriff stood in the dust, still polishing his badge.

Rose felt a warm, fragrant breeze across her face as movement rocked her into consciousness. There was a weight on her shoulders that wasn't there earlier. She could hear men's voices, but when she opened her eyes to see who it was, the light hurt her head too much. "I'm so cold."

She hadn't realized she had spoken the words aloud until the wagon stopped and she felt a gentle hand on her cheek. "Rose, are you awake?"

She shivered. "I'm so cold."

Miles frowned. "She's even hotter than she was at the station. She needs a warm bed and lots of rest. Daniel, let's take her to my place. You know Ma will be more than happy to take her in until she gets better."

"Well, it would make it easier on Abbie, with her expecting and all. Just until Rose is better, of course. We don't want to be a burden on you."

"Of course." Miles settled next to Rose in the wagon bed. "Neither would she."

10

Rose woke to the sun streaming across the bed where she lay in an entirely unfamiliar room. Calico curtains hung in the window, and a beautiful pieced quilt lay over the back of a rocking chair next to the bed. Another quilt covered her, and a colorful braided rug took up a large part of the floor. Rose lay still and wondered where she was and why she couldn't remember getting there.

Her nose started to tingle and she knew tears were next. *Did Uncle Daniel meet me at the wagon?* She remembered having a headache and feeling ill, but nothing else.

The door opened and Rose held her breath but didn't look up. She heard someone walk to the side of the bed and then felt a warm hand touch her head. "Are you awake, Rose?"

Turning, Rose saw a handsome face she knew well. The large brown eyes looked at her with such compassion that the tears overflowed and spilled down her cheeks.

"Miles, where am I?" she asked hoarsely.

"Let me get you a drink." From a pitcher on the bedside table, he poured some water in a glass.

She tried to sit up but found her arms shaking underneath her weight and her head reeling with dizziness.

"Take it easy. You've been ill. We tried to keep liquids in you, but you haven't had anything solid to eat for at least four days." Miles supported her head and held the glass to her lips so she could sip the cool water.

"Where am I?" she asked again.

"Spring Creek. At my parents' ranch."

"Where is Uncle Daniel?" Rose pulled the quilt closer around her shoulders.

A small woman entered the room and smiled warmly at her.

"Let me answer your questions, dear, since Miles seems to be a little on the slow side this morning." She patted him on the shoulder. "Go get some breakfast, Son. I think you've done your part here. Now it's my turn."

Miles shrugged and gave Rose a wink. Then he was gone.

"All right, dear. Now we need to get some food down you and get you better. Let me help you." The woman put an extra pillow behind Rose's back and rearranged the quilts. "I'm Elizabeth Crandall, and that big lug is my oldest son."

Elizabeth looked at her with large blue eyes surrounded by laugh lines. Rose envied the older woman's sleek blond hair and reached up to brush back her own stray curls. Once Elizabeth had Rose sitting up in bed, she placed a tray holding a bowl of hot porridge on Rose's lap.

"You most likely won't want too much this morning, but we'll fill you up eventually." Elizabeth pulled the rocking chair close.

"Where is Uncle Daniel?" Rose slowly took a bite of the oatmeal and felt her stomach rumble.

"Well, dear, you got sick during your journey. By the time you got to Spring Creek, Miles couldn't rouse you. Do you remember being unwell?"

"I think so, but I don't recall anything else." Rose wrinkled her brow and put the spoon down. "Didn't Uncle Daniel meet me? What am I going to do?"

Elizabeth picked up the spoon and handed it back to Rose. "Now you just calm yourself, dear. Daniel did meet you—he just arrived a little late. Of course, that is understandable, since Beans is always late anyway. When Daniel saw how ill you were, he was quite concerned, and he knew Abbie wouldn't take kindly to him bringing a sick girl home. Miles offered to bring you here until you recovered so you could meet your aunt on better terms."

"He just let Miles take me? You aren't even family." Rose pushed the tray away. "It's bad enough getting sent away from my home, but now I'm with strangers and I have no way to pay you for your kindness." Rose wished she could simply disappear.

Elizabeth stood up to her full height. "You listen here, young lady. I won't take any payment for doing a Christian thing. You were alone and ill. I would hope if my daughter were in the same situation, somebody would do the same for her."

"I'm sorry. I—" The tears wouldn't stop and Rose covered her face with her hands. "I just miss my mother," she sobbed, "and she seems so far away."

"There, there now." Elizabeth wrapped her arms around Rose and held her. "These things happen and there is no harm done. I dare say you had someone watching over you. How else do you explain traveling here with the new Spring Creek doctor?"

Rose heard the pride in the woman's voice. "Mama knew he would make sure I arrived safely."

"Well, he certainly did that," Elizabeth replied. "He is such a capable and responsible young man. Spring Creek has been without a doctor since old Doc McTavish passed on, and that was over two years ago. It is so nice to see that in addition to getting a good education, Miles has met such a nice girl."

"Oh, no," Rose protested. "I'm like an annoying little sister to him."

"We'll see," Elizabeth said just before she left the room.

Rose wanted to get up and follow her to clear up any misunderstanding about Rose's relationship with her son, but her body wouldn't cooperate and she drifted off to sleep.

When she woke up, Rose carefully got out of bed. Her trunks sat in the corner and she replaced her nightgown with a brown woolen skirt and a calico blouse. She heard a quiet knock on the door and opened it to find a young woman about her own age. She looked like a younger Elizabeth, blond and blue-eyed. Rose could only assume Miles got his dark good looks from his father.

"Hi, I'm Katie. Mama says if you feel like getting up you should come eat supper with us." Katie held her hand out in invitation.

Rose hesitated in the doorway, but a growling stomach made her decision for her. "That would be nice."

"Don't worry about the boys," Katie advised. "They're loud but harmless."

"I'm a little nervous to meet everyone." Rose blushed. "I'm not so good around strangers."

"The more you get to know us, the stranger we'll be." Katie laughed. "You may as well jump in with both feet." She took Rose's hand and led her down the stairs and into the cozy kitchen.

A fire burned in the stone fireplace on the far wall. The large table, set for the evening meal, dominated the center of the room. Rose counted eight places. Elizabeth rushed across the room with a basket of rolls in one hand and a pot of coffee in the other. A cast iron stove held steaming pots, and the aroma of cooking food was just about the sweetest thing Rose could remember in a long time.

Katie led her to a chair on the side of the table furthest from the door. "You better sit here so you are out of the way when the stampede begins."

"Come stir the stew, Katie," Elizabeth said, then sat next to Rose. "How are you feeling?"

"I'm hungry," Rose admitted.

"Well, of course you are." Elizabeth smiled and patted Rose's hand. "The boys will be in shortly."

Miles saw Rose sitting at the table when he came in the door, and she looked more than a little lost as the room filled with people. He tried to imagine how she must view his family. Elizabeth moved through the room as if there weren't anyone else in her way, smiling at her husband and laughing with the boys. Miles realized how much he had missed his mother and her no-nonsense ways.

Katie stood at the stove, stirring sauce for the cake. Watching her, Miles realized how much she had grown up in his absence. Some lucky young man would try to steal his sister's heart, but whether Katie could ever find anyone good enough for her family remained to be seen. Miles grinned as he imagined some innocent young man trying to get past three overprotective brothers.

Then there were the twins. Opposites in so many ways, they barely appeared to come from the same family. Ian's short stature and blond hair made him resemble his mother, and he could make anyone laugh with his teasing and jokes. Zach stood tall and dark like his father and older brother, his hair just lighter than Miles's. Katie always said Zach got all the looks and her other brothers would just have to get by. Miles knew she was teasing, but all the girls did follow Zach around.

Miles noticed Rose staring at Zach and sighed. Though Zach was good looking and a hard worker, he had a troublesome streak as well. Miles quickly sat next to Rose, hoping to distract her.

"How is my patient?" he asked.

Rose looked at him as if coming out of a trance. "Is that your brother?"

"Yes, that's Zach. The other one is Ian. You know Mother and Katie. Pa will be in soon with Abe, the hired hand. That's all of us."

"I think that's enough," Rose said.

"You didn't answer my question. How are you feeling?"

"A little better." Rose looked at her hands. "Thank you for helping me."

"You're welcome."

As she looked up at him, he allowed himself to get lost in her eyes and knew his heart would never be the same. All the extra time he'd spent watching over her during her illness had somehow changed him. He should continue caring for her like an adopted sister; after all, he had promised her mother to look after her. But he couldn't deny the attraction he felt for Rose.

"Thank you all for taking me into your home," she said suddenly, blushing and looking away from Miles. "I'm feeling so much better."

Just then, John Crandall entered the room and sat at the head of the table. "Can't help feeling better when Elizabeth is the cook."

"Hear, hear!" Ian said cheerily.

The laughter resumed as the Crandalls ate their evening meal. Katie chattered on about dances, socials, and introducing Rose to everyone, and Ian teased his brothers about an incident on the ranch earlier that day. Miles ate silently, only responding to the occasional question from his mother or father. He caught Rose casting discreet glances at Zach and wondered how long it would take for the two to become a couple.

"Rose, tell us about your family," Zach said.

Other conversations stopped as the entire family waited for her answer. "I grew up in the Cache Valley with my sister Carrie and my brother Sean. My father farmed. He passed away last month."

Miles's heart clenched at the pain in her eyes.

Rose continued, "Mother sent me here to help Uncle Daniel and his family. I'll go back to live with my mother after Aunt Abbie has her baby and Uncle Daniel doesn't need me anymore."

"Well, I hope he needs you for a long time," Zach said.

Rose froze, her mug halfway between her mouth and the table. Miles could tell the casual comment had surprised her.

"We hear it is thanks to your brother that my son has joined your strange religion." John looked at Miles.

Grateful for the change in subject, but hoping Rose wouldn't sense the tension between him and his father, Miles responded softly, "Not now, Pa, please."

"I just don't understand a religion that won't even let a man enjoy a cup of coffee with his dessert." John punctuated his statement with a loud slurp from his mug. "Now my son sits there and drinks milk like a toddler."

Miles shrugged and took an equally loud sip from his mug of milk. He heard Rose giggle as she grabbed the napkin from her lap and pretended to wipe her mouth.

"Maybe you'll find a reason to stay here in Spring Creek," Zach said, changing the subject and winking at her.

Rose's cheeks flushed a deep scarlet and Miles knew he wasn't the only one in the room who couldn't take his eyes off her. The subject of the Mormon Church frustrated his father and bored his brother, but he could see Rose didn't want the conversation to focus on her or her future, either. She pushed her plate away.

"Please excuse me." Rose stood, hardly noticing Miles right beside her, pulling her chair out. "Thank you, Elizabeth. The meal was wonderful."

"Excuse me, Pa. I think I'll just go make sure our patient is as well as she thinks she is." Miles followed her out of the room. "May I suggest some fresh air?"

"As my doctor?" Rose challenged.

As much as he wanted to answer differently, he knew what she expected. "Yes, of course." Miles took one of his mother's shawls from the peg by the front door. "Come outside and sit with me for a while."

Rose sat on the porch swing, using her foot to put it in motion as the crisp, fragrant night air invigorated her with every breath. She could hear the murmur of conversation coming from inside the house, but outside it was peaceful. In the distance, the mountains shaded the horizon, silhouetted by the sunset. The house sat in the center of a large yard surrounded by a fence made of pine logs. A freshly tilled and planted garden showed signs of spring, the green shoots just starting to push their way through the dark soil.

"It sure is pretty here."

"It beats the city." Miles sat on the step and rested his chin on his hand.

Rose closed her eyes and hugged the shawl closer around her, letting the motion of the swing carry her back to memories of her own family, especially her father. *He would love it here,* she thought. She missed her family and wondered what they were doing at that moment. Granny probably loved the chance to nag someone other than Aunt Jane every day. Rose smiled and imagined Carrie nagging Granny right back.

Looking up, Rose watched Miles stare at the distant mountains and wondered how John Crandall really felt about the Mormons. When she was a child, her father had made sure she knew the story of the persecution of the Saints and the exodus to the Salt Lake Valley. Her birth happened long after the family had settled in the Valley, so she hadn't experienced the same trials as her parents who had crossed the plains as children. But she knew the Latter-day Saints still weren't accepted everywhere.

Rose wanted to talk to Miles, but he was so quiet she didn't know what to say. Her experiences with Karl had only made her leery of men. She thought of him and how he showered her with wildflower bouquets and stolen kisses. She had pushed and prodded him until he swept her off her feet and promised her the world, offering to marry her and love her forever. And she had encouraged it all. But those promises had shattered around her, and they were both to blame.

The moment Zach had walked into the kitchen for dinner, he had impressed her with his youthful good looks and easygoing personality. She had stared at him, knowing it would give him the wrong idea, but unable to stop herself. He had stared back and Rose recognized the glint in his eyes. She knew he would be more than willing to entertain her until she could return to her family. *After all, I'm almost twenty-one, and Mama wants me to marry.* It was all so complicated. How did someone know whom to encourage and whom to avoid?

A soft sound came from Miles and Rose realized he was dozing, his head leaning against the rail on the porch. He had probably been working hard with his family as well as doctoring her. No wonder he slept. The tense lines in his face had relaxed and his hand rested on his leg, his long fingers curled around his knee. She watched him. Before he had died, her father had asked Rose to give Miles a chance as a suitor. But how could she do that if he never paid her any mind? She decided she would only think of him as an older brother to fill in for Sean. As soon as she felt better, she could move out of this house and away from its variety of menfolk.

Rose sighed and tried to get out of the swing quietly. It creaked slightly and Miles stood up, tripping on the stair. Rose held out her hand to steady him, stifling a giggle. "Guess you need sleep as well, Doctor."

He studied her and Rose knew that for a moment, she wasn't just a patient. The short nap had left his emotions unguarded, for she saw a tenderness in his gaze that surprised her. "Is it safe to walk around the yard?" she asked.

He shrugged. "Safe enough. Once in a while we see wild animals, but the dogs will warn us if something comes."

"You're tired," she said as he walked down the steps. "I can walk on my own."

"It's getting dark and the ground is unfamiliar." He held out his arm for her.

She took his elbow. They descended the porch steps and she stepped carefully onto the path, her legs shaking beneath her. It would take time to completely recover from the illness.

They walked in silence. "I see why you love this place," she finally said as they followed the fence line encircling the house. "I don't understand how you could want to give this up."

"As much as I love the old place, working in the community interests me more than ranching. I feel most satisfied when I help someone else." They went around a mud puddle and stopped in front of the porch. "But I'll never completely give up ranching, even if it is just helping my pa and brothers once in a while."

Rose realized she still held tightly to his arm, so she dropped her hand quickly to her side. "I wish you luck, Miles."

"I wish you luck too."

"Why do I need luck?" Slowly ascending the stairs, she waited for the answer.

"You have never met Abbie Weaver, have you?"

11

Miles's comment about Abbie kept Rose awake half the night worrying about what the next several months would hold. She wished her mother weren't so far away, but no amount of wishing would change things now.

As soon as the sky began to grow light, Rose got out of bed and packed her bags. She walked to the window, looked out on the yard, and watched the sun rise over the tops of the trees. The smell of bacon cooking made her stomach rumble in anticipation.

A knock on the door startled her. "Come in." She turned from the window as Katie entered the room.

"Oh, you're already up. Ma sent me to see if you would like to join us for breakfast. If you aren't feeling up to the company, I can bring you a tray." Then Katie noticed the trunks packed and sitting in the center of the room. She folded her arms in front of her and looked at Rose. "Are you coming?"

"Yes, I'll be just a minute." She waited until Katie left and then checked her hair in the mirror once more. She tucked a stray curl back into her braid, straightened her collar, and sighed. She still looked pale, and dark circles shadowed her eyes. Feeling so worn out didn't give her any confidence in her ability to help her aunt and uncle, but nothing could be done about that. She would just have to do her best.

As she approached the kitchen, she heard Katie talking to Miles. She entered the room as he pushed his chair back from the table and stood. "She won't be going anywhere for a few days," he said just before he noticed Rose standing in the doorway. He turned to look at her. "You need to get your strength back before you go to the Weavers'. You know how much energy it takes to care for a home, and you're not ready to take it on yet."

"I won't argue." Rose sat in the chair Zach held out for her. "I do feel rather done in, and the morning is just getting started."

Miles raised his eyebrows and looked closely at her. She ignored him and smiled as she nodded at Elizabeth. "Breakfast smells wonderful."

Zach sat across from her and began to eat, hardly taking his eyes from her. "I'll finish up the fence in the south pasture today," he said to the other men. "Abe'll come with me."

Ian and John announced their plans to check cattle on another part of the ranch. The men ate quickly, then excused themselves, leaving the table in a state of disarray. Before he followed his brothers outside, Miles instructed Rose to rest. But the work on the ranch wouldn't stop for her, and she wondered how to occupy herself as she waited for the okay to move to her uncle's home. Soon the meal was over and despite Rose's intentions to help clean the dishes, she found herself sitting at the table as the chores went on around her. Elizabeth and Katie worked smoothly together, and Rose felt sure she would just be in the way.

"I'm so pleased you are going to stay with us a few more days," Katie said. "The minute Miles brought you home, I knew we could become great friends."

Rose stood. "I'm glad you'll have me, but I don't want to be a burden anymore. Is there anything I can do to help?"

Elizabeth chuckled. "The garden needs to be weeded and the chicken coop needs to be cleaned, but if I let you at any of those jobs, I'll never hear the end of it. Miles insists that you don't overexert yourself."

"She could help me with my quilt," Katie said, putting an arm around Rose and looking at her mother with a pleading expression.

"That's a fine idea. But don't think I'll let you out of the weed-pulling for too many days." Elizabeth put on her bonnet and tied the strings beneath her chin. "I'm sure by tomorrow we can convince Miles that a little sun might do our guest some good." She grinned at the girls and then left them on their own.

Katie stood and tugged Rose up behind her. "We'll definitely be outside tomorrow. Ma will have her way on that one."

"I don't mind," Rose said quietly. "Mama always kept a big garden and I enjoyed helping her with it."

"Well, not today. Come in the other room with me. I've been piecing this quilt for ages. I just have a little more to do and then Ma will plan a quilting bee so we can finish it." Katie motioned to the rocking chair and pulled a stool next to it, then reached into the large sewing basket on the floor and pulled out several squares of colorful fabric. "Ma tried to talk me into a double wedding-ring design, but this Jacob's ladder pattern has always been my favorite."

Rose took the needle Katie handed her and threaded it. Then she took several of the pieces and started sewing them together with tiny stitches. She bent to the task and hardly noticed Katie watching her.

"You do beautiful work," Katie said when Rose held out the two squares she had joined.

"Mama is quite accomplished with a needle. She insisted Carrie and I work hard to learn the skill, although nothing I've done rivals Mama's work." Rose picked up a new set of squares and began joining them.

Katie started working on her own pieces and the two girls sat in companionable silence. Rose finished another set and handed them to her new friend. Finally, she spoke the question that had been bothering her all night. "Last night, Miles said something about my Aunt Abbie that didn't make any sense. I've never met her and know nothing about her, but he seems to think living there will be a challenge."

"I don't know Mrs. Weaver all that well." Katie shrugged. "Whenever I see her, she seems to be scowling at something. Her little girl, Diana, is the cutest thing, though. Sometimes Daniel will bring her and Tommy over for some of Ma's cookies. I don't think Mrs. Weaver spends much time in the kitchen. She's not from around here, so I don't know much else about her. Ma thinks she puts on airs and considers herself better than the rest of us, but don't tell Ma I told you that."

Rose's mother's reminder not to gossip flashed through her mind. "I'm sure I'll be just fine."

"Well, Pa sent Abe down to the Weavers' with a message that you had mostly recovered but would stay a little longer. I don't expect she will reply, but I'm sure Daniel will show up today to say hi. He's been by several times already just to check on you."

"I look forward to that. Mama always talks fondly about Uncle Daniel." Rose put another set of squares together and began stitching.

"You've never met your uncle, either?"

Rose shook her head. "We get occasional letters from him, but he hasn't been to Utah since I was just a little girl. I don't remember him at all. But Mama sure loves him."

"You'll like Daniel. He always seems ready to laugh, though living with Mrs. Weaver, I'm not sure what he has to laugh about." Katie looked up at Rose and blushed. "Sorry. I shouldn't have said that."

Rose smiled and put down her sewing. "Well, Mama always preached against gossip, but I appreciate the advance warning anyway." She leaned back in the chair and looked out the window. The ranch house sat at the edge of a grove of trees, and Rose could see robins hopping around underneath the branches. "I need some fresh air."

"Let's take the sewing onto the veranda. We can get a little more done before Ma needs help with dinner."

The two girls moved to the porch swing and sewed quietly. Rose couldn't help but wonder about her aunt and what she would expect of her. She didn't have long to think about it, because Katie's prediction came true. Just after the noon meal, Rose's uncle showed up and they were properly introduced.

Daniel greeted her with a grin and a twinkle in his eyes as he scooped her into a hug. "You look just like your mother."

When he released her, she studied his face and decided he looked a little like Mama too. Rose smiled. Katie had been right. Daniel seemed like a kind, good-hearted man, and she liked him right away. Rose listened as he talked to Elizabeth and ate a handful of gingersnap cookies.

"You're too good to me," he said as he swallowed the last bite.

Elizabeth shooed him away. "I'll be out in the yard if you need me." She motioned for Katie to follow her.

Daniel sat across from Rose at the table and sighed, his smile vanishing briefly. Rose glimpsed a man who hid behind good humor, but deep in his eyes she saw how tired he was. "Are you all right?" she asked.

"Just worn out. I'm trying so hard to keep up with everything at the house, but one man just can't do it all. Abbie hasn't been well for some time and needs all the help she can get. I'm so glad you agreed to come."

Rose wondered guiltily if her mother had told Daniel about her reluctance to move to Montana. It didn't really matter, she decided. She was here and he seemed to need the help, so she would make the best of it.

12

It had been three days since Rose had come out of her fever, and she had spent every waking moment with Katie and Elizabeth. Though she found him handsome and fun to talk to, Rose had decided to avoid Zach and his flirtations. She didn't want to form any romantic attachments in Montana; she only wanted the months to pass quickly so she could return to her family.

Before he left to visit patients that morning, Miles told Rose she was well enough to move to the Weavers'. Rose had hoped John would take her, but Zach had offered, so his father assigned him to drive her and her trunks to Daniel's. Katie insisted on coming with them, which pleased Rose.

The day before Rose's departure, Katie had shown her the path between the Crandall and Weaver homes, a shortcut that took only twelve minutes to walk. The road between the two houses wound through the hills and took twenty minutes by horse and wagon in good weather.

Now, on their way to the Weavers' house, Katie squeezed Rose's hand. Rose was glad her new friend understood her nervousness about meeting her aunt. She had been a little surprised that her aunt hadn't come by to meet her. She hadn't expected royal treatment, but she knew if she were in Abbie's situation, she would want to meet the niece who would be moving into her home.

Katie will be a good friend, she thought as she squeezed Katie's hand in return. Rose still missed her family and suspected that, even though time would ease the pain of being sent away, she would always long to see her mother. Elizabeth made a good temporary substitute, however, and Rose had appreciated her mothering ways as she recovered from her illness. Katie seemed excited to have a friend live so close, and Miles was determined to watch over her like a brother. Zach was still a bit of a mystery, and her avoidance of him hadn't stopped him from watching her whenever they were in the same room.

She put away her thoughts of the Crandalls and turned her focus to the road before her. Zach stopped the wagon in front of a small, simple house. The garden plot blended into the landscape—a small rectangle of lumpy soil and choking weeds—and begged for attention. A tabby cat lounged on the steps, and a little girl sat under a tree, playing with a rag doll.

Zach helped his sister down from the wagon and held his hand out for Rose. Katie started up the walk and called to the little girl, "Hello, Diana. Where is your mother?"

Diana looked up from her doll and shrugged. "In the house, I guess."

"Come on. Zach will bring your bags." Katie took Rose's hand and led her up the stairs into the log house.

Rose took in her new home. Like the outside of the home, the inside was simple, with nothing to make it cozy or homey. The curtains consisted of old flour sacks nailed to the window frames. The floors were bare except for one braided rug under the rocking chair, and even though the supper hour was near, the house was cold and she smelled nothing cooking.

"Mrs. Weaver, it's Katie Crandall. Are you here?" Katie waited and listened.

"Maybe she's asleep," Rose said.

"Maybe."

At a shuffling noise behind her, Rose turned to see Diana standing in the doorway. Rose guessed her to be about five years old. Her wispy, blond hair looked uncombed, and brown spots on her knees revealed that she had knelt in the dirt. Rose was surprised at how dirty and unkempt the child looked. *Wherever Aunt Abbie is, she has obviously let this child run wild.*

When Daniel had come to the Crandalls' home and talked of his family, Rose felt sure he did his best to care for them and that he loved them dearly. It didn't make sense that such a good father would let his daughter look like this.

"Sometimes she goes for a walk," the little girl said.

"Where is your father or Tommy?" Katie crouched down to look Diana in the eyes.

"Working."

Katie sighed. "Well, this is some greeting you get. I wish I could stay for a while."

"I'll be fine. You better get back."

They walked outside. "See ya soon, Rose. It isn't that far of a walk if you cut through the pastures."

Rose hugged her friend. "Thanks, Katie. I'll be fine."

"Do I get a hug too?" Zach asked.

"Stop it." Katie pulled his hat over his eyes and winked at Rose. "Bye." She waved as Zach jumped into the wagon and they pulled out of the yard.

Rose stood for a few moments in the doorway, shutting her eyes to imagine living at the Crandall ranch. At least she knew where she stood in the midst of the warm family who had taken her in and made her feel at home. As Rose turned and looked in the house again, wondering what to do first, she saw a woman standing in the center of the room.

They just stared at each other for a moment. Rose knew this was Aunt Abbie because the woman's blouse stretched over a stomach that bulged with new life. Her long, blond hair hung in a thick braid over one shoulder, the color like golden straw. Rose thought she saw fear in the other woman's eyes.

"Hi. You must be Aunt Abbie."

"You must be recovered from your illness."

Rose bit off the rest of her cheery greeting. "I'm feeling much better, thank you. Miles says it will take a little while for me to get back my full strength after the pneumonia."

"I'll show you your bed." The pregnant woman turned and led Rose through a door on the other side of the room.

Diana ran ahead of her. "You get to share a room with me."

"We really don't have much extra space," Abbie said. "I don't know what Daniel was thinking when he asked your mother to send you."

The venom in her aunt's voice stunned Rose. Despite the warnings, she expected more of a welcome than this. Following Diana into the small bedroom, she saw that its sparseness matched the rest of the house. A plain cloth quilt covered each of the twin beds—no fancy piecing or quilting, just solid tufts of wool holding the layers together. The same type of flour sacks that covered the windows in the kitchen covered the bedroom window.

"I hope I can be of some help to you, Aunt Abbie."

"Well, you may as well make yourself busy. I have a headache and Daniel will be hungry when he comes in from the fields." With that, Abbie disappeared back into her bedroom.

"I'll go wait for Papa." Diana gave Rose a timid smile, then took her doll back out under the tree.

Rose stood by herself in the silent, lonely kitchen and wondered again if being sent to Montana was some sort of punishment. Whatever the reason, she couldn't change the situation, and she was getting hungry too. Grateful her mother had taught her to cook, Rose searched the kitchen for something to make for supper. The least she could do was work hard until she figured out a way to return to Utah.

By the time Daniel and Tommy arrived home for their evening meal, thick slices of ham sizzled on the griddle and the kitchen smelled like homemade bread. Tommy ran into the house with the exuberance of a young boy.

"What smells so good? Things ain't smelled so good in a long time." Tommy peeked in the pan and then tried to take a slice of steaming bread from the cutting board.

"Go wash up, Son." Daniel smiled at Rose. "Sorry for Tommy's lack of manners. I think I worked a good appetite into him today.

"Hello, Uncle Daniel."

"Now enough with that. Just Daniel will be fine. I'm not much older than you, and 'Uncle Daniel' sounds strange." He sat at the table and pulled Diana onto his knee.

"Sure am glad to see you looking well, Rose. You scared me the first time I saw you. I thought I would have to write another letter to your mother."

"That's done with, thank goodness" Rose said. "I'm feeling much better. The Crandalls are nice people."

"You won't find any better in all of Spring Creek, that's for sure."

Tommy came back into the room with his mother in tow. "Doesn't it look good, Mama?"

Daniel reached for his wife's hand and gave it a squeeze. "Abbie hasn't felt well in a while. We've been keeping things pretty simple. This is a real treat tonight."

They sat around the table. Daniel said a prayer and then the children dug in, but Rose held back and observed the dynamics of the family. Diana watched and copied everything her brother said and did. Nine-year-old Tommy ate enough for two children and told tales about his day through a full mouth, even though his mother glared at him every time he did. Daniel listened to his children and enjoyed their banter. Every so often he would reach over to touch Abbie on the shoulder or squeeze her hand.

Clearly, Daniel loved his wife. Rose thought of the hints from the Crandalls that Abbie was difficult, and she thought of her own cool reception at the house. Rose's mother had always taught her that God made everyone good in some way, but some people made it more difficult to find than others. *If Mama can find the positive in everyone,* Rose decided, *so can I.* Maybe she could even find something to like about Abbie Weaver.

Rose's arms ached. They had been immersed in the laundry water for hours. Abbie never gave her instructions for the day's work, so Rose finally decided to follow her mother's routine for a good spring cleaning. Rose stripped all the beds and took the flour sacks down from the windows. Everything needed a good washing and airing.

With Diana's help she hauled the big washtub outside and filled it with water heated on the stove. Rose scrubbed until her hands were raw, glad she had some of her mother's special hand cream packed away in her trunk. Sometimes she looked up to see Abbie watching her through the kitchen window. The first few times, Rose waved, but her aunt would turn quickly and give no response. Rose finally just ignored the other woman and continued with the housework.

On her first evening in the home, after Abbie shut herself in the bedroom, Rose asked Daniel what was expected of her.

"Do whatever you see needs to be done. If you are anything like your mother, you know how to keep a home running smoothly. Diana could use some company as well." He sighed. "Abbie has difficult pregnancies. If you could just take over some of her responsibilities, my mind would be more at ease."

"What can I do to befriend her? She's so distant."

"I don't know how you can reach her, but I think you will find a way," Daniel said, patting Rose's hand. "She really does care about how things go here."

The house had been neglected for some time but Rose finally felt like she was catching up. She quickly established a routine for chores and even enlisted Diana's help. Rose had hoped to see some glimmer of friendship or even appreciation from Abbie, but several days passed without a change. She found herself missing her new friends and wishing Katie would visit.

After she hung the last of the towels on the clothesline, Rose sought out her aunt to make another attempt at breaking through her shell. She found Abbie sitting on the rocking chair in the front room, but her courage failed as she looked at the obviously miserable woman. At a loss for words, Rose got her sewing basket from the bedroom. She went back into the front room and sat in the straight-back chair next to the fireplace. Many items of clothing needed mending, but they all hung wet on the line, so Rose pulled out her half-finished sampler.

Her mother had been teaching her a new stitch, and Rose focused her mind on the motion of the needle and thread. The sampler she had been working on for months finally took shape before her eyes. Just last week she had added her father's name, and she paused and ran her finger over the fine stitches. *How would Papa handle this situation?* She closed her eyes and prayed for an answer, but her mind remained blank. She pulled a new color of thread from her basket and felt a movement at her shoulder.

Diana stood behind the chair, her eyes wide with curiosity. "You make such pretty things."

Rose took Diana's hand and guided the child onto her lap. "Sit here and I will show you." She took a few stitches and then gave her the needle. "You try."

"Oh, no, I'll wreck it!"

"No, Diana, I'll hold your fingers and help you." Rose gently held the child's small hand in her own. "Pinch the thread into the needle and don't let it slip out."

"She's too young for that," Abbie said.

"Let her try. She can't hurt anything."

Abbie stood and fled the room, slamming the bedroom door behind her.

Rose stared at the closed door and sighed. Daniel and the children seemed to appreciate her, though Diana fought her every time Rose tried to wash her face. If only Rose could figure out what made Abbie so prickly.

She took a deep breath and took Diana's hand again. "I was four when my mother first taught me my stitches." Rose helped Diana move the needle up and down through the fabric. "Would you like to learn?"

The look of excitement on her cousin's face was all the answer Rose needed. She found a new piece of fabric for Diana and helped her plan a simple sampler. They worked at it until Rose needed to start preparing for supper. The little girl continued sewing on her new project as Rose started cooking.

When the outside door swung open an hour later, Diana jumped off her chair. "Papa, look what Rose is teaching me." She carefully carried the fabric to her father.

"Diana, let your papa wash up for dinner." Rose put the last bowl of soup on the table. "You may show him after you eat."

"It's okay. Let me see." Scooping his little girl off the floor, he made the appropriate comments on her work and then deposited her in front of the sewing basket. "On Friday the town is getting together to raise a new clinic for Miles. It will be a good chance for you to meet some of the young people."

"Will you be going?" Rose asked.

Daniel washed his hands and dried them on a tea towel. "The kids love these events and I need to help with the clinic. We'll make a day of it. Abbie won't come, though."

"Are you sure you don't need me to stay here?"

"You aren't supposed to be tied to this house every minute. A day out will be good for you."

Abbie entered the room at that moment, so Daniel stood to hold out a chair for his wife. "Besides that, my sister would never forgive me if I made her daughter a prisoner in my home." He winked at her and then bowed his head to bless the meal.

Rose couldn't concentrate on the words her uncle spoke. She did need to take some time away from the house, and she missed the frequent social activities she had enjoyed in Logan. "I think I would like to go," she said after the prayer ended. She took the plate of bread and passed it around the table.

"Then it's settled. Why don't we walk over to the Crandalls' tomorrow? Diana loves to visit Elizabeth."

Diana started bouncing on her chair. "Mrs. Crandall makes the bestest cookies in the whole world."

Throughout the exchange, Abbie hadn't said a word. Daniel reached over and squeezed her hand and she gave him a tight smile in return. Rose's heart ached for the lonely woman sitting across the table from her. *There must be something I can do to befriend her,* she thought. But the smile she aimed at her aunt faltered under the other woman's cool glare.

13

The day dawned bright and clear, and Diana and Rose hurried through their chores. Diana insisted it would be a picnic, so Rose packed some sandwiches and dried apples in a basket.

Tommy was waiting by the barn when they came outside. "Pa said we should start walking and he will catch up. I know the way."

Rose turned and looked back at the house. Holding a small bouquet of wildflowers in one hand, Daniel opened the kitchen door and went into the house. Rose hoped this small act of love would leave Abbie in a better mood when they returned from their day out.

The path through the pasture curved along the edge of a fast-running creek. The birds sang as if they were trying to outdo each other, one louder than the other. Butterflies fluttered through the meadow, and bees hummed their own sweet tune. Rose couldn't keep it inside her anymore. She started singing out of pure joy. It was an old hymn she learned from her father when she was a child. Even though she felt a little short of breath and knew she had more recovering to do before her voice was back to normal, she let the music flow and stopped in the middle of the path just to feel the emotion of the words.

When the song ended, she opened her eyes to find three pairs of eyes staring at her in wonder.

"That was like an angel, Papa," Diana said in awe.

Rose blushed, realizing she had lost herself in front of three people who were almost strangers. Ducking her head, she started walking quickly in the direction of the Crandalls'.

"Rose."

She stopped but didn't turn around. She had never enjoyed singing for anyone other than her immediate family. Occasionally, she had sung to the Primary class she had taught, but they sang along with her, which made it easier. Just being out of the house and surrounded by God's beautiful creations helped her forget she wasn't alone, and she had sung her joy without thinking.

"That's the most beautiful thing I ever heard," Daniel said.

"Thank you." Rose started walking again. "I forgot where I was. I didn't realize you had caught up with us."

"Does it make a difference that I heard it?"

Rose shrugged. "It's just easier to sing in front of children. I used to sing with Mama and Carrie. Papa liked to hear us harmonize together."

"Don't ever be embarrassed about that voice. You remind me of Maggie. Your mother has a beautiful voice too. If you could sing for Abbie sometime, I think she would love it. She misses that type of thing."

The thought terrified Rose. Singing for Abbie would be more difficult than singing for anyone else. Rose could just imagine her aunt's cool glare. "I'll think about it," she said as they continued walking.

When they entered the Crandalls' yard, Katie ran out the door. "Rose, I'm so glad you came today."

Rose smiled at Katie's enthusiasm. The girl's round face beamed through a smattering of freckles, and Rose found her energy contagious. They headed toward the river and left the others standing there.

Miles watched Katie haul Rose off. He marveled that anyone could keep up with his little sister. Rose giggled as they ran past him into the grove behind the house. He heard his mother welcome Daniel and the children into the kitchen for some cookies and decided he would rather follow the girls. He could always tell Rose he was checking on her health.

The path curved around the edge of the pasture. His father always called the small stand of trees on the edge of the creek "the grove" because he said it reminded him of his childhood home. The voices of the girls carried through the trees, and Miles was about to make himself known when he heard a male voice join the conversation.

Clearly, Zach was smitten with Rose. Since the day she left for the Weavers', he'd kept up a constant conversation about her. He was always dreaming about her black hair and the way it framed her beautiful face. Miles heard reference to her emerald green eyes at least once a day, and while he thought her eyes were more the color of moss on the north side of trees, "emerald" sounded so much better.

As quietly as he had come, Miles turned and walked back to the house. He and his brothers had always been taught to respect each other, and they would never fight over a woman. This was the only time in his life he had been tempted to do so, but he knew he wouldn't win, not with Zach's good looks and charm.

He would simply have to banish Rose from his thoughts. Surely at the clinic-raising the next day there would be some young woman who would find Miles acceptably handsome and who would appreciate his quiet personality. Yet he wanted to marry a Church member, and his options in Spring Creek were limited. Perhaps he had made the wrong decision in returning to Montana. He had seen what he wanted in Rose, and he wondered if it would have been easier if he had never met her.

One moment they were in the grove, two girls giggling about dresses and boys, and the next minute Zach was there. Rose wanted to leave before he started his flirting, but then she remembered her resolve to be friendly toward him. The three young people visited for several minutes. Then Zach hit his forehead with his hand.

"Katie, I'm supposed to tell you that Ma wants you to come to the house and make some sandwiches. Daniel invited us on a picnic this afternoon."

"All right. Rose, are you coming?" Katie asked.

"She'll be along soon." He pushed Katie lightly on the arm. "I'll make sure she gets back."

With her eyes, Rose pleaded with Katie not to leave, but Katie winked at the two of them and then hurried down the path toward the house. Rose sighed heavily.

Zach looked at her until she met his eyes. "It does just make you want to breathe deeply—the summer air I mean."

Rose blushed. *He is so handsome.* But Karl had been handsome, too. Then she remembered her determination to befriend Zach. "Will you be in town building the clinic tomorrow?"

"Sure," he answered.

Walking to the bank of the creek, Rose stooped to pick a wildflower growing in the grass. "This reminds me of home. We had a creek running through our property. As a girl I fell in the water far more often than my mother thought ladylike."

Zach took a few steps and grasped her elbow. "I certainly would enjoy tomorrow more if the prettiest girl in Spring Creek agreed to give me a few dances after all the work is done."

Rose gave him her most innocent smile. "I'm sure Katie will dance with you, although there must be other young men she would rather spend the evening with."

"I meant you," Zach said. "There isn't anyone else I would rather dance with."

The intensity in his voice stunned her into silence. He gazed into her eyes, then squeezed her arm gently and walked away. Silence fell around Rose, and her heart pounded. She couldn't decide if Zach made her nervous enough to stay away from the dance or excited enough to wish the event was tonight. *No attachments,* she reminded herself.

As Rose headed back down the path, she heard doors close at the house and voices outside. Tommy called her name. They were probably looking for her so they could leave on their picnic. She hurried toward the ranch house and saw the group waiting for her.

"Elizabeth, aren't you coming with us?" she asked when she saw the older woman still standing in the doorway.

"This is an outing for you young people. Besides, how often do I get the house to myself?" Elizabeth gave Rose a hug. "Now you all go enjoy yourselves."

Miles held back as the group left the yard. He felt tempted to remain behind, yet it would be cowardly to be afraid of such a slip of a girl. He waited until everyone else had passed through the gate before he started after them. As much as he wanted to race to Rose's side and escort her up the trail, he knew his brother would see it as a challenge. *If I don't show any interest, Zach will get distracted by someone else sooner or later.*

He only hoped Rose had learned from her experiences with Karl to be more careful in her choice of suitors. Next time she might choose someone more stable, someone she had known over time and could trust. Still, Miles knew Rose saw him only as a substitute brother and as her doctor, and perhaps she was right. Perhaps he was overprotective of her because she seemed so alone and because of his friendship with her brother. Perhaps Miles's feelings for her weren't romantic at all. At this thought, he lagged behind the group even more.

"Where are we going?" Rose asked after they had walked for a few minutes.

Daniel led the way with Diana on his shoulders. "There's a beautiful picnic spot about halfway between our houses. The water is slow in that part of the river, and it's a perfect place for wading and fishing."

Tommy tried to match his stride with Zach's long legs. "It's the best place for swimming, Rose, although you're a girl so you probably can't learn."

She chuckled. "For your information, my father made sure my sister and I could both swim very well."

"Tommy, you know I can swim, don't you?" Katie asked.

"Aw, that's just cuz you have a bunch of brothers. Myra Jenkins doesn't swim. Her mother told her it isn't ladylike."

Daniel smiled at his son. "When do you take the time to talk to Myra? Aren't you a little young to start courting?"

The men all laughed at Tommy, and soon he joined in.

They reached the picnic spot and Katie spread out the quilt she'd brought.

Zach took Tommy by the shoulder. "Hey, let's see if we can catch some fish. You coming, Ian?"

The men headed to the river, leaving the girls to set out the meal. Miles sat on a log and watched the men walk into the trees. Rose didn't seem to notice him, although Katie gave him a funny look.

"I hope they catch a few. That would make for a nice meal tonight." Katie took Diana's hand. "Let's go pick some wildflowers to make our picnic pretty."

Rose hesitated. "You two go ahead. I'm a little tired from all that walking."

Miles jumped up and reached her side in an instant. "Are you feeling all right?"

"As a doctor or a friend?"

"How about a little of both?" He took her hand and led her to the log. She sat and lifted her face to the sun. Miles drank in her beauty and wished again that Zach's intentions weren't quite so obvious. Putting away the tender emotions, he stood a little straighter and assumed his best doctor voice.

"How are you really feeling?" he asked.

"Much better. Sometimes I get a little short of breath or cough a little."

"The effects of the pneumonia will bother you for a while yet." He put his hand across her forehead, relishing the excuse to be close to her. "Keeping busy will do you good, but sit down and rest when you need to. You'll continue to feel better with a little more time."

"You really seem to care about people. Spring Creek is lucky to have you."

"Even though I couldn't heal your father?"

Rose blinked away tears, and Miles caught one with his finger as it spilled down her cheek.

"I'm sorry I treated you so poorly," she said. "You stayed in Utah longer than you planned just to help my family, and then you took care of me. You're a great doctor."

"Thank you and you're welcome." Miles let his hand fall to his side, then squatted and straightened a corner of the picnic cloth.

Rose fiddled with her skirt. "Zach said there's a dance after the building is done tomorrow night."

"I suppose. There isn't much else in the way of entertainment around here."

Rose stood and spread her arms wide. Then she spun around. "It seems so long since I've danced. I love music." She tipped her head at him and twirled again. Her black hair flashed almost blue in the spring sunlight, and Miles caught the clean scent of it as it brushed his face. She laughed and spun again, this time losing her balance. As she fell against him, he felt his arms wrap around her of their own accord.

She stopped and held perfectly still. Miles didn't dare move for fear of losing the moment. He looked into her eyes and felt the world stop turning. Unsure if his heart still beat, he realized he was holding his breath. This certainly wasn't the annoying little sister he claimed her to be, but he wasn't sure what that meant for either of them.

"Miles, if you want to dance with me," Rose said quietly, "you just have to ask."

Tommy shattered the moment as he raced back to the picnic blanket. "Hey, Miles, you should have come with us. Ian and Papa caught a huge bunch of fish. They're really biting today. Zach is grumpy cuz he didn't catch any."

Miles released Rose and squatted near Tommy. "Did you?"

"Just one but it got away."

Watching Rose walk toward the others, Miles replied, "I know what you mean, Tommy. I know what you mean."

Diana opened the picnic basket and began handing out the sandwiches. Everyone laughed, joked, and enjoyed the good food. Sitting silently and speaking only when spoken to, Rose watched the two families interact. Zach followed her every movement with his eyes, and she got the impression he felt she would be crazy not to return his interest.

Rose knew if she wanted him, he would be hers. She could be married by Christmas, and her mother wouldn't have to worry about her anymore. Plus, it would be fun to have a beau again. She smiled as Zach started a game of tag with Tommy. *Maybe I should give him more of a chance.* Miles had joined the Church, and with a little patience, the rest of his family might see the truth. If Zach was baptized, there would be nothing to keep them apart. *You're being silly,* Rose told herself, taking another bite of her sandwich. *He is only flirting with you, and here you are planning a wedding.* Her cheeks flushed and she hoped no one noticed the sudden rush of color.

Her real confusion came in regards to Miles, who now watched his brothers entertain their young neighbor. In her mind, he was still her doctor. He was also her brother's friend, so she was comfortable with him and thought of him almost as an extra brother. When she had ended up in his arms, the sudden rush of emotion had surprised her. Even the time or two she had let Karl kiss her had been nothing compared to gazing into Miles's eyes for just those few moments.

118

14

"Lift her up, boys!" Rose heard as she watched the south wall of the clinic rise. She loved how buildings grew when men worked together in harmony. They obviously enjoyed the task, she thought as the sound of pounding hammers almost drowned out the cadence of their voices. Zach handed a plank of wood to Miles, and the two brothers laughed at something Ian said. Daniel waved at Rose.

She stood behind an overladen table and inhaled deeply. The mingled aromas of the food made her mouth water. Moving her apple pie half an inch over and re-adjusting another bowl kept her looking busy, but she knew she couldn't hide behind the table the entire day. In the churchyard next door, a quilt took shape under the able hands of the married women.

Katie's voice floated on the breeze, tempting Rose's gaze away from the circle of older women. Her friend stood in the midst of a group of young women her own age, their attention held by the young men working on the clinic. Rose hid a grin behind her hand. They were so obvious! Katie called to her, so Rose started walking toward the group of young women. She hadn't had many female friends, and as she approached the group, she struggled to think of something clever to say. Katie saw her coming and grabbed her elbow, steering her to the center of the group.

"Everyone, meet Rose." Katie started motioning toward individual girls and introducing them. One caught Rose's attention. "This is Mary Larson. She's sweet on Ian."

Mary blushed but didn't deny it. Rose smiled at her. The focus of the girls shifted, and Rose turned to see who had distracted them.

His badge flashed in the sunlight, and he rubbed his thumb across it, cutting the glare momentarily. "Good afternoon." The sheriff bowed slightly, and one of the girls giggled. "Thought I might say hello before I lend a hand on the doctor's fine new clinic." He continued to polish the star on his shirt with absentminded determination.

Rose wondered what he hoped to remove from the already shiny metal. She looked around for Diana, hoping to find a reason to escape, but the little girl played happily underneath the quilt with a friend. The other young women began flirting with the sheriff, but he ignored their attentions.

"Miss Sterling, you are looking much better than when we first met," he said.

"We've met?"

"I happened to be at the station when you arrived with Beans and Dr. Crandall."

"I'm sorry, I don't remember."

Small lines appeared around his eyes as he smiled at her. He removed his hat and tipped his head toward her. "Arthur Gibb."

She smiled at him. "It's nice to meet you."

His gaze didn't leave Rose as he addressed the group. "I just thought I would pass on some information. We will be looking for a new schoolteacher in the fall. I thought there might be one or two of you who might be interested in the position." He tipped his hat at them and headed for the building.

The girls began discussing the sheriff and how they thought he would make a good catch. Rose paid little attention to the comments about his good looks and eligibility, but his announcement had caught her interest. Abbie's baby would be born before the summer was out, and Rose had her teacher's certificate. As much as she wanted to return to Utah as soon as possible, Rose didn't want to be a burden on Aunt Jane and Granny. This job might be just the answer.

A shout from the building caught her attention and she looked to see the men descending the ladders. After a long day of work, the building stood new and proud in the deepening shadows. The women gathered around their husbands and sons, applauding. Miles stood in the center of the crowd as men slapped him on the back. With a clinic, his doctoring could begin in earnest.

Rose knew his practice would be much easier now that he could stay in town and be available for patients. She brushed a tear away as she realized she wouldn't see him nearly as often. *It's like missing my brother all over again,* she told herself as she watched Miles accept congratulations from the members of the community.

Soon, the group of young women dispersed and Rose found herself standing alone. Daniel came toward her, and she forced Miles to the back of her mind.

"Abbie's tired and would rather not stay for the evening festivities," he said. "She would like to leave as soon as the children have finished eating."

That morning her aunt had surprised them all, declaring she would attend the raising after all. Rose looked around and spotted Abbie sitting under a tree with eyes closed and an empty plate on her lap. "I'll get my shawl and ask Elizabeth if she will bring our dishes home."

"You don't have to come now. The Crandalls can bring you later." Daniel held up his hand as Rose shook her head. "Don't. You deserve some fun. I'll see you later." He waved as he walked away, collecting Diana and Tommy as he made his way through the crowd.

"Guess Daniel told you we'd take you home." Zach took Rose's arm, his eyes gleaming with pleasure.

"It looks like you'll get your dance after all," she said.

The musicians tuned their instruments and the lively sound of a fiddle beckoned the young people to the schoolhouse where the dance would be held. The one-room school brought back memories of Rose's own education. The stove in the corner, which would hold a warm fire during the cold winter months, now stood empty, but enough people filled the room so a fire wasn't needed, even on the cool spring night. The girls were a garden of color, and as they swayed and dipped to the music, Rose closed her eyes and pictured the wildflowers on the hill behind Daniel's house.

"Is there anyone you wish would court you?"

Katie shrugged. "Most of the men seem like brothers because I grew up with them.

"I'm surprised. I thought you would have beaus all over the place."

"I think they still see me as the little sister of their friends. The new sheriff is awfully handsome, though."

"He seems a little old." Rose smoothed her floral skirt and adjusted her mother's lace collar around her neck. She knew the yards of cotton fabric in the green skirt would swirl nicely with the music. Katie wore a yellow dress that reminded Rose of the flower that dotted the hills, which Miles called buffalo beans.

"I don't think he's that old. Anyway, it just makes him so much more mature than the boys just out of school." Katie adjusted a curl in Rose's hair. "You're going to be the belle of the ball."

Rose shook her head, but an hour later, her feet were starting to hurt. Most of the young men appreciated having someone new to dance with, and she didn't have a chance to sit down. Each time it looked like she would get to rest her feet, Zach would be at her side, ready to take another twirl around the floor. She enjoyed flirting with all the young men, but it hurt more than she wanted to admit that Miles hadn't asked her to dance even once.

She remembered her father's advice to choose her companions more carefully. Only Miles shared her family's beliefs, and Rose knew anything less would disappoint them. But she would only be in Montana for a year, and then she would go to Canada and marry a nice Mormon boy. A brief pang of regret over Karl dampened her mood for a moment.

Just then, Sheriff Gibb entered the room and made his way across the floor. Rose curtsied as he held his hand out to her. "May I have this dance, Miss Sterling?" He led her to the dance floor. "So how are you enjoying our little town?"

She tried to figure out whether his eyes were gray or brown. "It seems nice enough. I haven't been in town much, since I have been recovering from my illness." Hazel, she finally decided as the light shifted. Her hand rested on his shoulder and she could feel the muscles under his shirt flex as he moved her around the dance floor.

"It is nice to know those Mormons let some of their young women escape," he said suddenly.

"Is that what people are saying?"

"Don't worry, ma'am. People aren't discussing your religion. But I am the sheriff and I make it a point of knowing what goes on in my town. When I heard our doctor took a long detour through Utah on his way home from Boston, I got suspicious and did a little checking. I will have to keep my eyes on him just to make sure he understands that around here we believe in one woman per man."

"We don't practice polygamy anymore, Sheriff Gibb."

"Yes, I had heard that, but we can never be too careful." He laughed at the expression on her face. "I'm just kidding with you, Miss Sterling." Looking away, he said, "If you ever need anything, please don't hesitate to call on me."

They danced in silence until Zach interrupted them with a tap on the sheriff's shoulder. "May I cut in?" Zach proceeded to whirl Rose out of Arthur Gibb's arms and across the dance floor.

In spite of her frustration with Zach, who had cut in on several of her dance partners, Rose laughed. She was actually rather relieved not to be dancing with Sheriff Gibb anymore, after their odd conversation.

Only two weeks before, Rose had come into town ill and unaware of her surroundings. Now she looked around at all the people she'd met while the men built the clinic, and she grinned at some of Katie's friends. She tried to smile up at Zach, but her legs started to shake and an invisible band around her chest seemed to tighten as her breathing became more constricted. The previous day's walking had caused a sharp pain every time she inhaled, but even though Miles regularly asked about her health, she hadn't said anything. She hadn't wanted to worry him on such a glorious afternoon.

The music ended. Zach offered his elbow and she took it, holding on tight to keep her balance. She was worn out, but as they approached Miles and Katie, Rose hoped Miles would ask her to dance. But when he looked at them, some unspoken communication passed between the two brothers. Miles turned on his heel and stalked off as Zach pulled her closer in a possessive grip. Rose yanked her arm from him.

Obviously startled, Zach let go.

"Sorry," she said, putting her hand to her throat. "I need to sit for a few minutes."

Zach quickly led her outside into the cool evening air, then turned to her. "You could have just said something to me quietly instead of making a scene. You do realize half of the people in the room were looking at us."

"Isn't that what you wanted, Zach? You take every dance you can with me, and even when I am enjoying a rare turn around the floor with someone else, you have to come along and cut in."

He grimaced at her words. "Sorry. I thought you liked me."

"I didn't mean to lead you on. It was just so nice to listen to the music and to dance again. I have to keep reminding myself that I'm just here until my family comes to get me, so I can't get tangled up with anyone right now."

"Not even the sheriff? He couldn't seem to keep his eyes off you."

Rose concentrated on breathing. "I think he is just interested in me because I'm new in town."

"Stay away from him, Rose." Zach guided her to a bench against the side of the school building. "He's always at the saloons and has been seen frequently with the women who work there. He doesn't seem like someone your father or brother would approve of."

"Well, my father isn't here to give me advice, and I don't need it from you." The words came from Rose's lips almost of their own accord. "A sheriff would have to be in unseemly places sometimes to keep an eye on things." Dizziness blurred her vision, and Rose put a hand to her chest. "Zach, I really need to sit down. I'm not feeling very well."

He steadied her as she sat on the bench. "Do you want me to get Miles?" He lifted her chin and looked closely at her.

"No." She leaned against the rough white walls of the schoolhouse.

"It's getting cool out here. I'll get your wrap for you."

Zach wasn't so bad, Rose thought. He just had so much enthusiasm he forgot to think of anything else except what involved him at the moment. His attention really was flattering, but it didn't seem real to her. She wrapped her arms around her shoulders and tried not to shiver. The hot spring days still gave way to cool night air. The tightness in her chest eased, but her head still felt like she had been holding her breath. Rose hoped Zach would get back soon with her shawl. Trying to slow everything down, she closed her eyes.

A gentle and familiar voice penetrated the dark. "Rose, wake up."

She opened her eyes to see Miles kneeling over her. "What happened?" she wondered aloud.

"That's what I was going to ask you. I saw you leave with Zach and then he came back in without you and started talking to Katie."

"He was going to get my shawl for me. I must have fainted." Rose realized she was lying on the ground, so she tried to sit. Miles helped her back onto the bench. He took his jacket off and wrapped it around her shoulders. She closed her eyes and let the warmth envelop her.

"What's wrong?" he asked.

"I think I just got overheated in there."

"You were quite ill. It will take some time for your strength to return." He pulled the jacket tighter around her and began buttoning it. "Can I give you a piece of advice as your doctor?"

She nodded.

"Maybe you should refrain from wearing a corset until you are completely recovered. With your waist tucked in so tight it's a wonder you can breathe at all. I should have said something yesterday, but you seemed fine and I knew you were excited about the dance."

How dare he mention my undergarments? How dare he even think *of my undergarments?* Rose buried her blushing face in his jacket collar. Was she just a patient and Sean's sister? Is that why Miles didn't dance with her? "Miles . . ."

Her thought remained unfinished as Ian, Zach, and Katie came around the corner.

"Are you all right?" Katie asked, concern etched in her face.

"She's fine. A small fainting spell. She's just doesn't have all her strength back yet." Miles stood, pulling Rose up with him.

Rose smiled weakly at her friends. Even though the night air was cool, she felt warm and secure in their company. She held Miles's jacket to her and inhaled deeply until Zach placed a possessive hand on her shoulder. His touch jerked Rose from her thoughts. "I'm sorry to be a spoil sport, but I think I should probably go home," she said.

Zach's eyes grew dark as he looked at Miles. "And what does the good doctor think?"

The unmistakable challenge made Rose cringe. Miles held his hand out for his coat and Zach draped her shawl around her shoulders. It was fun flirting with Zach and he was certainly more entertaining than Miles, but she didn't know if she wanted to be known as his girl quite yet.

Rose brushed the thoughts from her head and stood as Ian brought the wagon around. Zach helped her and Katie onto the bench seat and then climbed into the box with Miles. Rose gladly sat next to Ian and Katie, happy she could stay warm next to her friend and keep her back to the two brothers. Zach sat behind her, dominating the conversation. He mentioned a few girls by name and asked Rose several times if she had enjoyed the evening.

Rose was too tired to care about much of anything. She leaned against Katie and listened to the banter of the siblings as the horses pulled the wagon home. Ian teased Zach about the size of his ego and wondered how he would ever manage all the girls who batted their eyelashes at him. Miles sat silent and Rose could feel his eyes boring into her back. Katie took her hand and squeezed it.

Rose knew she had worried everyone. What a way to ruin her first outing with the Crandalls! If only her mother were waiting at home to give her a hug and help her make sense of things. Tears stung Rose's eyes, but she bit her lip and held them in. *I won't cry in front of them,* she decided.

The wagon stopped in front of the Weavers' cabin. Rose took Ian's hand and he helped her down from the wagon before any of the other young men could. She thanked them for a wonderful time and said good night. Standing on the front step of her uncle's home, she watched the dark shape of the wagon disappear into the dark. She could hear the jangling of the harnesses even after the wagon faded from sight. She entered the quiet house and found a kerosene lamp glowing on the kitchen table. Taking up the light, she went into the room she shared with Diana. She put away her dancing dress, blew out the lamp, and cried herself to sleep.

15

In the weeks following Miles's return to Spring Creek, Sunday morning had quickly become his favorite time. The Church had opened a mission in Montana, but so far no missionaries had come to the area and the only ward in Montana was in Lima, several hours south. Since no other Mormons lived in Spring Creek—and, truthfully, they weren't very welcome—Miles had started coming to the Weaver home on the Sabbath so they could share a simple service together. It upset his mother that he didn't just attend the church in town, and he couldn't seem to get his family to understand that his new religion made him feel better than any minister he had ever talked to.

Miles dismounted his horse, tied him in the yard, and walked to the house. Before he could knock, the front door opened and Tommy held out his hand. "Good morning, Brother Crandall."

He shook the extended hand and nodded seriously at the young boy trying so hard to be a man. "Good morning, Brother Weaver." Miles took a seat near the fireplace and smiled at Rose as Daniel began the meeting.

They started with a hymn; Rose sang softly in the corner and Abbie harmonized with her. After Diana said a short prayer, Daniel and Miles prepared the sacrament for the small group. It was much different than taking the sacrament in the ward he attended in Utah with the Sterlings, but the Spirit of God was there just the same.

Daniel taught the family about honesty. Tommy blushed through much of the sermon, and Miles hid a grin. He looked across the room and noticed Rose having a similar reaction. There must have been some trouble with the boy during the last week.

Suddenly, Diana blurted, "Tommy shouldn't a said he was going to do chores when he was really swimming, right Pa?"

Abbie shushed the little girl, but even Tommy grinned at her contribution to the meeting.

After they worshipped, they gathered around the table for a simple Sunday meal. Miles knew the food was Rose's work, since Abbie didn't cook. "The meal is delicious."

"Thank you."

"Have you heard about the latest news in town?" Miles turned to look at Daniel. "One of George Larson's hired hands was beaten two nights ago."

Daniel's chair came forward with a thump. "What happened?"

"George said the hand was rounding up some cattle when he came upon two men dumping something in the well." Miles paused. "He tried to stop them, but ended up with a good beating for his efforts."

"Is he all right?" Rose asked.

"He'll be sore for a while, but George Larson is a good boss and will make sure he gets better before putting him back to work." Miles pushed away his empty plate. "I've heard all sorts of stories from my patients. In the last few weeks there have been reports of cattle disappearing, and the girls working in the saloon refuse to go too far from home because one of their own disappeared and another was badly beaten."

Abbie wrinkled her forehead in distaste and motioned for Daniel to change the subject, but he ignored her. Rose leaned in closer when Miles continued.

"Well, Sheriff Gibb is not sure whether one of them disappeared or just left town on her own. The other reported being chased by two men when she went for a walk outside of town."

Daniel stood and went to the window. "It almost sounds like it could be Butch Cassidy and his gang, although they don't generally resort to that kind of random violence."

"They have been mentioned once or twice, but Sheriff Gibb doesn't believe it. He's trying to convince everyone it is just a bunch of foolish kids, and that the girl ran away." Miles took another bite of pie. The crust melted on his tongue and he closed his eyes, savoring the tart apples. When he looked up, he found Rose watching him and grinned. "Good pie, Rose."

She blushed and busied herself clearing up the table. Daniel stepped in to help.

"I hope Sheriff Gibb puts a little more effort into solving the problem," he said as he handed a stack of plates to Rose. "We don't need those kinds of things happening here."

"The mayor kindly pointed out that the trouble didn't seem to start until I returned to town." Miles pushed away his plate.

"That's ridiculous," Rose exclaimed.

Miles shrugged. "You know how rumors are."

Daniel put his hand on Rose's shoulder. "Until the problem is solved, you better stick close to home."

Abbie stood and stretched, her hands supporting the small of her back.

Daniel jumped immediately to her side. "Are you okay?"

"I just need to stretch my legs."

Handing a towel to Miles, Daniel chuckled. "I guess you get to dry the dishes. I'm taking my wife for a short walk around the yard." He led Abbie outside with a gentle arm around her waist.

Miles started drying a plate and watched Rose, her hands deep in the soapy water. "How are things going?"

She didn't answer for several seconds. "I still haven't made any progress with Abbie. She never seems to want to be in the same room with me." Rose looked over at Diana, who sat in the corner playing with her dolls. "Tommy and Diana feel just like my brother and sister. I'd do anything for them."

"Including stay here?"

"Where else would I go?" Rose picked up the pan of dishwater, but Miles took it from her and emptied it out the back door.

He put the washbasin away and turned to Tommy. "Watch your sister for a bit."

"Yes, sir," Tommy replied.

Miles took Rose's hand and pulled her out the door. "Let's go for a walk. You could use fresh air just as much as Abbie."

The July sky held no trace of cloud, and the air felt warm and pleasant against Rose's cheeks. As she and Miles took the shortcut toward the picnic spot, Rose wanted to skip and wished it weren't Sunday. She would love to race Miles and feel the wind against her face. Instead, she walked demurely along the path like a refined lady. Watching Miles out of the corner of her eye, she wondered what he was thinking.

Every Sunday they followed the same routine. Miles would show up at the Weavers', worship with them, eat with them, and then walk with Rose. Their conversations usually centered around the weather, the latest news in town, and how the new medical practice was coming along. Sometimes Rose would talk to him about Abbie and how she wondered if she would ever reach her.

Miles and Rose had almost reached the picnic spot when she remembered teasing him about dancing. "You're one of the best friends I have," she said out loud. *I wonder if there could be anything more.* The errant thought surprised her and she walked a little faster.

Miles lengthened his stride to keep up with her. "Thank you. That means a lot to me." He took her hand. "Come here. I'll show you some of the river's secrets."

Rose could hear the water before they reached it and shut her eyes to listen. "It's so pretty."

"We used to play up here all the time as kids, but you have to be careful." His tone became somber. "Sometimes flash floods come through so quickly they take everything in their path." He watched the water silently until Rose tapped him on the shoulder.

He shook his head as if pulling himself back to the present. "Let me show you our old hideout." He took her hand and they walked back toward the path. "If we go toward Daniel's house a little way, there is a stone overhang. It used to be big enough for all four of us kids, but it probably only fits a couple of adults."

He pointed to a large rock suspended above a dip in the grass. Rose could see how it would be an interesting area for young imaginations. She tripped as she walked towards it, but Miles caught her in his arms before she landed.

"Watch out for that tree root. It's become much bigger in the last few years." He set her down but didn't let go of her arms. "Are you all right?"

She could hear the doctor in his voice. The close contact made her want to forget everything else, but he would only ever see her as a patient. "You need to stop worrying about me," she snapped. "I'm fine." Hurt filled his eyes and she twisted from his grasp. "I'm fine," she said again, climbing around the depression in the ground and up onto the rock.

"Katie says you are getting quite a string of beaus."

Rose sat down, swinging her legs over the edge. "She shouldn't gossip. Anyway, I haven't been here long enough to have any beaus."

Miles grinned and shook his head. "Well, most of the unattached men in town have asked me about you at least once. The clinic is a great place to hear all the news. Just figured you might want to know what people are talking about."

Rose shook her head. "Not really."

"Well, Katie thinks you and Zach would make a charming couple, and she would love to have you as a sister." He climbed up and sat next to her on the rock.

Her legs stopped and she looked at Miles. "Katie would be a great sister, but I hardly know Zach." Rose wanted to scoot closer to him, but the subject of Zach made the space feel enormous. "I do have fun with him." She picked up a pebble from the ground and tossed it, hearing the soft *plunk* as it landed in the creek. "What do you think?"

Miles scowled. "I think you should hold out for a Mormon boy. You know how your mother feels." He sighed. "I suppose if you're patient, Zach might have a change of heart. Sometimes he talks about coming to the Weavers' for church."

Rose wondered why Zach hadn't shared that with her. True, they hadn't known each other for long, but surely he would use that to help win her over.

A memory of her mother's face brought her back. Miles was right. Her mother would never approve of her marrying a nonmember. "Maybe I'll just marry you." She bit her tongue to stop the words, but they had slipped out of her mouth before she realized they had even been a thought.

"Don't do that, Rose."

"Do what?"

"Flirt with me. You don't really mean it." He jumped from the rock and held a hand out to help her down from the overhang. She grabbed his fingers but he dropped them as soon as her feet touched the ground. "You're getting yourself tied up in Zach, and yet you turn around and tease me."

"Zach and I are just friends. I like talking to him. He's fun and doesn't scowl as often as someone else I know." Rose shook her skirt and smoothed out the wrinkles. "There's no harm in a little fun, Miles. Maybe you ought to relax a little."

"He's falling in love with you. You're all he talks about."

Rose raised her eyebrows, wondering if Miles had exaggerated the situation. She grabbed his hand. "I'm leaving for Canada when my family comes. He knows that. We're just having fun."

Miles gently took his hand from her. "Messing with people's emotions—you think that's fun?" Miles voice grew soft and thoughtful. "I thought you were better than that." With that he started back to the Weavers', Rose hurrying to catch up with him.

"I'm sorry," she said sincerely, but the only response was the swishing of their feet through the grass. "Thank you for showing me your old haunts."

When they entered the Weavers' yard, Miles just nodded, mounted his horse, and rode away.

16

The letter to her family was almost done, and Daniel said he would take it to town to mail. Rose reread the words of the last missive from home:

Dearest Rose,

We are all well. The neighborhood is the same. There is always a birth, death, or wedding to report. I won't bore you with the details, because Carrie let me read her letter to you and I know she has filled you in on everything. Aunt Jane seems to appreciate us being here. It helps take some of the load off her shoulders. Granny is as stubborn as always and Carrie is sure she will outlive us all.

Sean is quite good at writing regular letters. He says the plans for the canal are progressing well.

He found a room to rent and enjoys working for Brother Card. He thinks most of the Saints who come will end up living in tents or dugouts while the canal is built. I'm glad we stayed behind. I know I should be stronger and more faithful, but I'm quite happy to stay with Granny and Jane in their cozy home for now. Sean promises to have a house built before we come. I wonder if he'll still want his mother to come live with him or if he'll find some young lady to marry. Only time will tell, I suppose. I still feel like I need to go to Canada, and I hope the year passes quickly so we can reunite our family.

I can't believe you have been gone for almost two months already. We think of both you and Sean often. Carrie says she misses walking along the river with you and playing chess with you and Papa. I miss your cheerful smile and wish I could give you a hug. A mother's arms are always empty when her children are too far away, but I know you will do fine wherever you are.

You are always in my heart, dear daughter.

Love, Mama

P.S. I heard rumor that Karl is planning to wed a girl from Salt Lake this fall.

Tears that had been near the surface all week threatened to spill again. Rose missed her family every day and wished time would speed up. The last line of the letter left her hurt and frustrated. Even though she knew she didn't love Karl, she had imagined he would show up and declare his undying love. It hurt to think he could let her go so easily and already be courting someone else. Then Rose pushed her prideful emotions away. Besides, her parents had been right—she was better off without him.

Rose added a few more words then sealed her reply and went out to find Daniel. She heard him whistling in the barn and saw the wagon hitched up to the horses and ready to go. Tommy and Diana sat in the wagon box, bouncing up and down with excitement. She remembered how much she used to love going on outings with her father.

"Are you coming, Rose?" Diana asked.

"Not this time. I need to stay and help your mother."

Daniel came up behind her. "I appreciate you giving up a trip into town. I worry about leaving Abbie alone, her being so close to her time and all."

"Katie and I are planning on going tomorrow to help Miles spruce up his new clinic."

"I thought he had been using it for some time already."

"He has. But he wants to start living there, and Elizabeth thought the building needed curtains and some of the other comforts of home."

Rose looked behind her, feeling uneasy at the idea of being stuck in the house with her aunt all afternoon. But she had plans, and they didn't involve being ignored by the other woman.

Daniel took the letter from her hands and jumped into the wagon. "We'll be back for supper."

When Rose turned and walked back to the house, she noticed Abbie watching from the sitting room window. In the weeks Rose had lived there, Abbie had spoken only briefly to her and never once lifted a finger to help. Rose decided since they would have several hours together with no one else around, she was going to talk to her aunt.

She entered the sitting room and stood behind Abbie. "Can we talk?"

The other woman didn't turn, so Rose said, "We can't keep tiptoeing around each other. You haven't said three civil words to me since I came, and I am worn out trying to keep up your home without any help from you."

Abbie whirled around. "I can't give you any instruction!"

"I don't need instruction," Rose said, "but it sure would be nice to be acknowledged once in a while."

Abbie turned back to the window, but not before Rose saw the tears in her eyes. "I am not fit to be a wife or mother, and I can see how much more Daniel values you than me."

Rose's mouth dropped open. "There's nothing between Daniel and me! He's my uncle." She went to the window so she could see Abbie's face.

Abbie laughed bitterly. "Oh, I know Daniel loves me more than anything, but he values your competence and strength. I feel like I'm only a pretty picture to grace his home." Tears started rolling down her face. "I'm good for nothing else."

Finally, Rose began to see why Daniel had asked her here. If his wife couldn't care for a home, he wouldn't want to embarrass her by telling anyone. As family, Rose could come in and help without the whole community being told. When her family arrived in the spring, she would go to Canada, and Abbie's secret would be safe.

"I didn't know. Daniel didn't say anything." Rose put her hand on Abbie's arm and led her to the rocking chair. "I just want to help."

The chair squeaked as Abbie sat in it and started rocking. Both women were silent for several minutes before Abbie spoke.

"I was raised in a home where we had everything. Mother passed on when I was just four, so my father and I lived by ourselves with a cook and a maid to help out. The cook didn't like children, but Father kept her on because she did her job well and she had been with the family forever.

"While all the other girls I knew learned household skills, I helped Father. He taught me how to read and do my numbers, and I spent many evenings helping him with the books from his business. I fell in love when I was eighteen and married my first husband. Nothing changed when I moved into his home. His cook and maid took over where my father's left off."

Rose watched Abbie's face soften as she spoke of her father. Rose pulled a chair from the kitchen table and sat next to the rocking chair.

"Two years after we married, my father's business failed. Christopher, my husband, was on his way to meet with my father and discuss our options when his carriage overturned. They brought him back to the house on the verge of death. He had enough time to say good-bye to me and Tommy and then he was gone. Father stepped back into my life and we tried to make everything right.

"A year later our money ran out. My father's solution was to go west. He heard about opportunity in California, so we sold everything we had and joined a wagon train. I met Daniel the first day on the trail and by the time we reached Salt Lake, I'd been baptized and we had fallen in love. Father continued west. I married Daniel and stayed with him in Utah."

Abbie looked at Rose pleadingly. "I was so unprepared to be the kind of wife Daniel needed. Back east I had someone to care for all my needs. Here, I'm supposed to manage so many things. My attempts at sewing have been disastrous, and poor Diana would never have had any nice clothes if your mother hadn't sent old dresses from you and Carrie. I'm surprised my family hasn't starved to death. Daniel suffers through my cooking with a brave face. I guess Tommy doesn't know any better."

"But you could learn." Rose reached forward and placed a hand on her aunt's shoulder.

"I guess I never learned how to ask for help." Abbie stopped rocking. "I know we are judged for our religion here, and I've never felt comfortable approaching any of the women. Daniel tells me all the time that Elizabeth would be more than happy to teach me everything I need to know. But I just can't admit to her how helpless I am."

Rose took the other woman's hand.

"I'll never live up to the standard you have set since you came here." Abbie still sounded bitter, but she didn't jerk her hand away.

"Maybe we could start by being friends," Rose said.

Abbie brushed a tear away from her cheek and stood. She walked over to the wooden chest under the window, opened the chest, and took out a small box. When she took the lid off the box, laces and ribbons spilled out, tumbling across her round stomach. Rose could see little bits of thread through some of the pieces as though they had been used on something and painstakingly removed.

"They're so pretty," Rose said.

"I did try." Abbie laughed sadly. "This is what's left of my efforts to sew baby clothes when I was expecting Diana. Now this baby is on its way, and we've had a hard year. There are some things but . . ."

"Oh, Abbie, do you really want to sew some baby clothes?" Rose clapped her hands. "What fun it will be! I'll teach you." She started sorting through the laces, her mind already envisioning the things they could make. She knew there would be enough to make something new for Diana as well. Rose couldn't contain her joy at having a real conversation with Abbie and finally having a purpose to her days.

"Papa tried to get Mama to have some help, but Mama always refused, saying she had girls who needed to learn to run their own homes," Rose explained. "I guess she was right. What do you want to do first?"

Abbie put the laces back in the box and set it on the table. "How about a cooking lesson? I'm famished, and we need to start dinner soon anyway."

Rose stood and put her arm around the lonely woman's shoulders. "Sounds like a great place to start."

17

Rose awoke early and helped Abbie make a simple breakfast of pancakes. A few times, Rose had to bite her tongue as her aunt struggled with even that simple task. Abbie's mood soured quickly when she burned the first half of the batch, and Rose couldn't wait to get out of the house. She watched through the window for Katie as she braided Diana's fine hair. "Go play now," she said to her cousin. The little girl bounced off the stool and ran out the door to play with her favorite doll under a tree.

Soon Katie arrived and the two girls were on their way. Elizabeth had worked hard making curtains and blankets for Miles. The Crandall men had also been busy, and the finishing work on the clinic was done. The two girls planned to spend the day helping Miles prepare the inside of the building so he could move into town and have some measure of comfort.

When they arrived at the clinic and walked in, Rose was impressed. The main room held several chairs, and a small stove sat in one corner. Just off the waiting room was a slightly larger room with a couple of cots. A large cupboard with glass doors sat empty, waiting to be filled with medical instruments, which Rose assumed were in the crates stacked on the floor. At the back of the building, a bedroom, a kitchen, and a sitting room made up the living space. Rose knew Miles planned on staying there whenever patients needed him, but would still spend much of his time helping out on the ranch.

After donning their aprons, the two girls set to work turning the empty building into a warm, inviting place of business. Rose swept the floors, getting the sawdust out of the corners, while her friend washed the windows. The clean, white curtains they hung gave the room a finished look, and Katie even had a vase of dried wildflowers for the desk in the corner. It wasn't long before the exam room was made up with several warm blankets on the cots, and sheets and bandages stored in the cupboard. The homemade quilt they put on the bed in the bedroom provided the finishing touch.

"Mother wanted me to take a loaf of fresh bread to Mrs. Larson," Katie said as they finished hanging the kitchen curtains. "Do you want to come with me?"

Rose pulled another loaf of bread out of the basket. "You go ahead. I'll stay here and finish putting these things in the icebox for Miles." She watched Katie walk away from the clinic and turned back to her task. Elizabeth had sent a variety of foods for her son. *I guess she thinks he will starve to death if she doesn't feed him.* Rose smiled and lost herself in thought, imagining what it might be like having someone to worry about.

The sound of the front door opening interrupted her daydreams. Putting down a jar of preserves, she started to open the door between the kitchen and the waiting room but then stopped as she heard Miles speak to someone. Not wanting to intrude on his work, she stepped back into the kitchen and proceeded with her task.

Trying hard not to eavesdrop, she hummed quietly to herself, but the voices in the other room grew louder. Now concern outweighed propriety and she moved over to the door and leaned toward it to hear better. She didn't recognize the other voice, but the words carried a subtle threat.

"I suggest you keep yourself busy with doctoring. You are naive and don't understand the workings of this community."

"How am I supposed to keep quiet when I have to keep bandaging up unfortunate men who have been beaten or shot?"

"Some of our citizens believe you might be involved."

"That's ridiculous!" Miles said, his voice rising.

"I don't know. Doesn't it seem odd that we have a peaceful town until the new doctor shows up? Maybe you're trying to drum up patients for yourself. Maybe you're just a little insane. Whatever it is, I'll be watching you."

"Those accusations have no basis in fact."

"I'm just telling you what others are saying. I don't necessarily believe them." The other voice sounded as if it were trying to sooth Miles's temper. "This is a rough country. Men have guns. That is a fact of life. They drink and get a little rough. That, Doctor, is a fact of life." Rose heard the front door open. "And it is a fact of life that doctors should stick with healing. Let the sheriff take care of the bad guys. Good day, Dr. Crandall."

Rose backed away from the door, then reached again for the bottle of preserves and busied herself putting them away. The front door opened again and when it latched, she knew she was alone. She pondered the conversation she had just overheard. During their Sunday meals, they often talked about some of the things Daniel and Miles thought were wrong with the politics in Spring Creek. They had spoken of injuries, but Rose didn't know who had been shot or beaten up. She wondered who the other voice belonged to.

Katie burst through the kitchen door, startling Rose. She had Mary Larson in tow and the two girls began laughing at Rose's shocked expression.

"Sorry. We didn't mean to scare you." Katie grabbed the ties on Rose's apron and removed the white garment. "Mary was on her way to the store and I knew you needed to pick up some things for Abbie. Are you ready to go?"

Rose nodded, then followed the two young women out of the clinic and down the street. They continued to giggle and talk about Ian's courtship of Mary. Rose smiled.

The door of the general store stood open and the three girls soon found themselves surrounded by a wide variety of foods and dry goods. Rose went right to the counter that held bolts of fabric. Abbie wanted something to make curtains for all the windows in the house. Rose looked at the array of cottons and finally decided on a blue gingham, because it reminded her of her mother's kitchen at home. After she purchased several yards, she turned to see the other two girls examining a new shipment of bonnets.

As Rose walked toward them, she heard a familiar voice. She changed direction and went out onto the wooden sidewalk, almost running into Sheriff Gibb.

"Miss Sterling," he said, standing aside for her, "how delightful to see you."

With a smile, Rose adjusted the packages in her arms and looked to see if her friends were coming. They were still trying on bonnets. Sheriff Gibb held out his hands to take her packages.

"Please let me carry those for you." He took the fabric from her and started walking toward the clinic. "I noticed you come into town with Miss Crandall and hoped I would get a chance to speak with you about the teaching position."

Rose took two steps for every one of the sheriff's and finally touched his arm to slow him down. She listened closely to his voice but couldn't decide for sure if he'd been the one talking to Miles in the clinic.

Sheriff Gibb looked down at her. "I'd be pleased if you would allow me to come calling some evening, Miss Sterling."

Rose stopped and stared at him in surprise. *He must be at least fifteen years older than I am,* she thought. His average height allowed her see the intensity in his dark eyes. She realized he was waiting for a response and blushed.

"Sheriff Gibb, I'm surprised you don't have a wife waiting at home for you," Rose teased, pushing away a memory of Miles telling her not to be a flirt.

"Please, call me Arthur," he said as he placed her packages in the wagon. "The title of sheriff sits uneasy on my shoulders." He ducked his head. "I'd really like to discuss your qualifications for teaching. I hear you have some schooling."

She ignored his false modesty. "I attended Brigham Young Academy and received my teacher's certificate."

"So how did you convince your parents to let you escape from the Mormons? Weren't you in line to be someone's second wife?" Arthur leaned against the wagon and stared off at the mountains.

"Like I told you before, we don't practice plural marriage anymore, and I wasn't escaping." Rose knew the time wasn't right to get into a religious discussion. "Tell me more about the school." She heard the door to the clinic open behind her.

Suddenly, the sheriff looked tense. "I will see you soon, Miss Sterling. I'll be up to talk to your uncle in a day or two." His stride took him away from her even as Miles called her name.

She turned to face him, a grin playing on her lips. "Is something wrong with the clinic?" She put on her most innocent look. "I think Katie and I finished everything before we went to the store."

Stopping right in front of her, Miles just looked at her. Rose flinched under his gaze.

"Your brother warned me about you. He said you would need watching." He pulled a hand across his eyes. "I had no idea you would prove him right so quickly."

"I did nothing wrong. Can't I have a conversation with someone other than you or Zach?"

"Well, you don't tend to have good judgment when it comes to men. Karl proved that."

Rose balled her hands into fists. "So your assignment is to be my keeper?" The words escaped through clenched teeth.

"Rose," he said quietly.

The pain in his eyes stopped her for a moment, but she buried the desire to please him. "Just leave me alone." She whirled away before he could see the tears on her face.

18

Zach reined in his horse and waited for Rose to catch up. She laughed and rode past him. After the clinic was set up, the rest of the week had been quiet. Rose's bonnet, which she had so carefully tied beneath her chin before they left, now flopped against her back, doing nothing to protect her face from the sun. She slowed her horse and turned to look at Zach. "Thanks for asking me to go riding today."

"I heard about the sheriff asking to call on you. Figured I should keep you too busy for him."

Rose brushed off the comment and shrugged. "He hasn't been up to see me even once. Besides, I don't have a lot of time for callers. Abbie and I are working hard to get ready for the baby."

They rode along the side of the road, and Rose listened to the twittering of the birds. The summer sun lost some of its intensity as the breeze rustled Rose's skirt and the sun slipped behind a cloud. She noticed the long prairie grasses were yellowing in the heat and remembered hearing the men talk about the danger of prairie fires. Zach stopped his horse next to the river and dismounted. He held his hand up for Rose and she slid off her horse.

"Can I ask you something?"

"Sure." Rose gave her skirt a shake and led her horse to the water for a drink. When the two horses stood side by side, Zach took Rose's hand and led her to a fallen log. She sat and looked up in anticipation.

"Why did Miles join your church?"

The question surprised her. Even though Miles hinted that Zach wanted to worship with them on Sunday, he still hadn't joined them once. "He believes it's true," she answered.

"But why? We were raised as Christians. Ma always insisted we pray and read the Bible. Why did he have to go and join the Mormons?" Zach stood and began pacing back and forth in front of the log. "Pa's angry with Miles for falling in with your church, and Ma's angry that Pa is angry. It's a real mess."

"I didn't realize everyone felt so strongly about it. You're all so nice to me." She took Zach's hand as he walked past her and pulled him to the log. "Stop pacing."

He sat and put his head in his hands.

"You say everyone is upset, but exactly what are they upset about? Has Miles changed for the worse?" Rose picked a buffalo bean growing next to the log and twirled it absently between her fingers, watching Zach as she waited for his answer.

"He has changed. I can't put my finger on it, but he seems calmer somehow. The past doesn't seem to haunt him like it used to." He took the flower from her hand and put it behind her ear. "He seems at peace with himself, but I can't figure out why it bothers my parents so much."

Rose picked another stem. The yellow blossom cheered her and she felt a peaceful, calm warmth. "Zach, how do you feel?"

He looked like the question had never occurred to him. "I don't know. My parents are already frustrated with Miles for not attending Sunday meetings with them, so I've just left things alone."

"Miles said you might want to join us at Uncle Daniel's on Sundays."

Zach shrugged and looked the other way. "I borrowed that Book of Mormon Miles brought home with him. I don't read very fast, but I'm working my way through it. He said I could keep it. When I protested, he told me he had complete passages memorized and would just remember them in his head until he could get a new copy."

Rose felt a guilty tug at her conscience for not sharing her joy in the gospel with Zach sooner. The feeling grew stronger. "Zach, I've read the Book of Mormon too. I know why Miles joined the Mormon Church. It is true. I know it in the deepest part of my soul." She took a deep breath. Living in Salt Lake, surrounded by other members of the Church, the opportunities were rare to bear testimony to a nonmember.

Zach sat for a while and then threw down the blade of grass he'd been chewing on. "Enough serious talk." He placed a finger against her lips to silence her protest. Rose thought he might kiss her as he leaned forward, but he just took her hand, led her to the horses, and helped her mount. "Tell me more about the sheriff. He seems mighty interested in you."

"I'm sure it's only for my teaching skills. Miles told him I graduated from Brigham Young Academy last year and am qualified to teach school." Rose guided her horse across the river and into the meadow.

"Have you taught before?"

"I hadn't found a job before my father decided to move to Canada. Then everything just got pushed aside once he got sick." She said the words quietly, trying to hide her sadness.

"Are you so hard to convince that Gibb must call on you personally?" Zach took his hat off and wiped his brow.

"He talked to me about the job, but he struggles with my religion, just like you do." She grinned at him. "Anyway, I don't want to commit to teaching until I know how much Abbie needs me after the baby comes. Why, are you jealous?"

Zach reached into his saddle bag, pulled out two apples, and handed one to Rose. "How are things with Abbie?" he asked, ignoring her question.

Rose shrugged her shoulders. "We talked about things. She is more pleasant these days, although sometimes she still gets a little grumpy." She took a bite of the apple. "We are both learning to be more patient with each other."

The two friends rode in silence, enjoying the summer day. The schoolhouse stood in the distance and Rose decided it would be nice to see the building where she might work in the fall. "I'll race you to the school," she said to Zach as she spurred her horse on. *What would Mama say?* The thought didn't slow her down and she laughed as the powerful stride of the horse carried her to the imaginary finish line.

Suddenly, a scream pierced the air and her horse shied away from the noise. Rose reined the mare in and patted the animal's neck. Zach stopped his horse beside her and listened. Another quieter sound, more like a sob, moved him to action.

"Stay here," he said.

As he rode toward the noise, Rose followed right behind him. They came into a small clearing just off the road and found a woman crumpled on the ground. Rose slid from the horse and ran to her. She lay face down, her shoulders shaking with sobs. When Rose reached to touch her, she flinched and screamed again.

"It's okay, I want to help you," Rose said softly. Then she looked up at Zach, who reached down and gently helped the woman to sit. Rose gasped. The face looking back at her was covered with blood, and the eyes were swelling shut. The woman held one wrist gingerly and Rose could see it swelling also. "Let us get you to Dr. Crandall."

Zach brought the horses near and helped the injured woman onto his mount. They rode slowly into town and headed for the clinic. When they arrived, a small crowd followed them as the people on the streets noticed the bloody woman.

Rose quickly dismounted when they arrived and ran to the door. "Miles." She knocked but no one answered. "I don't think he's here," she said to Zach.

"He rode out of town half an hour ago," a neighbor offered. "He said he had to check on the new Standish baby."

With a key from his pocket, Zach opened the door to the clinic. Then he deposited the injured woman onto the exam table. "I'll go find him. You do what you can for her." He touched Rose's cheek and rushed out the door.

Rose went to the pump and filled a basin. Clean rags made a neat stack on a shelf in the room, so she took one and dipped it in the cool water. Carefully, she began cleaning the blood off the woman's face. The water quickly turned pink and Rose took the bowl to empty and refill it. The woman kept muttering quietly, "I'm okay. I'm okay."

With the face in front of her cleaned off, Rose recognized Sarah Turner, the wife of the blacksmith. "Mrs. Turner?" Rose waited for a response, knowing Sarah was having a hard time seeing her through her swollen eyes. "It's Rose Sterling."

Sarah grabbed Rose's hand and gave it a squeeze. "Thank you." Tears seeped from her eyes and Rose cried with her while they waited for Miles.

The visit to the Standish home had been short and Miles was already on his way back to town when Zach found him. The two brothers raced back to Spring Creek. Miles jumped off his horse and threw his reins at Zach, then ran into the clinic. There he saw two weeping women huddled together.

"Rose, what's wrong? Are you hurt?" As he said the words, he crossed the room and began examining Sarah Turner's face.

"I'm fine."

He held a hand out to Rose and she handed him a damp cloth. He dabbed at a wound just above Sarah's eye. "You should leave. I'll take care of her now."

Rose put the bowl down on a table and turned toward the door.

"Please stay," Sarah pleaded.

Rose looked to Miles for direction.

"If it will put you at ease, Mrs. Turner."

Rose walked back to the exam table and took Sarah's uninjured hand.

Miles prepared to stitch the wound above her eye. "Tell me what happened."

Sarah sighed. "I don't really know." The tears started flowing again. "I was walking out to the farm after visiting in town. I thought I would stop and pick some huckleberries to make Jake a pie for dinner.

"I'd nearly filled my basket when I heard someone behind me. He grabbed me by the neck and told me he wanted my money and jewelry. I had a few coins in my bag but the only jewelry I was wearing was my wedding ring and a brooch from my husband.

"I guess I hesitated too long. The other man hit me across the face with his fist and ripped the brooch from my throat. I asked him to stop and that just made him angrier."

"There were two of them?" Rose asked.

"I think so." Sarah wiped a tear from her cheek.

Miles shook his head and clenched his teeth. He'd heard too many stories lately about senseless violence, and often for even less than a brooch and a few dollars. "Did you recognize them?"

Sarah shrugged. "One wore a bandana across his face, but he seemed young."

Miles cut the thread and put away the needle. He carefully examined Sarah's wrist and then asked Rose to get a bandage from the cupboard. "I think your wrist is severely sprained, but if you take it easy, it should be fine in about a month." He took the bandage from Rose and carefully wrapped the wrist. "Rose, please go tell Zach who we have here, so he can fetch her husband."

After Rose left the room, Miles washed his hands and made some notes in his record book. "Are you sure there is nothing else you can remember?"

"I'm sure if I see him around, I might recognize him," Sarah said. "He seemed familiar. And like I said, the one with the bandana seemed young—maybe even still a teenager." She shrugged. "I'm afraid that's all I can tell you."

Miles put his notebook back in the desk drawer.

"I'm just so glad your brother and Miss Sterling were riding in the area when it happened. I think they scared them off."

Miles frowned. He had no claim on Rose, but to hear that she allowed Zach to court her tore at his heart. Realizing Sarah was still talking, he shook the thoughts from his mind and tried to focus on what she said.

"She's such a pretty girl." The injured woman shifted on the bed and pushed a strand of hair out of her face. "Miss Sterling and your brother make a right handsome couple." She smiled at him nervously.

Miles smiled back and then walked toward the door. "You just rest. I'll go see if there is any word from your husband yet."

He closed the door behind him and turned to find Rose sitting on a wooden chair in his waiting room. She held her head in her hands and her shoulders shook with sobs. Miles knelt at her feet in an instant.

"Talk to me. Are you sure you're not hurt?"

She lifted her head and looked into his eyes. "It was so terrible. She was so terrified and there was so much blood."

Miles took a clean handkerchief and gently wiped away the river of tears on her face.

"It's good you heard her and brought her in." He stood and moved to look out the window. The people who had gathered outside when he arrived at the clinic were gone. The streets were quiet, and he could only hear Rose crying behind him. Clenching his fists, he sighed. "You and Zach seem to be getting awfully close."

"He's a good friend. I enjoy his company."

"Just remember that he doesn't share your faith," Miles continued before she could speak. Then he leaned forward and gripped her shoulders. "I'm not trying tell you what to do. I care for you and I love my brother."

She stood and looked up at him. "Anything else?"

The challenge in Rose's eyes left him weak in the knees. She could be so infuriating. He wondered if Zach ever saw the serious side of her that he loved. He wondered if she shared her thoughts and dreams with Zach the way she did with him on their Sunday walks. She seemed to wear her heart on her sleeve, but he couldn't be sure. If only he knew how she really felt about him. "What do you want? Is it Zach?"

Her gaze faltered and she looked down at her hands. Miles pulled her closer and forced her chin up so he could see her eyes. She blinked back more tears. "I want to be happy. I want to be loved."

"Can Zach give you that?" He dropped his hand from her and stepped back. "I want you to be happy, too. If you love my brother, I'll support you."

She opened her mouth to answer but the door flung open before she could get anything out. Jake Turner burst into the room. "Where's my wife?"

"She's fine, Jake. Come in here." Miles pointed the upset husband toward the exam room, taking a last look at Rose and wishing he had the nerve to say what he really wanted to say.

19

After two months of Rose's tutelage, Abbie was thrilled with her newfound skills. She loved the smell of bread fresh from the oven, and how the aroma of hearty meals filled the house. Rose spent hours teaching her to make tiny stitches, and even though nothing Abbie made rivaled Rose's fine work, she improved every day. Rose busied herself knitting a warm blanket for the anticipated arrival, and Abbie put the finishing touches on a baby's nightgown.

There were still moments when Abbie snapped at Rose or ignored her completely, but her unfailingly patient niece just smiled in response. Just once, Abbie had caught Rose glaring at her, but the look had disappeared quickly. Abbie wished she could control her temper. She resolved to treat Rose better and to let her know how much she appreciated the help.

Now, Abbie stood and looked out the kitchen window. Rose promised her they would work up some pretty curtains to frame the marvelous view when they finished sewing clothing and blankets for the baby. Abbie's new skills opened up a world of possibilities in her mind, and she spent hours dreaming about her next projects.

She watched Diana run around the yard, playing some imaginative game with her dolls. The child had been so much happier since they resolved the tension in the home and made Rose a part of the family.

"I'm going now," she heard her niece say.

"Have a good time."

The door to the kitchen closed and Rose headed across the yard to the meadow. She planned to meet Katie Crandall for a picnic to discuss the upcoming harvest dance. After the fainting incident at the last one, it had taken some convincing to get Rose excited, but Miles told her she would be fine if she took it easy.

Abbie patted her stomach. "Come along little one," she said softly. "Once you make your appearance and I can get around again, I think I would like to finally get to know the neighbors." Noticing the dark clouds on the horizon, she went outside to take the wash off the line.

Rose watched the same dark clouds as she wandered down the path towards the Crandalls'. The clouds were quite distant and she guessed the storm was a few hours off. Further along the path, she saw Katie coming towards her carrying a quilt.

They met and spread the quilt in the shade of a large tree on the bank of the creek. Katie told Rose about Ian and Mary and her mother's excitement over a potential wedding in the family. When she finished, Katie looked closely at Rose.

"What's wrong? You don't seem your usual happy self."

Rose and Katie had grown close and Rose trusted her, but the words to explain her feelings wouldn't come. "How is Miles?"

Katie smiled. "He's getting busier, and the people in town seem to trust the so-called 'young doc' a little more."

Rose sat in silence as Katie continued to talk about her brothers and parents. Then Katie commented on the change they'd all noticed in Abbie. "She is starting to seem downright friendly, Ma says."

With Abbie gaining a little self-confidence, people already perceived her differently, and Rose was happy for her new friend. She was grateful for Katie, too, but she suddenly realized how much she missed her own family. "I want to go home."

Rose didn't realize she had spoken out loud until Katie said, "We just got here. Are you feeling all right?"

"Oh, I'm fine. I just meant that I just miss my family. I wish home wasn't so far away."

"It must be hard to be so far away from them, but it must be some comfort to have Zach wrapped around your little finger."

"I don't know if I want him wrapped so tightly."

Katie looked shocked. "Why ever not? You could even have Miles if you had half a mind."

Still unable to explain her feelings, even to herself, Rose started cleaning up the picnic. Even if Miles did set her heart fluttering, he insisted on being so serious all the time, and sometimes he even seemed to avoid her. She loved their Sunday walks, but they were just good friends, and he had never tried to be otherwise.

"I wish someone would look at me the way they look at you. How are you ever going to decide between the two of them?" Katie asked Rose. "And then there is the sheriff. Tell me more about him."

"There is nothing to tell." Rose picked a wildflower and twisted it around her fingers. "I'll only be here for a few more months and then I'll be going to Canada with my family. Zach and Arthur will forget about me before I even leave Montana. And Miles? Well, you're wrong about him. He's not the slightest bit interested in me."

Katie took the flower from Rose's fingers and placed it behind her own ear. "If you say so. I'm still jealous that you have so many men who want to be your beau."

The dark clouds Rose had noticed earlier continued to build. "We should probably get home," she said, folding the quilt. She and Katie said good-bye and headed in opposite directions on the path.

As she walked, Rose felt the stillness around her and noticed that even the birds were silent. The hot air had become humid with promised rain, and Rose saw lightning flash against the black horizon. Picking up her skirts, she walked a little faster. She had hated thunderstorms ever since she was a child. The memory of Sean teasing her and Carrie as they huddled under one of their mother's quilts waiting for the fury to pass still made her shudder.

Soon, she ran into the yard and grabbed Diana's hand. "Time to get inside, little one. It's going to rain."

Abbie met them at the door just as a clap of thunder shook the house. The look on her face told Rose all she needed to know.

"Diana, go into the kitchen and get yourself a cookie," Rose said, then turned to Abbie. "Is it time?"

She nodded and Rose saw the fear in her eyes.

"Diana was a hard birth. Old Doc McTavish said they almost lost me and the baby." Abbie's chin quivered. "Rose, I'm scared."

Another clap of thunder and the slamming of the kitchen door set Rose's heart racing. Daniel came into the room, shaking the rain off his shirt, followed by Tommy, who was doing his best to copy his father's every move.

Daniel took one look at Abbie and turned to the boy. "Go saddle the horse, Son. Your mama is going to have this baby and we're needing the doctor. Ride into town as fast as you can and go to the clinic. Find Miles and tell him to hurry."

Tommy straightened his shoulders. "I'll hurry, Pa. Don't worry, Ma, I won't be long."

Shuddering at the thought of someone going out in the storm, Rose went into the kitchen to boil water. It was the only thing she knew to do, since she had never been involved in birthing a baby. The ride into town took twenty minutes at a brisk walk, but if Tommy kept the horse at a gallop, he would make it in a fraction of that time. From what Rose had heard, labor could take several hours or more, so Tommy and Miles should be there long before anything else happened.

Diana finished her cookie and started tugging on Rose's skirts, looking for something else to eat. Rose dished the little girl a bowl of the stew on the stove and cut her a slice of bread. Between mouthfuls, Diana explained all the games she had played with her dolls that afternoon.

Rose half listened as she picked at a piece of bread and butter. As soon as the meal was done, Rose cleaned up Diana's messy fingers and took her into the bedroom to say good night to her parents.

Abbie lay on the bed, clearly tired and strained. Daniel sat holding her hand and whispering words of love and encouragement. She smiled at her daughter. "Come and kiss me good night and then get to bed. Tomorrow you will have a new baby brother or sister."

"G'night, Mama."

After Rose tucked Diana into bed, she walked to the window in the sitting room. Every few minutes, thunder crashed and lightning illuminated the room. Rain pelted the earth and the road looked slick with mud. Rose watched, hoping Tommy and Miles would arrive safely—and soon. She could hear Daniel speaking gently to Abbie in the other room. From Abbie's pained response, Rose knew nature would progress with or without the doctor.

"Rose!"

The urgency in Daniel's voice brought Rose running into the bedroom. Abbie lay on her side clutching her abdomen, her face red with exertion and pain. Rose's heart went cold and her hands began to shake.

"Rose, listen to me," Daniel said. "Something is wrong. Even if the roads were good, we couldn't expect Tommy to return with Miles for at least another thirty minutes. And Miles may be out with another patient. I need to run through the meadow to the Crandalls' and get Elizabeth. She has helped birth many babies. Stay with Abbie and try to keep her comfortable."

Abbie grimaced in agony and Rose saw her own panic reflected in her aunt's eyes.

"Daniel, please don't go," Abbie said. "I need you here!" Tears now ran down her face.

Daniel looked torn. As he hesitated, Rose spoke. "I'll go." She started toward the sitting room. "Stay with your wife, Daniel."

"Hurry," he begged.

She tried to laugh, but it came out sounding more like a sob. "Believe me, I'll run the whole way."

After wrapping a thick shawl around her shoulders, Rose opened the front door. She closed it behind her and then leaned against it for a few seconds. A flash of lightning showed her the path and set her heart pounding. Steeling herself for the race through the meadow, Rose took a deep breath and made her way carefully across the farmyard. There was too much mud to run here, but she knew once she reached the grasses in the meadow, she needed to move faster than ever before.

Quickly soaked by the rain, Rose's long skirts hampered her movements as they wrapped around her and stuck to her legs. She gathered the heavy fabric in her arms, glad the weather would keep people inside so there would be no witnesses as she ran across the meadow with her bloomers flashing.

As she moved along the path that followed the creek, she heard the rushing water between claps of thunder. The trees along the water's edge provided little shelter from the pelting rain. Rose knew it was ridiculous, but at times she felt all the monsters from her childhood lurking in the darkness. She forced herself not to cry and reminded herself that this was about Abbie and a new little life. *Lord, help me do this,* she prayed.

When Rose saw the picnic spot in front of her, she knew she was halfway to the Crandalls' house. The fallen log next to the fire pit was shiny with rain, and Rose stopped and leaned on it to catch her breath. When she stood to continue on, she saw two dark forms coming toward her. She froze in place, holding her breath. The figures moved closer and she recognized Elizabeth's stout form and Miles carrying his black doctor's bag.

Rose gasped in relief. "How did you know to come?"

"Tommy came to the house about five minutes ago," Miles said. "He said the baby is coming and they need the doctor."

"What are you doing out in this maelstrom?" Elizabeth asked Rose.

"Daniel sent me. There is something wrong with Abbie or the baby, and we didn't expect Tommy back from town for quite some time. How did he end up at your house?"

"He met Ian going into town and Ian told him Miles was at the house. Don't worry about Tommy. Katie is getting him some warm, dry clothes and a hot meal." Elizabeth squeezed Rose's shoulder. "Let's get going. Babies don't wait for anything, not even a storm."

Rose tried to move but her chest felt tight and her knees weak. Miles hurried along, clearly focused on the doctoring ahead of him, and Elizabeth followed close behind him. As hard as she tried, Rose couldn't keep up with them.

"I'll catch up to you later," she called out to them. "I need to walk for a minute."

Lightning struck again, giving Rose a final view of Miles and his mother just as they rounded a curve in the path. She was soaking wet and exhausted, and she had never felt more alone. She thought of finding a nice thick tree to sit under, but then she remembered her father telling Sean, who loved storms, to stay away from trees during a lightning storm. Then Rose realized she must be near the large, flat stone Miles had shown her. It would still be wet under the overhang, but at least she could hide from the storm a little.

Another flash of lightning lit the scene and Rose could see the flat rock just in front of her. If she sat for a few minutes and caught her breath, she decided, she could be back at the house before anyone missed her.

Suddenly, Rose tripped over a tree root, going down in the mud and twisting her ankle. Pain jolted through her leg. She pulled herself to her knees and dragged her body under the overhang, then sat shivering and crying. After several minutes, she took the wet shawl from her shoulders and squeezed out as much water as possible, then wrapped it around her shoulders again. Concentrating on taking slow, deep breaths took her mind off the storm, and she could feel the vice around her chest ease slightly. Rose laid her head back against the wall of dirt under the stone, closed her eyes, and tried to think of anything but the rain and her ankle.

She had no idea how long she sat huddled under the overhang, but she finally realized the baby must have already arrived. Rose's breath started to come a little easier, but she knew the slightest exertion would only make it worse. The frantic dash to get help had worn her out, and her eyes felt heavy. As she drifted off to sleep, she didn't notice the sound of the rain beginning to taper off and then the silence after the storm.

20

In the Weaver home, Abbie still strained against her burden, making no progress and getting progressively weaker. Diana had been awakened by a thunderclap and sat in her bed, screaming for her mother. Daniel stood at Abbie's side, wringing his hands and telling her to hold on.

Miles and Elizabeth walked into the confusion and immediately took things in hand. "Mother, get him out of here, please."

Elizabeth took the upset father out of the room. "Tend to Diana, Daniel. Calm her down and calm yourself down." She patted him on the shoulder. "Things will work out."

When she returned to Abbie's bedside, Miles spoke quietly to the expectant mother. "The baby is in the wrong position, Abbie. I need to turn it."

Elizabeth took Abbie's hand. "Now you just look at me, dear, and everything will be fine." Using her free hand to stroke Abbie's damp forehead, she looked at Miles for confirmation that she spoke the truth.

Miles hid the worry from his mother even as his face tensed with concentration. He had done this before and was confident in his skills. He worried about Rose, though. When he and his mother had made it to the house, he'd thought Rose was right behind them, but she still hadn't arrived. With a sigh, he decided she would be there soon. Then he focused on the situation at hand.

It wasn't long before a healthy baby girl lay in Abbie's arms. Relief washed over Miles. The baby was beautiful the way only newborns can be, with a tuft of blond hair to match her mother's. He could tell his mother was instantly enchanted and guessed that if Abbie welcomed it, Elizabeth would become a surrogate grandmother to the infant and spend all her spare time at the Weavers'.

The door opened behind them, and Miles heard Daniel enter the room. "Oh, Abbie," he said. He knelt at the side of the bed and put his large, weathered hand on his wife's cheek. "You did it, sweetheart."

Miles left the room silently and looked at his pocket watch. Over an hour had passed since he and his mother had met Rose on the trail. Even if she walked, she should have arrived long ago. Worry hit him with full force.

His dripping coat hung on the back of a chair near the fire and was starting to steam from the heat. Looking outside, Miles saw the rain had stopped. He took a quilt from the back of the rocker and wrapped it around his middle so his body could warm it. Then he put on his heavy, wet coat and let himself out of the house.

It was nearly midnight, and Miles felt the fatigue as he started back along the well-worn path between the two properties. He listened as he walked, hoping he would hear her cry out for help. "Rose!" he called, but he heard nothing in response. The world rested, still and hushed except for the water dripping from the trees flanking the river.

Miles walked all the way to the picnic spot with no sign of Rose. That meant she had left the regular path, perhaps to find some shelter. Then he remembered showing Rose the large stone overhang he and his siblings had played under as children.

After stopping to get his bearings in the dark, Miles finally found the outcropping. He tripped over the old tree root and dropped to his hands and knees to look under the stone. There lay Rose, huddled in an uneasy sleep. Miles moved closer, softly saying her name. When he touched her icy hand, she didn't respond, so he removed the wet shawl from her shoulders and replaced it with the warm blanket from his middle. She sighed in her sleep but didn't awaken.

He lifted her and carefully stepped over the tree root, then returned to the main trail. The slight body in his arms weighed no more than a child. She turned her face into the warmth of his neck and said something he couldn't hear.

"Rose, are you all right?"

"Thank you," she whispered a little louder. "Thank you for coming to find me." Then her eyes closed and she rested her head on his shoulder.

Miles marveled at the tender feelings she brought out in him. He only wished she would see him as something other than a friend.

The house came into view and Miles saw his mother watching from the window. They would all be worried about Rose, and he had left without a word to anyone. He quickened his step as he saw his mother open the door.

Rose stirred in his arms, then looked up at him and smiled. "You do take delight in rescuing me, I believe." She sounded weak and tired, but Miles was relieved she was conscious.

"Not really. I would rather see you well all the time. Why didn't you come back to the house? Did you have trouble breathing again?"

They were in the house before she could answer.

"Oh, Rose, where were you?" Elizabeth stroked Rose's damp hair off her face. "I'm so sorry I didn't notice you weren't right behind us."

Miles started to put her down. As Rose's foot touched the floor, her ankle buckled. He caught her before she fell and eased her onto a chair. She blushed and held her foot out. The skin bulged above her shoe, purple and swollen.

"I had trouble breathing after all the running. You didn't hear me when I tried to call to you. I thought if I could just sit for a minute and get my breath back, the pain would go away a bit and I could get home."

"How did you hurt your ankle?" Miles asked.

"I tripped on that darned root. You told me to be careful of it, but with the lightning and thunder, I panicked and forgot."

"I'm so sorry." Daniel put his hand on her shoulder. "I forgot how frightened you are of storms, and I sent you out in one."

"I'm fine. I'm sure the next storm won't seem so bad." Rose smiled at her friends. "Although now I think I may have a healthy fear of tree roots."

21

The baby sighed softly in her sleep and Rose held her close, snuggling the warm body under the shawl. Abbie and Daniel had named her Tempest Rose Weaver. Elizabeth said a name like Tempest was just asking for trouble, but Abbie insisted that Tempest sounded like a much better name than Storm. Daniel chose Rose because of the bravery of their very own Rose going out to face her fear of storms for the baby's sake.

During the week since Tempest had entered the world, Rose spent most of her time in Abbie's rocking chair, holding the baby. Her ankle was badly sprained, and Miles insisted she keep it elevated. She hadn't argued with him because the foot wouldn't bear even the slightest weight for the first few days. Now she could get around a little, but she still took every opportunity she could to hold the baby.

Rose's injury had almost been a blessing for Abbie, who got out of bed in no time to ply her new skills in her home. The yeasty aroma of fresh baked bread filled the air, and at every meal a variety of dishes tempted the family. The occasional burnt offering made its way to the table, but Abbie's cheerful attitude never wavered.

Without Rose's constant help around the home, Abbie's confidence in her own abilities had grown. Rose knew her aunt didn't need her anymore and wondered exactly how she would fit into the family now. In Abbie's spare moments she played happily with Diana, and she had even invited Elizabeth over for tea twice, baking a variety of cookies and cakes to the delight of her neighbor.

With the baby clothes done, Rose and Abbie started on the curtains for the kitchen. Abbie cut them out on the table under Rose's watchful eye, and Rose sat in the rocking chair sewing the gingham. The curtains would have ruffles like the cheerful curtains Rose remembered from her own mother's kitchen, and she couldn't wait to see them hung in place.

Now, Abbie stood at the sink doing the noon dishes. "There's someone coming up the road. It's probably for you again." She turned and winked at Rose. "You have more male callers than I know what to do with."

Rose rolled her eyes. Abbie's temperament had improved during her recovery, but Rose's had soured, and almost anything could push her into an ornery mood.

"It looks like Zach." Abbie reached for her daughter. "Let me take the baby and you can have a visit with him. She needs to eat anyway."

Rose handed the sleeping infant to her mother and arranged her skirts to cover the ankle that rested on a low stool. She picked up the curtain she was working on and began making tiny stitches. Zach spent time every day at Daniel's house, and, of course, most of it was with Rose.

The kitchen door burst open and Daniel and Zach blew in with the gusty Montana wind. "Got a caller for you, Rose."

"Still sitting around, letting people wait on you?" Zach removed his coat.

That had been his greeting all week, and Rose tired of the constant reminder that her injury placed a burden on the very people she had come to help. Abbie was much more competent around the house and Rose could still help with the mending and holding the baby, but that didn't make her feel any better.

I'm just used to keeping busy, Rose reminded herself. Her mother always made her children work hard, as much as she let them play hard. Most of the chores took the form of games because Rose and Carrie had invented ways to make the work fun. Their mother had finally despaired of getting them to concentrate without playing and had joined in the fun herself. Rose missed her childhood home and wondered if Carrie had as much fun doing chores on her own.

"Rose?" Zach looked at her expectantly, and she realized he must have asked her a question.

"I came all this way to see you. The least you could do is listen when I talk to you."

She looked at Zach and shrugged as Daniel headed out the door again. "Sorry. I guess I'm getting a little stir-crazy."

"What does Miles say about your foot?"

"He hasn't been by for a few days. My ankle tires easily, but I have been walking on it a little more."

"You'll be back to your normal self in no time. When you're up to it, we should go riding again." Zach smiled at her and then continued to talk about the ranch and the latest gossip in town.

Rose watched him get lost in his own words, his straight, dark blond hair sticking straight up on the crown of his head. She had heard some of the other girls dream about smoothing his wild hair, but she thought it gave him a boyish look that suited him. His brown eyes were a shade lighter than Miles's and always sparkled over some secret joke. Rose could never be sure if he was laughing at her or not.

He went on about his fishing trip the previous day, and the harvest social scheduled for the weekend. Rose silently held out the basket of cookies Abbie had placed by her chair. Zach took one and managed to eat it as he continued talking.

"Are you going to let me say anything at all?" Rose blushed at her own boldness.

Zach looked at her with his mouth open. He put the cookie down and stood. "I thought you liked my visits."

"I'm sorry, Zach. Your visits really are welcome. But I hear just about the same news from Sheriff Gibb and Daniel and Abbie. You come to visit me, but you never let me say anything. I feel like all I am to you is a captive audience."

"You've been in this house for a week and I thought you would be interested in what's going on." Zach looked at her as if waiting for an apology.

He doesn't realize he's being inconsiderate, even when I point it out! Rose thought. "I think you should leave, Zach. I'm tired."

She looked out the window and ignored the man in the room as he put on his coat and left. She watched him ride his horse out of the yard and stomped her good foot on the floor. Zach was fun and good looking but so self-absorbed that he didn't even sense her need to talk about something other than him. On the other hand, Miles never stayed in the same room with her long enough to have more than a short conversation about her health.

The sound of another horse caught her attention and she looked out the window to see if Zach had come back. He really wasn't bad company, she thought. Maybe she was just tired of sitting and that was why she kept snapping at everyone. She glanced out the window and recognized Sheriff Gibb's horse. The curtain lay in her lap, and she knew she wouldn't get anything done at this rate.

Daniel let her caller in the house.

Rose smiled at the sheriff. "What a surprise, Arthur."

"How is the foot?" He removed his hat and took her hand.

She gently slid her fingers from his grasp. "It is improving daily. Thank you for asking."

"I saw Zach leaving and took the opportunity to ask if he would become a deputy." After putting his hat back on, the sheriff leaned back in his chair. "I've been thinking he'd be perfect for the job for some time now."

Rose frowned. "Why do you need a new deputy?"

"Deputy Sykes quit. His wife has been begging him to stay home more and work the land. Truth is, I think they're both running a little scared." The sheriff sighed. "But there's been too much trouble in the town, and without Sykes, I need someone else I can trust. Zach accepted the job."

Rose picked up the curtain and began to stab the fabric with her needle. "Just seems like putting him in a lot of danger when there is so much going on right now. He's just a rancher. He doesn't have any experience that would make him a good deputy."

"Should I be a little jealous, Miss Sterling? You seem awfully worried about Mr. Crandall. Do you worry about me at all, since I am right in the thick of things?" Arthur began polishing his badge with his finger.

Rose glared at him.

A nervous look crossed Sheriff Gibb's face. "I'm also here on other business." He leaned forward on his chair. "Fall is almost here and your aunt seems to be getting on just fine. The town needs a new schoolteacher. We hoped you might agree to take the job."

Rose let the fabric fall into her lap. "I have the training, but I've never taught before. And I didn't plan on staying long in Montana. Isn't there someone else who could do it?"

"There really isn't, Rose. I'd like you to seriously consider the idea."

She had already done so. Both Abbie and the baby were healthy, and it would be a blessing for Rose to be out of the house every day. Still, Rose was about to protest, but then she remembered the warm feeling that had washed over her after she prayed about the teaching position. "I think I could do it. I'll talk to my uncle, but I think the answer will be yes."

The sheriff grinned. "I'm sure you'll do just fine." He put his hat back on and stood. "My son will be in your class and I'm sure he'll learn a lot from you. He's had a hard time since his mother died. And, for my part, I'll look forward to seeing you more often." With a wink and a smile, the sheriff walked out the front door.

Rose sat in the rocking chair, marveling at the turn her life had just taken. This would give her a purpose since she couldn't go back to her family yet, not while they were still crowded into a tiny house in Utah.

The door opened again and Diana came into the house. Dragging her rag doll behind her, she crawled up into Rose's lap and started to cry. "Tommy won't play with me."

"Go get your mother's writing box," Rose said, "and we'll play a game."

Soon, Diana returned with the flat box that held all the writing implements in the house. Rose selected a sheet of paper and a sharpened pencil. Then she closed the lid of the box so it could function as a table. "Let's learn how to write your name." She wrote "DIANA" in block letters and explained the sound each letter made.

The lesson enthralled the little girl. She took her turn with the pencil and practiced writing her name over and over again. When she tired of that, Rose wrote the name of each member of the family, and Diana practiced those, her wobbly letters dipping and dancing across the page. Both girls laughed.

Rose looked up to see Abbie watching them.

"I was going to teach letters to her this winter," Abbie said a bit crossly. "I wouldn't neglect to give her some learning."

"I thought I could just practice with her. Sheriff Gibb offered me the teaching position in the school this fall." She handed the box to Diana and carefully rose from the chair, then limped over to Abbie. "I've never taught anyone, other than my sister, a few things here and there. I wanted to give it a little try before school starts."

Abbie blushed. "Sorry. I didn't mean to be so touchy."

Rose hugged her aunt, realizing Abbie's confidence was still tender. "Maybe you could help me figure out the best way to go about some lessons."

"I taught Tommy how to read and write. He learned real fast." Abbie handed the baby to Rose and went to start preparing the evening meal. "He'll be excited when he hears that you'll be his teacher."

The next morning dawned bright and clear. The sun slanted through the window and warmed the quilt Rose had tucked around her shoulders. She stretched and turned to look at Diana, who lay asleep in the next bed. Easing out of the warm blankets, Rose put her feet on the cold floor and tried putting some weight on her sprained ankle. It hurt, but by putting most of her weight on her good foot, she found she could limp across the room at almost a normal pace. She dressed quietly so as not to wake Diana, then slipped out of the bedroom.

Abbie sat in the rocking chair feeding Tempest. Rose knew Daniel was outside doing chores and would come back soon for breakfast.

"What can I make for the morning meal?" she asked Abbie.

"You shouldn't be on your foot. Miles said another few days."

"Well, that was several days ago and he hasn't been to see me for a while. I'm tired of spending all my time in that rocking chair." She pulled her hair back and tied it with a ribbon. "Are we still going to the social tonight?"

Abbie smiled. "If we missed this one, Diana would be sad until Christmas. I think I'm actually looking forward to visiting with my neighbors for a change."

"I'm glad." Rose took an apron off the hook on the wall and wrapped it around her waist. "Now about breakfast . . ."

"You're about as stubborn as your uncle. All right, why don't you make up some pancakes while I finish feeding the baby?"

Rose mixed up the batter and set the griddle on the stove to heat. She put some brown sugar into another pot and added an equal amount of water and put it on to boil. Diana loved hot syrup on her pancakes. Rose wondered if Daniel could get some real maple syrup for Christmas.

When the pancakes were steaming on the griddle, Daniel came in with Tommy on his heels. He gave Rose a protective fatherly look that made her duck her head, but he didn't say anything. She limped to her place at the table and sat with the family as Daniel prayed over the food.

Tommy took big mouthfuls of pancakes but managed between bites to tell everyone how excited he was for the social that evening. Diana squirmed in her chair and Daniel teased her about using up all her dancing energy before the evening arrived. Rose smiled at the easy banter in the family. If she couldn't be with her own family, this had to be the next best thing. Even though she still missed her mother, she found herself sad at the thought of ever leaving the Weavers. *I guess Papa was right. As long as I have family, anywhere can be home.*

After breakfast, Abbie assigned Diana the job of cleaning up the dirty dishes. Then she looked at Rose. "Since you insist on being up and about today, we'd better get to work on making up the food for tonight. But promise me you will sit if your ankle gets to bothering you."

Rose agreed and started making a cake. She made her mother's recipe from memory and knew it would take a good part of the morning just to beat the egg whites until they were stiff enough. At least her arm wasn't injured. Abbie had made a batch of bread dough when she first got up, and now she started shaping the yeasty mass into rolls.

The two women chatted easily in the warm kitchen as the smells of baking surrounded them. Every woman in the area would bring her best dishes tonight. While no official prizes were awarded, everyone would talk about who made the best pickles and preserves, whose bread was the lightest, and who made the tastiest sweets.

Abbie had never attended the harvest dance before and wanted to make a good impression on everyone with her new skills. Rose wanted to impress one certain young man, and she just didn't want to admit to herself, let alone Abbie or Katie, who he was.

"How can you tell when you're in love?" Rose asked Abbie.

"Well, that question came out of nowhere!"

Rose beat the egg whites a little harder to hide her embarrassment. "I, uh . . ."

"It's fine to wonder. Is it Zach you're thinking about?"

"I don't know. He can be so much fun and he's so handsome. But I sometimes feel like I'm only a decoration on his arm. I don't think he really sees me at all."

"He seems to like you well enough," Abbie said.

"He thinks he does. We've had a few good discussions, but he hasn't really taken the time to get to know the real me. He never asks me what I think, or what I would like to do. When we sit and talk, it's always about him." With a sigh, Rose put the mixing bowl on the table.

"Some men are just like that. It doesn't mean they don't love you."

"Abbie, you've been married twice. How did you know you were in love?"

A faraway look crossed her aunt's face. "When I met my first husband, it was sparks all the time. We always disagreed about something, but he challenged me to grow, and at the same time he liked me for who I was. My friends didn't think he was especially handsome, but in my eyes he was the best-looking man in the room wherever we went. I suppose we were just comfortable together. And one day we realized we loved each other. Because he worked with my father it was an easy situation and getting married just made it more comfortable."

The egg whites stood in stiff peaks, and Rose carefully folded them into the cake batter. She poured the batter into a greased pan, put it into the oven, and then turned to peel some potatoes over the sink. She hadn't thought of love as being a comfortable feeling before. From what the other young women said, she thought everyone fell fast and hard when the right person came along.

"What about Daniel? Did you know you loved him right away?" Rose put the knife down and rested her chin on her hand.

Abbie finished forming the rolls and put them under a tea towel to rise. "Oh, no. Daniel was very different. He tried to sweep me off my feet. He brought me a handful of wildflowers every night when we stopped the wagons. He complimented me on everything from how I did my hair to what a good child Tommy was. I would have been turned off by all of it, except I could tell he was sincere. I found him charming enough and pleasant company. He wanted to hear what I thought about everything, and we spent hours talking."

"But the way the other girls talk about fluttering hearts and weak knees . . ." Rose shook her head. "I am so confused. How can a person really know?"

"You'll just know. I knew Daniel was my friend. He sought out my company, and I sought out his. I started to fall in love with him the first time he said hello to me, but I knew I loved him when he would take my arm and all those warm, friendly feelings would make me 'weak in the knees,' as your friends say. So I guess it's a little of both."

Abbie wrapped her arm around Rose's shoulder. "Love needs to be based on respect. All the warm, tingly feelings in the world can't make the relationship good if that is lacking."

"Thanks, Abbie." Rose stood and hugged her aunt. With all Abbie had given her to think about, the rest of the day would fly by.

22

People filled the schoolyard, and trestle tables bowed under the weight of the food. Daniel and Abbie took their contributions to the tables while Rose stayed in the wagon, holding the baby and watching Diana. She had worked hard all day, and now her ankle throbbed. Perhaps she should've stayed home to rest. Then again, attending the harvest dance was better than spending the evening alone, even if she couldn't dance. Rose decided to use the occasion to get to know some of their neighbors better. She already looked at the members of the community differently, especially watching the children that would become her pupils in a few weeks.

After Abbie returned and took the sleeping baby from Rose, Daniel helped her down from the wagon and carried her over to the rocking chair he had brought.

"I feel like some old lady holding court." Rose did her best elderly woman voice and Diana giggled.

"You are too pretty to be an old lady," the little girl said, "and you don't have any white hair."

"I agree," Zach said from behind Rose's chair, then sat on the ground next to her and began talking about his day.

She listened enough to respond in the right places, but her mind began to wander. Elizabeth and Katie stood by the tables, helping to arrange the food. When they were done, they would be over to say hello. Ian and Mary hardly noticed anyone else around them, but Rose smiled at them anyway. She couldn't see Miles anywhere. Finally, she heard the clang of metal against metal and turned to see him and his father playing horseshoes with some of the other men.

"How's your foot?" Zach eventually asked.

Rose turned to him. "A little sore today. I helped Abbie in the kitchen for too long, and now I'm paying for it."

"Well, I hope it feels better soon," he said. "I won't be able to stop by nearly as often. Sheriff Gibb wants to hire me on as a deputy."

"He told me." Rose bit her lip. Did he think enough of her to listen to her opinion? "I don't think you should do it."

"Why not? It sounds exciting. Miles gets to help the community. Shouldn't I get a chance to do the same?"

"I thought you loved ranching." Rose shifted in the chair and stretched her foot.

"Maybe. You know, Rose, I used to dream of joining up with the Hole-in-the-Wall gang. Ma would kill me, though. But this would be almost as interesting. Sheriff Gibb is excited to hear my ideas about how to catch whoever has been robbing and beating people." He put his hat back on his head. "It's time for me to be my own man."

"So you go from having your mother and father telling you what to do, to having the sheriff telling you what to do." She purposely baited him, but he only shrugged. "Go play baseball if you want," she said, trying not to sound frustrated.

"Talk to you later," Zach replied with a grin, then hurried off.

Sometimes Zach was just like a little boy, Rose decided. She wished he would be sensible and not take the deputy job. He was just going to get hurt.

She sat quietly and watched the community she had grown to love. The married women buzzed around in little groups that shifted and changed. The single women stood in a cluster watching the young men play baseball. Rose was older than most of the single girls, and she knew her mother would be thrilled if she settled down and married. Zach caught a ball in the outfield and Rose wondered how her mother would feel if she allowed a nonmember to truly court her. Her father had always preached about the importance of building Zion, and Zach had shown some interest—at least more than anyone else.

The men played hard and Rose took the opportunity to observe them. The only two she really knew were Ian and Zach. Zach played like he did everything else, with great enthusiasm. Rose had never seen anyone with so much energy. Ian planned to be married by this time next year, since he had been courting Mary Larson for several months. The prospect of a wedding and future grandchildren excited Elizabeth, who, of course, wanted to see all her children married.

There were other attractive young men, but Rose hadn't had the chance to get to know any of them. Zach made it clear to everyone that Rose was his girl and therefore off limits. Not one of the other young men fought him for the privilege. But Rose supposed it was only to be expected, because by the time she attended that first dance, the Crandalls and Weavers had totally absorbed her into their families. Now Rose worried she would always be just a warm, comfortable fixture in the Weavers' home.

Katie came over and handed Rose a plate of food, then sat beside the rocking chair with her own plate. They watched the baseball game in silence while they ate.

"Why do the other girls avoid me?" Rose finally asked.

"They are a little mad at you for taking Zach out of circulation."

"Out of circulation?"

Katie giggled. "Zach has a bit of a reputation around here. He will court one girl for a little while and then move on. I think he has called on just about all the girls here. Sometimes, he will go on to a new one, and sometimes he will go back to one he has already courted. The girls don't seem to mind. He is good looking, and they all know he will get part of Papa's ranch someday. They're just waiting for him to make up his mind."

"But I haven't stopped him from seeing anyone else. We have no agreement."

"Well, since you came to town, he hasn't called on any of the other girls. Before you arrived we thought he might be serious about Emma Watt, but he hasn't stopped to see her in months now." Katie winked at Rose. "We think maybe you would make a good Crandall, so we just keep encouraging him to see you."

Rose stood, her face red. "Did anyone think to ask what I wanted?" She started to limp away from Katie.

"Come back, Rose. I'm sorry." Katie caught up with her and took her arm. "You didn't seem to mind his attention. We just thought you would be so good for him."

"I don't want to just be good for someone. I want to find someone who is good for me, and I'm not sure Zach is that person." Rose sighed. "I'm almost twenty-one years old, Katie. Mother is worried I will never marry. She thinks I'm too flighty and too stubborn, and maybe she's right. I'm sure part of the reason she sent me out here was to learn some responsibility."

"I think Zach would marry you in a second if he thought you wanted it." Katie laughed. "Wouldn't it be great to be sisters?"

"It would be great to be sisters." Rose saw Miles walking towards them. "We'll have to see what happens."

Katie looked at Miles. "I don't think he's mad at me, Rose, but he looks upset. You're on your own."

Miles watched Katie make her way to the other single girls, leaving Rose standing alone. She limped back to her rocking chair, clearly in pain, and he wondered what had possessed her to stand and put weight on her ankle.

His palms sweat as he approached her, but he wiped them on his woolen pants, determined not to let her get to him. *She is Sean's little sister. She is my patient.* Even as he thought this, he knew it was too late.

Little sister she might be, but she was also a beautiful, capable woman in her own right. He knew Abbie's story and had seen the change in her since Rose had become part of their family. The strength it took to go out and face her fears in the storm had made him even more aware of her potential. He mentally kicked himself. *Who thinks of a beautiful woman in terms of her potential?*

"What's wrong, Miles?" asked the object of his thoughts. "You look ready to take on a ferocious beast, but it's only me sitting here."

He squatted next to her. "If you can't stay off your foot, how do you expect it to heal?"

"I only took a few steps, Doctor."

"And stood on it all day helping Abbie." Miles sat on the ground.

"I can't believe she would tell on me." Rose gave him her best annoyed look.

"She wasn't telling on you. I only asked who made the best cake on the table, and she told me. As soon as she said it, she realized she had given away your secret." Miles took her foot in his hand and gently probed her ankle. She closed her eyes.

"It is amazing how you can compliment me on making the best cake, and make it sound like I committed a crime all at the same time," Rose said.

"I guess I can't keep you off it, can I?"

"It might be easier if I had more than Daniel, Abbie, and Zach for company. Even the sheriff comes by more than you." She adjusted her skirts to cover her ankle again as Miles put it gently on the ground. "You know, Dr. Crandall, you could come and visit your patient once in a while."

Miles lost himself in her eyes for one brief moment. "I just might do that."

She broke the gaze as the music started up. "Oh, I wish I could dance tonight." She sighed and looked up at him. "If you held me up, I could have one dance. Then I promise to be good."

As soon as she said it, she closed her eyes and blushed. Miles had never been asked to dance by a girl before. It just wasn't done. But this was more than just a forward girl. He watched as she swayed slightly to the music and remembered the first evening he had spent at the Sterling home. Peter had requested that his girls sing him a birthday song, and Mama had urged her daughters to stand with her and serenade him. The sound of angelic music filled the home as the three-part harmony of Rose, Maggie, and Carrie Sterling fit together perfectly. Miles and Sean had listened to the sweet tones for several minutes before the last note died away.

Miles knew how Rose felt about music. It was part of her, and sitting through an entire evening of dancing must be torture.

He reached forward and gathered her into his arms. "One dance, that's all."

Rose felt safe and protected as Miles carried her across the grass to the dance floor. She wished they could have stayed in the fading light by her chair with him gently massaging her ankle, but she knew it wouldn't be proper.

Miles chose a quiet corner and placed her gently on the floor. She rested most of her weight on her good foot and let him support and balance her. They stood in one spot and swayed as dancing couples whirled by them. Miles kept a suitable distance between them, talking about this year's crops. Rose couldn't have been happier, and she knew she couldn't blame her weak knees on her injury.

Sheriff Gibb approached them, swaggering with confidence. He tapped Miles on the shoulder. "May I cut in?"

"Not tonight, Sheriff. I am dancing with a patient and I want to make sure she treats this foot right so she can have many more dances next time."

A dark look crossed the sheriff's face. He hid it quickly, his hand coming to his badge, which he polished absently. "Of course, Doctor. Miss Sterling, have you made a decision concerning the teaching position?"

Rose nodded. "I'd be delighted to take the job."

Sheriff Gibb smiled. "Wonderful. I'm sure the children will love you." He tipped his hat at Rose.

Miles watched the man walk away. "Be careful around him." Miles said in a low voice. "I don't trust him."

"He's just lonely." Rose laughed as she tried to keep her balance.

Miles tightened his arms around her to keep her from falling. He watched her closely. "How's the foot holding up?"

"Oh, please don't make me stop dancing yet. This is the most fun I've had in two weeks."

He smiled and adjusted his arms.

"Ma told me you planned on teaching this fall."

"Word travels fast here." She tilted her head to the side. "What do you think?"

He gently whirled her around. "I think you will need a good horse to get you back and forth from school each day. We have a gentle mare you can use. I already talked to Pa about it."

"Thank you again. You always seem to be taking care of me somehow."

He pulled her a little closer. "I enjoy it."

Zach danced by them with Emma Watt. He winked at Rose and continued on his way.

Miles stiffened noticeably, and when the music stopped, Rose reluctantly pulled away from him. He scooped her up and deposited her in the rocking chair, which Daniel had moved to the edge of the dance floor.

"Thank you, Miles," she said.

Without a word, he tipped his head to her, turned, and walked away. As Rose watched his retreating back, she decided he was the most aggravating man she had ever met. But somehow she would break through his walls. After all, it was her father's dying wish that she allow Miles Crandall to court her.

23

The last of the children ran outside, and Rose waved at Tommy and Diana as they headed toward home. Then she noticed a few snowflakes falling. Daniel had predicted the season's first snow that morning at breakfast. *I'm glad Abbie insisted I bring my heavier shawl*, Rose thought as she shut the door and began tidying the room for the next day.

The seventeen children she taught in the little one-room schoolhouse wore her out. Rose sat at her desk and sighed, then rested her head on her arms and shut her eyes. She knew if she stayed long enough Zach might show up to escort her home. During the two months since the harvest dance, she had tried to get closer to Miles, but he had made every effort to avoid her. Zach was more than willing to fill the gap.

A knock on the schoolhouse door startled her and she jumped from her chair. The door opened and Sam Gibb walked into the room. He kept his gaze on the floor as he walked toward her, and Rose wondered why he always acted so shy around her. She had seen him lead the games with the other boys. She smiled at him and sat back down in her chair. "Can I help you with something, Sam?"

The boy lifted his chin and looked beyond Rose at the chalkboard. "I need some help with the math problems we worked on today."

He sunk into one of the desks and lowered his head again. Rose knew the fourteen-year-old didn't see his busy father much, and she never heard him mention his mother. Then she remembered the sheriff saying something about his wife dying. The boy probably just needed a little more attention than he got at home.

"Sure. I'll help you." Rose picked up a piece of chalk. "Show me which problems are giving you trouble." For the next half hour she helped Sam with his homework.

By the end of the session, he understood the assigned equations, so Rose wrote him a list of new ones to practice on. "Can I help you with anything else?" she asked as she handed the sheet of paper to the boy.

The sound of his tapping foot filled the room and Rose wondered what made him so nervous. "I hear you hold Mormon services at the Weavers' house." Sam stood up suddenly, knocking his pencil to the floor. "I'd like to come."

"Why of course, everyone is welcome. What made you ask?" Rose sat in her chair, astonished at the request.

"She was Mormon." The words were whispered, and Rose struggled to hear the end of Sam's statement. "My mama, I mean."

Before he could say more, the door to the school swung open again. Sheriff Gibb walked into the room with a flurry of snowflakes behind him.

"You had me worried when you didn't show up, boy." He stopped next to his son, and Rose watched the boy hang his head again, but not before he caught her eye with a pleading look.

Rose remembered how much the sheriff seemed to dislike her religion. "He needed a little extra help on his schoolwork."

"I didn't think you would miss me, Pa." Sam ducked his head again and resumed tapping his foot on the floor.

"There's a storm coming in and I want you home before it hits," the sheriff said. He nodded at Rose and left the school, pushing the boy in front of him.

Rose shook her head, thinking she would never see that boy on Sunday. She had kept her promise not to teach religion in the school, even though she said her own silent prayer every day before lessons started. When she turned to put the math book away, she realized she still held Sam's paper in her hand. The decision to take it to him came easily. Sam needed his homework and needed to know someone cared.

It didn't take long to finish tidying up the schoolhouse. Rose made sure the fire in the stove was out, and then she ventured into the first snowstorm of the season. The flakes whirled around her and brushed against her cheeks. Rose tipped her head back and let the little frozen bits melt on her face. The gentle horse she had borrowed from the Crandalls plodded through the accumulating snow around the north end of town and across the river to the sheriff's farm.

The house sat back from the road, partially hidden by a large barn. The yard spread before her, silent and still, and Rose decided she was quite alone. She stopped and dismounted, tying her horse to a fence rail out of sight of the house. Lifting her skirt so the hem would stay dry, she made her way to the house. The buildings looked well kept and she could see through windows that were polished to a shine.

As she came to the front step, voices assaulted her ears. She recognized one of them as the man who told Miles to stick to his doctoring the day Rose had helped prepare the clinic.

"No son of mine is going to get friendly with those Mormons," the sheriff responded angrily. "They took your Ma—they ain't taking you too. You get your help during school hours and I'll answer any questions you have when I have the time."

Rose stopped on the top stair. In that instant, she knew she should turn and leave, but she ignored the feeling and raised her hand to knock on the door.

She stopped when the other man began to speak. "He don't need so much learnin', Arthur."

The tea kettle whistled and reminded Rose how cold she was, but her curiosity got the better of her. She tiptoed to the window and stood still as she listened further.

"My son will get an education. Just because you quit school after the second grade doesn't mean you should encourage your nephew to do the same thing."

"Aw, Arthur, I get by just fine. Look at all your book learnin'. All it got you is a two-bit sheriff job in a nothin' sort of town." Rose saw a hand reach forward and toss a log into the fireplace. "Who needs an education out here? All this land for the takin', and I'm here to take it."

"Pa, just let me quit school and help at the farm. I can get all the learning I need from you." The only sound for a few moments was the crackling of the fire.

"No, Son, you need to keep going to school. What will the community think if I won't even send my own boy to the school when I handpicked the teacher?" The steady sound of someone pacing across the room made the porch vibrate.

The other voice laughed, a dark sound in the deepening dusk. "Now, Sam, don't go gettin' any ideas about that little teacher of yours. She's much too old for you."

"I ain't interested in her like that. I just want to do well at school." Sam heaved a big sigh. "She reminds me of Mama."

"You stay away from her Sam. I mean it."

"It's just, well, she kind of looks like Mama."

"Stay away from her and all those other Mormons," Arthur Gibb said sternly. "I don't want you befriending them or defending them. I got you away once and I won't give you back."

Rose flattened herself against the wall, wondering if she should just knock on the door and hand them the homework. She turned and reached toward the door one more time, but stopped at Sam's words.

"Pa, let me work with you. I proved I could be tough when I stole Mrs. Turner's jewelry." The voice came soft through the glass and Rose felt her insides twist. She backed from the door and carefully made her way down the steps. Looking behind her, she realized a perfect little trail led to her cold feet. There would be no mistaking woman's footprints in the snow.

She turned her face toward the window and felt her heart stop. Sam Gibb stared through the panes of glass at his schoolteacher. He raised his eyebrows in question and with a shaking hand she pulled the paper from inside her coat. He turned back into the room. Rose lifted her skirts and hurried to her horse. She put a foot in the stirrup, but before she could pull herself up onto the horse, a hand grabbed her ankle.

Sam pulled her back from the horse and held his hand out for the paper. He smiled and stood watching her. Realizing for the first time how tall he was and remembering his comment about Mrs. Turner, Rose trembled.

"I hope your father won't mind me stopping by," she said, keeping her voice low.

"He won't know you did."

"Did you really hurt Mrs. Turner?"

The pain on the boy's face was obvious. "I didn't hit her. I only took her jewelry."

"But she was hurt bad. Zach Crandall and I picked her up and took her to the doctor." Rose wanted to believe Sam hadn't harmed the poor woman, but she had washed Sarah's bloody face herself.

Sam blushed. "I only took her jewelry," he repeated. "Uncle hurt her. He laughed at me and told me I wasn't a real man because I wanted to let her go without hitting her."

"Does your father know you did it?" Rose held her breath and waited for the answer. The door to the house slammed. Sam grabbed her waist and hoisted her on the horse without answering her question.

"Get outta here, Miss Sterling. They can't know you were here." He slapped the horse's rear and turned to go back around the corner of the barn.

Rose took one last look at the Gibb house and then let the horse run through the swirling snow toward home.

24

Snow was falling again and Rose wondered if it would ever stop. Outside the house she could see a winter wonderland. The icicles hanging off the roof almost touched the top of the snowdrifts. The drifts themselves lay three feet high in some places. But it wasn't a bitter cold, and she had spent the day with Tommy and Diana making snowmen and tobogganing down a nearby hill.

Now she stood in front of the stove warming her hands and watching the children drink mugs of hot cocoa. Abbie had a large pot of stew cooking and biscuits in the oven. The children chattered to their mother about their fun-filled afternoon, and as soon as they finished their cocoa, Abbie sent them to work setting the table for supper.

Christmas approached rapidly, and every day the children seemed more excited about the holiday. Abbie worked on Christmas gifts, and Daniel spent many hours hiding away in his wood shop. Rose tried to feel the joy of the season, but she missed her family. She took her own mug of hot cocoa and slipped into the bedroom she shared with Diana.

Since moving into the house, Rose had replaced the tea towels over the windows with pretty blue curtains. She and Diana hung some dried flowers along one wall to give the room some color and to make it pleasant and inviting. The warmth of the fireplace and stove in the main rooms didn't reach into the bedroom much, so Rose took an afghan her mother had made and wrapped it around her shoulders.

The Weavers had been wonderful to Rose, but she knew Abbie didn't need her help anymore. Her aunt had just needed a good teacher, and now she loved being in the kitchen. Her skill with the needle was evident around the house and in the new clothes her family wore. Rose sat on her bed and cried. The teaching job filled up some time, but in the last week there had been so much snow that she had canceled classes until after Christmas.

Rose worried almost constantly about Sam. He worked hard when he came to school and demonstrated a great love for learning. He'd even attended their Sunday meeting two days after she'd overheard the conversation in the sheriff's house. He'd hardly said three words, but Rose knew he felt at peace in the Weaver home. Still, it didn't matter what the boy felt; Sheriff Gibb's attitude hadn't softened toward the Mormons and she knew she'd best leave the boy alone, for both of their safety. She wanted to tell Miles what she had overheard, but at the time he was tending to a patient, another victim of a brutal beating. She hadn't seen Miles or Zach since.

I want to go home, Rose kept saying to herself. But she knew that even if the roads were passable, her family didn't have room for her at her aunt's home in Utah. They would be coming through Montana in a few months anyway. Rose took the latest letter from her mother and reread it.

Dearest Rose,

We are all well, although Aunt Jane has surprised us all and gotten married. We thought she would remain a spinster forever. She married a perfectly nice gentleman by the name of Oscar Powell. Because Granny won't move from here, Mr. Powell has moved in. They tell us we are still welcome, but the space feels even tighter than before. Carrie and I spend a lot of time in our small room just to stay out of the newlywed's way.

Granny Sterling is as feisty as ever. She keeps wondering when you will get married. She is worried that you will turn out like Aunt Jane. I don't have such great concern as she does, but you are twenty-one next month.

How is Miles? We are counting the days until we can leave for Canada and see you again . . .

Rose threw the letter on the bed. She had never wanted to get married; even her time with Karl had been more about finding an excuse to stay in Utah. Looking back she couldn't remember why she had been so reluctant to leave. Like Miles had promised, she had grown to love Montana and knew she could learn to love Alberta, too. But something else had changed.

Without her family to lean on every day, she felt indescribably lonely. It amazed her that Aunt Jane had stood it all these years, not having someone who loved her. It made Rose smile to think her aunt had finally found happiness. Rose wondered if some decent young man—someone who wasn't full of himself—would take serious notice of her.

Rose heard the kitchen door open and knew Daniel had come in for dinner. She stood and put the letter back under her pillow. The warmth from the main room washed over her as she opened the bedroom door. Zach stood there and she greeted him warmly.

After the meal, Zach asked her if she wanted to walk around the yard with him. He assured her it was still pleasant outside and they wouldn't be long. Rose took her heavy wool coat off the peg and followed him outside.

It was so peaceful under the stars. The blanket of snow muffled everything and crunched under their feet as they walked. Rose wrapped her shawl tighter around her head, glad for the warm pair of mittens her grandmother had knit for her.

Zach kicked the snow in front of him and Rose watched as it sparkled its way back to the ground. A branch snapped off a tree with the weight of the snow, and the cracking sound made Zach jump. They reached the fence line at the far side of the yard. The barn loomed dark next to them, and from inside the house, the kerosene lamps cast a warm glow in the snow.

"How's the teaching going?"

She turned to look at him and found him watching her in the moonlight. "You know I've shut down the school until after Christmas because of the snow." Then she swallowed the lump in her throat and put her hand on his arm. "I need to tell you something." The story of her visit to the Gibb ranch spilled out.

Zach listened intently, putting his hand over hers to steady her. "I've suspected he's up to something for a while now. I've talked to Miles about it, but we decided to see if we can get some more concrete evidence before we do anything. Right now it is just speculation and would be your word against his. Too many members of the community still think Miles is somehow involved."

"It doesn't make sense. What would Miles have to gain?"

Zach shrugged. "What would anyone have to gain? The few small things that have been stolen are of such little value it hardly seems worth the effort. I have noticed a pattern, though. The few families and landowners that have been involved all live west of town. Did you hear that the Turners are leaving? Mrs. Turner finally convinced her husband that Spring Creek isn't safe. They are going to San Francisco after Christmas."

"Sam did admit to robbing Mrs. Turner. If his uncle was responsible for the beating . . ."

Zach cut her off. "We can't accuse anyone without proper evidence. As hard as I look, I can't find anything to point to them."

"So you'll let him continue hurting people and breaking the law?"

"Until we can prove his involvement, there is nothing we can do. I wish there was."

"You really are taking this job seriously." Rose looked up at Zach. He had surprised everyone, proving himself to be a great deputy. Rose wondered if he would ever want to be sheriff.

Zach touched her hand. "Miles and I both feel rather powerless right now, but at least we can tell you to avoid Gibb and his son. The less you are around them, the less I have to worry.

"I'll try. But Sam needs a good friend and I am his teacher."

"Just be careful. Don't tell anyone else about this. The sheriff doesn't need to know you heard anything." Zach took his hat off and twirled it in his hands, and they watched the stars in silence for a time. Suddenly, Zach said, "Listen, do you think you might want to get married someday?"

Rose thought the situation would be funny if it were happening to someone else. The question didn't surprise her, but the joy she imagined she would feel if he asked her wasn't there. "I don't know, Zach, maybe. How about you? I hear you're walking out with Emma Watt these days."

He put his hands on her shoulders and pulled her close. "A man has to explore his options. I think you and I complement each other. You would be the kind of wife to make a man proud." He leaned in and she knew he wanted to kiss her.

She pulled away. "I need to think Zach. This is sudden."

"Give me a good reason not to decide this right now." He took her chin in his hand and turned her face so he could look into her eyes.

"Well, there is the religion thing. You know I would like to marry someone who believes as I do." Rose stepped back from him and leaned against the fence.

"I just couldn't get into that book, but I could try again if it is so important to you." Zach sighed. "I did enjoy the meeting I attended with Miles, but even though you all seem to believe, I don't really see how it is so different from the church in town."

Rose took Zach's hand. "If you gave it a chance, you would feel differently. I know you would."

"So if I joined your church, would the answer be yes?" The anticipation in Zach's eyes shone in the deepening shadows.

"You can't be baptized just so I will marry you. You need to do it for yourself." Rose looked across the snowy fields. "I don't love you yet. But I do like to be with you and we have lots of fun. I'm sure the love would come." She felt tears start to well in her eyes. Her mother would be so happy if she received a letter announcing a wedding, but she would be disappointed that Zach wasn't a member of the true Church.

"I'm not dumb," Zach said sadly. "I know you don't love me. I've even seen the way you look at my brother. But I love you and I figure we do have fun together, and if Miles won't act on his feelings, then you and I might as well get married." Zach bent and scooped up a handful of snow, then threw a snowball that hit the side of the barn with a dull thud. "Like you said, we could learn to love each other."

Rose could tell Zach believed he truly loved her. She just didn't love him. "Give me until after Christmas to decide, Zach."

"I'll expect an answer by New Year's Day," he said, taking her hand and walking her back to the house.

All Rose could do was wonder what Zach meant about Miles not acting on his feelings.

"Rose, will you help me again?" Diana handed the handkerchief she was embroidering for her mother's Christmas gift over to Rose, who deftly untangled the knot in the thread. The gift was coming along nicely, the monogram in the corner of the fabric taking shape under Diana's chubby fingers.

Rose planned to give each of the Crandalls a small gift because of their kindness to her. For Elizabeth and Katie, she made sachets, and Rose's room was filled with the scent of the lavender she and her mother had grown and dried. She embroidered the sachets with little purple flowers entwined with an "E" and a "K."

The Crandall men were more difficult. Rose finally settled on monogrammed handkerchiefs for John and Ian. She made a small bag out of a piece of leather for Zach to carry his money in. As for Miles, she felt she owed him a great deal because of his constant care of her after her illness and injury. He had insisted that because Rose was Sean's sister, and because he had promised her mother he would take care of her, he wouldn't accept payment for his services. But when Rose allowed herself to think about it, she knew there were other reasons she wanted Miles's gift to be special. She tried not to think about those reasons as Zach's proposal weighed on her mind.

Now, Daniel came in the house, stomping the snow off his boots. He dragged a large pine tree behind him, followed by Tommy. Diana squealed at the sight of the evergreen, and Rose moved the rocking chair away from the window to clear a spot.

The night before, the family had spent the evening getting ready for the tree. Fluffy, white popcorn hung from colored thread, waiting to be draped over the green boughs. Abbie showed Rose and Diana how to make folded paper birds just like her father had taught her many years before. They tore pages from an old catalogue and fashioned scores of ornaments for the tree.

Once Daniel had the tree up, they wasted no time in trimming it. Abbie went into her bedroom and came back out with a simple wooden box. She opened it and took out a shiny tin star and matching ornaments. "They were my mother's," she said. After they hung the last ornament, they all stood back and admired their handiwork.

"Oh, I almost forgot to tell you. Tommy and I ran into the Crandall boys. They asked us if we would join their family for Christmas dinner."

Abbie clapped her hands. "Oh, it will be so good to get out of the house."

Rose agreed, but wished they were going somewhere besides the Crandalls'.

25

Christmas Day dawned bright and clear. Snowfall from the night before left a fresh, thick blanket of glimmering white covering the ground. Diana woke up before anyone else and ran into the sitting room to check her stocking. "Santa came. Santa came!" echoed through the little house, and soon everyone else was awake.

The children found peppermint sticks in their stockings as well as an orange. Tommy and Daniel were delighted with the new scarf and mittens Rose had knit each of them. Rose had made Diana two new dresses for her rag doll, and the little girl played happily with them all morning. For Abbie, there was a crocheted doily that immediately found a spot on the back of the rocking chair.

Rose was touched by the gift they gave her—a drawing of the three children in a fine wooden frame. "It is so beautiful."

"Thank you. I haven't done any sketching in a long time." Abbie put the baby down and stood to give Rose a hug. "Daniel made the frame."

"I will cherish it forever." Rose's eyes filled with tears.

Daniel chuckled. "All right, enough of this. We have a Christmas dinner to go to and we don't want to be late."

Everyone started bustling around. Tommy and Daniel went outside in their new scarves and mittens to hitch the horses to the sleigh. Abbie and Rose gathered the food they had prepared the day before.

Soon they were on their way, skimming over the snow on the way to the Crandalls'. Rose enjoyed the sleigh ride and loved holding little Diana close to her under the lap robe so they could share the warmth. *If only Mama, Carrie, and Sean were here*, she thought, *this would be perfect.*

The Crandall ranch came into view, a soft spiral of smoke curling out of the chimney. Soon, Rose could smell the roast turkey on the breeze, and her stomach growled in response. A large Christmas tree filled the front window, and someone had tied bright red bows on the porch railing.

When the sleigh stopped, the Crandall men spilled out of the house. Ian and Daniel took the horses into the barn, while Zach and Miles helped the women and children out of the sleigh. Zach gave Rose a wink as he lifted his arms to help her to the ground. She smiled back at him and wondered why she didn't feel more excited to see him.

She glanced at Miles out of the corner of her eye and found him studying her. Boldly, she turned her head to meet his gaze, giving him her brightest smile. He turned quickly and herded the young ones into the warm house.

Miles helped Diana out of her little coat and hung it high on a peg. A flurry of activity erupted behind him as the women greeted each other. With the heavy snows, most of the women in the area were housebound until the snow melted. Only those in town managed to get out with any regularity. Katie and Rose hugged each other and set to talking as only young women do.

Elizabeth soon called everyone to gather for dinner. Miles remembered the first time Rose had sat at this table. Still weak from her illness, she had been the picture of beauty and grace. He also remembered how she had looked at Zach. He watched them now and noticed that the looks Rose gave his brother were wary and guarded.

He wondered what had happened between the two of them. In the weeks before Christmas, he had noticed Zach's reserve when it came to discussing Rose. Whenever a family member had mentioned her name, he changed the subject, often to discuss Emma Watt. Yet Miles had seen the wink Zach gave Rose as he lifted her from the sleigh.

"The meal is wonderful, Elizabeth," John said to his wife as he sat back and patted his stomach.

There was a chorus of agreement, but Elizabeth brushed off the praise. "It wasn't just me. Abbie made a fine contribution herself. I declare, Abbie, I think you are becoming the best bread maker in Spring Creek."

It pleased Miles to see that Rose's journey all this way from her family had been so good for Abbie.

Rose looked up and met his eyes, catching him staring at her again. He didn't look away until she blushed and lowered her eyes.

"How many have you treated?"

Miles shook his head when he realized he was being spoken to. "I'm sorry," he said, unsure who had addressed him.

"Zach says the beatings are still happening," Daniel repeated. "How many of the injured have you treated?"

Miles found it difficult to focus on the conversation with Rose sitting across from him. "Six. Those I did treat were luckier than the ones who were beyond my help."

"Someone died?" Abbie's face blanched.

"Guess I forgot to mention that." Daniel frowned.

"It seems odd to me that we have a safe, good town until we get a new sheriff, and then we have a crime spree that no one can explain," John said.

"Just a coincidence, I'm sure. He seems to think he has it under control, plus there haven't been as many problems since the snow settled in. I guess it makes even criminals stay indoors." Zach pushed his chair back from the table. "I'm just glad we haven't been personally affected."

Zach looked at Rose, and Miles wondered how much she and Zach had discussed. She had seemed surprised at the mention of murder, but not surprised the sheriff might be involved.

"Hopefully they can solve this before we are affected," Daniel said as he stood. "Excuse me, Elizabeth. Thank you for the wonderful meal."

Elizabeth pushed her own chair out and started clearing away the food. "Enough of this depressing talk. It's Christmas and we're here to celebrate."

John laughed. "Your mother's spoken, boys. Let's get this meal cleared up so we can have us some fun."

The two families gathered in the sitting room and listened as John read the Christmas story as recorded in the second chapter of Luke. The familiar words were a balm to Rose, and when she closed her eyes, she could almost imagine her father reading the beloved verses. Everyone was quiet as John read the final verse.

"May I tell you another Christmas story?" Miles asked softly. Without waiting for an answer, he related the story of the signs of the Savior's birth in the Americas. He finished his story and looked to his father for approval. Tears touched Rose's eyes as John nodded at his son and smiled.

Out of habit, Rose started singing "Silent Night." She sang this song every Christmas Eve after her father read the Christmas story to his family, Once she realized she'd been carried away by the moment and should have asked the Crandalls' permission to sing, it was too late. When she reached the last note and opened her eyes, her planned apology lay unspoken on her tongue. The families around her sat in awed silence. She looked at Miles and noticed tears in his eyes.

Daniel wiped his eyes. "Rose, you sound like an angel."

"Please sing some more, dear." Elizabeth reached over and touched Rose's hand.

Rose blushed. "It's tradition in my family that I sing 'Silent Night' after my father reads from Luke. After that, the whole family joins in. I would love it if you would sing with me."

Protests filled the room. Rose shrugged her shoulders and sat back in her chair.

"I'll sing with you," Miles said.

She started the song again, singing the first line alone. Miles joined in with a mellow tenor, and soon everyone in the room sang together. After they got over their initial reluctance, the group sang every Christmas song they could think of.

Finally, Elizabeth held up her hands in surrender. "I won't have any voice left tomorrow." She laughed and stood to give Rose a hug. "Thank you for bringing music to our home, dear."

"Presents?" Diana couldn't keep still any longer. She ran to the bag hanging by the door and hauled it over to the center of the room. "Here, Rose."

Rose laughed. Diana had helped her wrap the gifts and acted more excited to see them unwrapped than she had been to open her own earlier that morning. The little girl handed out the cookies she and her mother made for the Crandalls. Then, Rose gave each member of the family the gifts she had carefully crafted. "I wanted to say thank you for your help when I arrived here so ill, and also for your friendship."

John and Ian loved their new handkerchiefs, Katie and Elizabeth exclaimed over the sweet smell of the sachets, and Zach looked pleased with the money pouch, bragging about how soon he would fill it. Rose saved Miles's gift for last.

"Miles, I wanted to say thank you for the help you gave me when I was ill and when I sprained my ankle. You already told me I couldn't pay you, but when Katie and I came to town and helped you set up your house, I noticed you didn't have many blankets. I hope this helps." She reached in the bag and pulled out a beautiful crocheted afghan. She had made it a deep blue and copied the afghan that lay on her own bed.

"I wondered what you had done with that," Abbie said.

"Rose, I don't know what to say." Miles took the blanket in his hands and held it to his chest. "Thank you."

Rose felt some deeper meaning in the words tonight.

Daniel pulled a watch from his vest pocket. "Well, we should probably head home. It will be dark soon."

"Will you stay the night?" Katie took Rose's hand and squeezed it tight. "We never get a chance to visit. We can get you home in the morning."

"Go ahead, it will be fun for you." Abbie kissed her niece on the cheek and then took the tightly wrapped baby from Elizabeth. She ushered the older children out the door. A few minutes later, over the bells on the departing sleigh, Rose heard her aunt call, "We'll see you tomorrow, Rose."

26

Katie drifted off quickly, but Rose lay in the bed wide awake. The moonlight fell across the quilts and she kept tracing the pattern of the log-cabin design with her eyes. Around and around the squares went. Finally, Rose decided she should do something productive rather than lie in bed unable to sleep. She put Katie's robe over her borrowed nightgown and tiptoed into the hallway. The cold floor stung her bare feet and she hurried across the room to put them on the braided rug under the rocker. The coals glowed in the fireplace and a few small flames still jumped in the dark. Rose curled her feet under her and picked up the family Bible.

She wanted to read the Christmas story one more time, but as she placed the Bible in her lap, the pages fell open to the center of the book where the family records were kept. She read the dates and names of the Crandall family but stopped short when she reached the entry for Miles's birth.

"Matthew Miles Crandall. Born 15 June 1874." Right below that entry was another. "Magdalena Crandall. Born 15 June 1874. Died 26 August 1883."

She looked up at the fire and tried to remember if anyone had ever mentioned another sister. As her gaze rested on the hearth, she noticed she was not alone. Miles sat on the floor near the fire, leaning back against his father's large chair. He had her afghan wrapped around his shoulders.

"Why didn't you say anything when I walked into the room?" she asked.

"I don't know." He reached behind him and placed another log on the fire. "I see you found the family history."

"I wasn't snooping," Rose said as she shut the book.

"I know."

Rose stood and pulled the robe tight around her. "I should go back to bed."

"Please sit down and let me tell you about my sister."

The rocking chair creaked in the silent room as she slowly sat down.

"She was my twin, and we did everything together. She was about as much a tomboy as is Katie, I guess." His fingers absently worked the edge of the afghan. "She could climb every tree I could and run faster most of the time. We loved to play at the picnic spot. We went fishing up there all the time, and when it was really hot we would go wading in the creek. Our whole life was about getting the chores done as fast as we could so we could play."

The fire sparked as the log shifted, illuminating the sadness in Miles's face. Rose wanted to reach out and ease his pain, but she sat still in the rocker and let him continue.

"It was August and as hot as I can remember. We were playing in the creek, skipping stones and getting our feet wet. I saw the dark clouds coming but didn't pay them much attention. We were having too much fun." Miles stood and started pacing in front of the fire. "The clouds opened on us suddenly and the heavens emptied every drop of water they had. Mama always warned us to be careful and watch out for each other. Lena had crossed to the other side of the creek when the cloudburst started. We knew Mama wouldn't be happy if we stayed out in the rain, so I hollered at Lena to come back so we could get home."

Rose noticed the tenseness in Miles's shoulders as he told the story.

He stopped in front of her and dropped to his knees. "She didn't make it across the creek. She wasn't even halfway when a flash flood came roaring through. The force of the water knocked her over and she hit her head on a rock. The water dragged her under a low-lying tree branch. She was unconscious and trapped under the water, and I couldn't get to her."

Rose reached forward and brushed a lock of hair off his forehead. "Oh, Miles."

"I watched my sister and best friend die, and I couldn't help her."

"It wasn't your fault. You were just a kid." She continued to stroke the hair off his forehead like she would to comfort a small child. He grew still beneath her touch.

"I know."

"Is that the other reason you became a doctor?" she asked.

"I suppose so. It feels good to help someone else, and I think Lena would have been happy I chose this path. But I want to be more like Zach, Katie, and you. You all seem to have such zest for life, but every time I try to have a little fun, I picture Lena." Miles reached up and stilled her hand by closing his fingers around hers. "Lately, she seems to be smiling instead of hurting.

They sat still with their fingers linking them, Rose watching the emotions play across his face. *How could I have ever thought him cold and arrogant?* she wondered. *How did I miss the pain in his eyes?*

212

Miles stood and pulled her up with him. He wrapped his arms around her and pulled her close. She felt the familiar thrill of just being near him and rested her head against his shoulder.

"You had better get back to bed," he said finally, then gently pushed her away and turned her toward Katie's room. "I'll see you in the morning."

"Are you going to stay out here all night?" Rose asked softly.

He grinned. "Zach and Ian both snore. It must be the twin thing. I'll get more rest out here by the fire."

She stifled a laugh with her hand. "Good night. Thank you for telling me about Lena."

"Good night, my Rose." She heard him whisper as she left the room.

Rose woke as Katie hummed around the room.

"It's about time you got up," Katie said as she playfully tugged on Rose's hair. "You would think we stayed up half the night."

Rose's cheeks went red. "We should go help your mother."

"She has given me the day off to entertain you, so we can do whatever we want. Breakfast is on the table, so come out as soon as you are dressed." Katie skipped out of the room.

Rose threw the blankets back and dressed in the brown woolen skirt and pink blouse she had worn to dinner the day before. The bedroom had turned icy during the night, so Rose couldn't wait to get to the stove-warmed kitchen. She remembered the first time she had walked into the same room to face a bunch of strangers. This time she ate with friends and looked forward to spending the day with them.

Zach waited for her in the hallway. "Good morning, sleepy head." He walked with her to the kitchen, talking the whole way.

When they entered the kitchen, Rose looked for Miles, but his place at the table was empty. His dishes had already been cleared, as had John's. Sitting next to Katie, Rose helped herself to some hot porridge and poured a small amount of fresh cream on top.

Zach continued his monologue about his excitement over working for the sheriff. Katie listened to her brother, injecting a word here and there about it not being a game and about how he should be careful. Soon, Ian finished with a "thank you" to his mother and left to help with the chores.

Rose had hardly paid attention to the chatter around her, and as soon as they finished eating, Elizabeth promptly shooed Zach from the room. "Katie, would you do the breakfast dishes for me? I want Rose's help with something."

Rose wondered what Elizabeth needed as she followed the older woman to Katie's bedroom.

Elizabeth waited until Rose crossed the floor, then she shut the door and turned to face her. "Now tell me what's wrong, dear. You look like a lovesick calf, and I think you need a mother right now."

Rose picked up the nightgown lying across the foot of the bed and folded it, weighing her words carefully. "Really, I just didn't sleep well last night."

"That's interesting. Miles told me the same thing this morning when I asked him why he was so fidgety." Elizabeth took the gown from Rose's hand and motioned for her to sit down. When Rose sat on the edge of the bed, Elizabeth pulled up a chair and looked at her expectantly.

"I guess we both couldn't sleep well at the same time. He told me about Lena."

Elizabeth turned her face away from Rose.

"Oh, I am so sorry. I didn't mean to bring up old pains." Rose twisted her skirt in her hands and then smoothed it. She repeated the action several times while she waited for Elizabeth to speak.

After wiping the tears from her face, Elizabeth looked Rose in the eyes. "He hasn't spoken about her since the day she died. We tried to get him to tell us what happened but he wouldn't. The story pieced itself together and we never blamed him, but somehow he blamed himself."

The revelation surprised Rose, and she wondered why she was the one he had chosen to share the story with.

"This morning he seemed lighter somehow, more free and at ease." Elizabeth took Rose's hand and gave it a motherly squeeze. "Thank you, for whatever you said to him." She started toward the door and then turned. "I can see how you are so good for both of my boys. I know Zach gave you some time to think about his proposal. Have you made a decision?"

"I don't know." Rose lifted her hands and shrugged. "I just don't know."

Later that morning, Katie and Rose helped Ian and Zach take down the Christmas tree. Then they put on their winter coats, hats, scarves, and mittens and watched the boys haul the tree to Miles, who was chopping wood in the yard. They waved and continued on to the grove. The day felt almost warm with the sun beaming down on them. The two girls followed the path and talked of fashions, and who would be marrying whom in the spring.

As they reached the end of the grove and turned to go back to the house, Rose noticed the chopping sound had stopped. She wondered what chore Miles had started now, and then chided herself for not wondering the same thing about Zach.

Katie grabbed her arm and startled her from her thoughts. "I think we might be in trouble. I didn't think they would do it with you here, but I thought wrong."

"Do what? Who?" Rose halted in confusion. "Katie . . ." The first snowball hit her and left a white mark on her dark skirt.

"Our annual day-after-Christmas snowball fight!" Katie bent over and scooped up two handfuls of snow, then packed a snowball and hurled it at one of her brothers as they emerged from behind the trees. "Come on. Don't make me win all by myself."

Rose laughed and grabbed her own handful of snow. Katie waved her over and they ran behind some trees to catch their breath. She could hear the brothers laughing and teasing. She glanced at Katie, who looked confused.

"Miles is out there."

"Well, he is one of your brothers, Katie." Rose continued to pack snowballs.

"But he never does the snowball fight with us. And Rose, I've never heard my brother laugh before."

The girls stopped their movement and listened. They heard Zach and Ian's familiar voices, but a third voice also rang through the air. Miles's laugh was contagious, and soon Rose and Katie were laughing as well.

Katie lifted the hem of her skirt and filled it with snowballs, so Rose copied her. They each came around a different side of the tree, throwing white missiles at their attackers. Katie started chasing Zach away and Ian went to his brother's rescue. Rose could hear them crashing through the trees and turned the other direction to find a better route.

She took the path she and Katie had just come down and hurried to go the long way back to the yard. The sounds behind her faded and she thought she might be home free, until a noise startled her. The snowball hit her throwing arm and she dropped the snowball she was about to launch. Before she could pick up another one, Miles stopped in front of her.

"Do you surrender?"

"Never," she said, laughing as she backed away.

"Be careful how you answer."

"Never," she said again as she lifted the hem of her skirt to run.

"The loser gets their face washed with snow!" Miles called after her as she dodged through the trees.

"You have to catch me first," she yelled back at him.

She focused on the way ahead of her and ran. She knew he was letting her gain some ground, and she ducked behind a tree to catch her breath. The familiar tightness gripped her lungs and she leaned forward, trying to calm down. She couldn't hear Miles behind her, so she sank to the ground. Laying her head on the tree trunk, she could hear Katie still battling with her brothers. Rose had never had so much fun.

The tightness eased a little and she opened her eyes, determined to pummel the boys with snow and help Katie. When she looked up, Miles knelt on the snow next to her. She had been so focused on drawing breath that she hadn't heard him approach. By the look on his face, Rose realized she had frightened him.

"I'm fine. I just needed to sit down for a minute."

"In a snowdrift? Come on, let's get you back in the house."

Rose answered him by throwing a handful of snow at him. It hit him squarely in the face. "You are not carrying me this time." He sputtered and caught Rose as she tried to get away. Laughing, she fell to the ground. As fast as she could, she threw snow at him. "I will not have my face washed with snow today, Miles Crandall."

Miles held his arms up in surrender. "All right, I guess I lost this time. Go ahead and do your worst."

She sat for a moment and just looked at him. His cheeks were red from cold and exertion. He knelt in front of her, his hair curling around the edges of his knit cap and his eyes happy.

"I won't wash your face on one condition," she said. "Keep laughing. It looks good on you."

"With you around, Rose, I can't help it."

He reached to her and helped her to her feet. She let her hand rest in his longer than necessary as she looked for the somberness in his eyes. But today it was gone, replaced by her reflection.

27

The week passed quickly. Rose alternated between considering Zach's marriage proposal and remembering the moments spent with Miles over Christmas. She knew she didn't love Zach, even though, as he'd told her, love might come eventually. It had happened for her parents. Still, Rose wanted more than an eventuality. On the other hand, Miles had made her no offer, and she was quite aware that an offer might never come.

Rose shook off her thoughts and turned back to the new dress she was hemming. A package from her mother had arrived several weeks before Christmas. The family had been excited as she opened it and found yards and yards of pale green silk taffeta. Under the fabric lay the latest *Ladies Home Journal*, small toys and candies for the children, a new book for Daniel, and a delicate pair of lace gloves for Abbie.

Abbie and Rose had spent hours poring over the magazine until they decided on a dress design for the fabric. Then, they had carefully cut out the pieces and stitched them together. Elizabeth had helped Abbie fit the gown until not a wrinkle could be seen.

Rose hoped to finish the dress in time to wear it to the New Year's Eve dance the following evening. She snipped off a piece of thread and re-threaded her needle. The soft fabric draped over her hands, and she knew the color would suit her dark hair and fair skin.

Holding the dress in front of her, she examined it with a critical eye. The voluminous skirt fell over her lap, and the silk caught the last of the day's light that filtered through the sitting room window. A few more stitches and the dress was finally done.

Diana rushed to the bedroom. Rose had been hiding behind the closed door for an hour, only letting Abbie in to do the laces on her corset. "They're here. They're here!" Rose could hear Diana jumping up and down in excitement.

Rose pushed a curl into place and looked at herself in the mirror. The bodice fit perfectly and emphasized her waist, and the skirt hung smoothly over her hips before flaring to the floor. Zach expected his answer tonight, and she still hadn't decided what to tell him. Even so, she wanted to look her very best.

She opened the bedroom door and grinned at Diana's excited squeals. "You look like a princess," the little girl exclaimed.

"She's right." Daniel helped Rose with her coat. "Have fun."

Abbie handed her a shawl for her head. "You'll do the right thing," she whispered in Rose's ear before giving her a kiss on the cheek.

Rose put on her mittens and then opened the door and stepped into the chilly night. Ian held the reins while Zach helped Rose into the seat next to Katie. Rose tucked the lap robe around her knees and huddled close to her friend. The night stretched ahead of them as they raced off to welcome in the year 1900.

Rose and Katie walked into the hotel and stood for a moment to look around. A large crystal chandelier hung from the ceiling and sparkled a thousand shimmers of light into the room. Tables circled the floor, leaving space for dancing. Each table was covered with a snowy white tablecloth and featured a centerpiece of pine boughs arranged as a wreath around a flickering candle. Red ribbons entwined through the greenery, matching the red ribbons woven through the stair railing.

Many young people stood talking in groups, and Rose noticed most of the town dignitaries in attendance as well. Even Sheriff Gibb had dressed up for the occasion and stood in the middle of the floor talking to the mayor.

Katie and Rose hurried off to hang their wraps and pick up their dance cards. They met Mary Larson in the cloak room.

"Have you seen Ian?" Mary asked.

Katie nodded. Rose removed her coat and scarf, hung them up, and turned around. "I am ready if you are," she said to Katie, who stared at her as if she had never seen her before.

"Oh, Rose!" Mary sighed. "That dress is beautiful. You are going to steal all the young men's hearts tonight."

"I only need one." Rose giggled and took Katie's arm. "I think Ian is safe with you, Mary."

Katie and Rose followed Mary into the ballroom. The trio of Crandall brothers fell silent as the girls made their way toward them. Rose glanced at Zach and then sought out Miles's gaze.

Ian broke the silence. "Well, boys, I think we are escorting the three most beautiful women in the room tonight."

"I'll say. You're all right pretty." Zach held out his hand to Rose. "May I sign your dance card, sweet lady?"

She started to hand him the card when she felt Miles's hand on her arm. "May I?" he whispered. He took the card and penciled his name into the first and last dance slots.

Zach glared at his older brother but didn't say anything as he penciled in his own name for several dances. He held out his arm to Katie. "Will you honor me with the first dance, dear sister?" Katie curtsied and allowed Zach to lead her away.

The strains of a waltz swelled through the room. Miles offered Rose his arm and they followed Zach and Katie onto the floor. As they swirled around the room, Miles never stopped looking at her.

"You dance well," she said finally.

"I had many opportunities to learn when I was at school in Boston. But I never danced with anyone as lovely as you." Miles said the last so softly that Rose strained to hear him.

"Are you still smiling?" she asked him.

He answered her with a silly grin that made her heart soar. Oh, how she wished she were considering a proposal from Miles instead of one from his younger brother! But Miles had never expressed any romantic interest in her, and she wondered if he ever would. Rose was almost twenty-one—practically a spinster—plus her mother desperately wanted to see her married. What if Rose never got another chance to marry and have a family of her own?

Miles relaxed into the dance, a smile playing on his lips. "What has got you concentrating so hard?" he asked Rose. They drifted past Ian and Mary but paid them no attention. "You should be enjoying the dance. You might even decide to try enjoying my company."

Katie and Zach had separated to find different partners. Zach held Emma Watt in his arms, but as they swung past Rose and Miles, Zach gave his brother a challenging look.

The answer to Miles's question stuck in Rose's throat. Should she tell him about Zach's proposal? She didn't want to come between the brothers, but as she moved around the room in one brother's arms, she knew she could never marry the other, even if she did end up like Aunt Jane. She smiled sweetly at Miles and kept silent, focusing on his eyes.

When the set ended, Miles escorted her to the table where their group sat. Ian and Mary laughed at something Zach said, but as soon as Rose came near, Zach stood and offered her his arm. "May I have the honor, Rose?"

Rose let him lead her away. She switched partners several times throughout the evening until she finally ended up in Zach's arms again. They took a few more turns around the floor, laughing and talking and greeting the other dancers. Zach drew others to him with his electric personality, and everyone had something to say to him. Rose noticed Emma watching them dance and saw the possessive look in her eyes.

They drew near the entrance of the ballroom and Rose gave Zach's arm a gentle tug. "Can we talk?"

Several small groups of people chatted in the foyer, where the music was quieter. Zach found a private corner and escorted Rose to a bench under the window. For several minutes, they listened to the music without talking.

Finally realizing Zach wasn't going to start the conversation, Rose turned to face him. "Zach, I've been thinking about what you asked me a few weeks ago." She took a deep breath and tucked her hands in the folds of her skirt to hide their trembling. "I love having fun with you and laughing with you, and I love your zest for life, but I think getting married would be the wrong thing."

She sighed. "I have tried to imagine us together—having a home and raising children—but I can't see any future for us other than as friends." Rose looked out the window at the darkness. She knew the last bit sounded cold, but she couldn't think of any other way to say it.

The music played on as Zach sat without a sound. She finally got up her courage and looked at him, but he had shut her out like she wasn't even there. "Zach," she said.

"This is about Miles." He looked at her. "Am I right?"

She turned away from him and felt the heat stain her cheeks. "I can't help how I feel, and right now I don't even know how he feels." Her hands stopped trembling, and as she felt warmth spread through her, she knew she was doing the right thing. "Even if Miles didn't exist, it wouldn't be right for you and me to be together."

"I wish you luck," Zach said resignedly.

Rose looked in his eyes and saw that he really meant it.

"Let's continue to be friends, please."

Zach stood and held out his arm. Just as they passed the main entrance of the hotel, the doors swung open and a disheveled young man ran into the foyer. "Where's Dr. Crandall? Luke Larson has been shot."

28

Shock spread through the room and Rose could hear people calling for Miles. Zach grabbed the young man's shoulder. "What happened, Bill?"

"Luke and I were a bit late getting here. We heard something over at the bank and went to see what was going on." Bill wiped a hand across his brow. "They robbed the bank and shot Luke. I left him in the road to come and find you."

Supported by Ian, Mary approached the group just as Bill finished telling Zach his story. When Ian and Miles left to tend to her brother, the crying girl buried her head in Rose's shoulder. Zach ran out behind his brothers, telling the girls to stay at the hotel. The sheriff tried to follow but the crowd hemmed him in.

The room buzzed with conversation and soon accusations flew. "Sheriff, how come you can't keep this town safe?" someone yelled. "Mayor Brown, how come we keep paying a sheriff that lets people die on his watch?"

Standing next to Sheriff Gibb, the mayor tried to fend off some of the questions, but Rose could see the situation was getting out of hand. She thought Sheriff Gibb looked pale and wondered what he might know about the robbery. Art Bradshaw, the proprietor of the hotel, tried to get the band to start playing again, but the musicians were as angry as everyone else and started packing away their instruments. Mary grew more agitated as the chaos built around them.

"Let's get a posse up and go after those thieves," someone yelled.

As more and more people got into the fray, Rose, Katie and Mary went to the cloak room to get their wraps. "We can't wait for things to settle down, and your brothers are ready to go home," Rose said. Zach had told them to stay at the hotel, but Rose felt sure they would be safer at Miles's office. Most of the other women were already being escorted to their homes.

"My brothers won't be going anywhere until this is solved," Katie said.

"We'll see," Rose replied. She knew if they left and the Crandall men saw them, one of them would take them home. They began crossing the street and met Mary's father coming from the clinic.

"There you are, Mary." He held out his arm for her. "Your mother needs you."

She slipped her hand around his elbow. "How is Luke?"

"Dr. Crandall thinks he'll be fine."

Father and daughter walked ahead of Katie and Rose. The two girls held onto each other's arms for support as they crossed the icy street. They arrived at the clinic to find the men of the town already gathering in front of the building, wanting to know how the injured man fared. Zach stood next to the sheriff, who tried to calm the angry crowd.

"We'll be organizing a posse," the sheriff said. "All able-bodied men need to get their mounts and meet at the livery stable in ten minutes. Bill here says they rode off to the south. Probably headed for Hole in the Wall."

The men cheered at the plan, and then there was a rush of bodies as each man hurried to get his horse. When Ian saw the girls standing on the fringes of the crowd, he strode over to them, pushing his way through men.

"I'll be riding with Zach in the posse. Miles will tend to Luke." He put his arm around Katie and gave her a squeeze. "You stay here."

Katie started up the walk to the clinic, Rose following her. They entered the building to find a tearful Mrs. Larson sitting on a chair by the window. Mary sat next to her mother, holding her hand. She looked up as the two girls entered the room.

"Miles says Luke is going to recover, but he won't let Mother see him yet. We don't even know exactly what is wrong."

Rose could see the tears in Mary's eyes and remembered how worried she had been every time Miles went in to see her father when he was dying. This must be far worse, Rose decided, not knowing what was wrong. She turned from the distraught women and walked across the room. She hesitated at the closed door of the exam room, wondering if she dare knock. She heard Luke moaning and had started to back away when the door swung open.

Miles stood aside. "Rose, come in here." He took her hand and pulled her through the doorway and shut the door.

Luke lay on the exam table, struggling to get up. He kept calling for his mother, and Rose felt her stomach churn at the sight of his blood. She leaned back against the closed door and took a deep breath. *Whatever Miles needs, I can do,* she told herself.

"I need you to talk to him and try to hold him steady. The bullet is lodged in his leg and I need to take it out."

Rose noticed that Miles had already secured one leg to the table. Luke continued to struggle and was clearly weakening. Rose went to him and started to stroke his forehead. At her touch, he stilled slightly. Miles nodded his approval and continued to secure Luke's arms and legs to the table.

The memory of doing the same thing for her father when he was in pain burned clear in Rose's mind. She began to talk to Luke about the same inconsequential things that used to comfort her father. Luke listened quietly, moaning occasionally as she told him about their Christmas and the package she received from her family. She talked about the music at the New Year's dance and all the types of elegant food the restaurant had served.

Miles quickly removed the bullet from the young man's leg and wrapped the wound tightly, then washed his hands in the warm water he had heating on the fire. Rose helped him undo the restraints, watched him clean up the blood, and then covered Luke with a blanket.

"He lost a lot of blood, but if he rests he should be all right." Miles sat down and leaned his head on the back of the chair.

"You look tired," Rose said.

"Please tell Mrs. Larson to come and sit with her son."

Rose hurried out of the exam room and knelt in front of the worried mother. "You can go in now. He's resting quietly."

Katie looked at Rose with great admiration. "I couldn't have gone in there."

"Sure you could have. I just helped calm Luke a little."

"No, she couldn't have," came the strained voice from behind her. "She faints at the sight of blood."

Miles sounded tired, but Rose could hear the laughter in his voice. She smiled at him. "I am glad I could help." Turning to Katie she said, "We need to get home. Your mother and father will be worried when we don't show up, not to mention how frantic Abbie and Daniel will be."

Katie frowned and pulled at the fringe on her shawl. "Isn't it dangerous?"

"The sheriff said the robbers went south. They should be long gone by now." Rose looked at Miles for confirmation.

"I don't want you to go," Miles responded. "It's very late and those bandits are still out there."

Rose brushed away his concerns with a wave of her hand. "We'll be fine."

Miles ran a hand through his hair. "I wish I could get you home, but I need to stay here and keep an eye on Luke."

"We'll be fine. After all, we are going the opposite way entirely." Rose picked her coat up off the chair where she had dropped it. "Come on, Katie."

Mary Larson grabbed her own shawl as the other two girls wrapped themselves against the winter cold. "Mother says to tell you that you are welcome at our house until morning."

Rose started to shake her head, but Miles cut in. "They would be delighted. You can keep Mary company while Mrs. Larson sits with Luke. I know Mr. Larson has gone with the posse."

The girls put on their mittens and opened the door. The gusty wind hit them and Rose shivered. The weather had taken a turn for the worse, and she worried about Zach and Ian out riding with the posse. With one last look at Miles, Rose followed the other two girls out into the night.

29

The Larsons' two-story home stood on the outskirts of Spring Creek. Rose, Katie, and Mary walked briskly across town as the wind become even fiercer and the temperature dropped. The girls linked arms as they walked down the dark, deserted street, partly for security on the ice, but also to ward off their fear.

Rose squeezed Mary's arm. "Thanks for letting us stay tonight." She couldn't imagine trying to get the sleigh home in the dark with a storm brewing. Suddenly, Rose thought she heard someone behind them, so she pulled the other two girls on a little faster.

"Rose, what's your hurry?" Katie slipped and almost fell on the ice.

"Sorry. Guess I'm just excited to get out of the cold."

Soon, the girls reached the house and hurried inside. Mary left her two guests warming their hands by the fireplace while she went to check on her younger brother and sister.

"They're sleeping soundly," she reported a few moments later.

Katie and Rose each slumped into a kitchen chair. "I'm so tired." Katie stifled a yawn.

"What a way to welcome in the New Year. Happy 1900, girls." Rose stood and curtsied to her friends, her silk skirt spreading around her.

"Let me help you get settled. Mama and Papa won't be home tonight. You can have their bed. I'll get you a nightgown." Mary stood up and blew out the lantern. She handed each of the girls a candlestick and started to lead the way out of the room. The sound of sleigh bells and then a soft knock on the door stopped them before they reached the stairs.

The girls looked at each other and hesitated. Rose kept thinking of the footsteps she thought she heard while they were walking home. "Don't answer it," she said to Katie. Another knock shook the door. "I thought I heard someone following us."

"Katie, Rose! It's Zach. Let me in."

Katie quickly opened the door. Zach entered the room, dusting the snow off his shoulders, his nose red from the cold. "Are you girls ready to go home?"

"Miles thinks we should stay here since it is almost morning anyway," Katie said.

"Pa is expecting me to help him with the chores. Besides, he will wonder why we didn't come home." Zach put his hand on Rose's shoulder. "Daniel and Abbie are probably worried sick. The sleigh is outside, all ready to go. I've got some extra blankets and a couple of lanterns. You girls can sleep all the way if you'd like."

Katie sighed. "I guess we shouldn't impose on the Larsons any more than we need to." She took her coat off the hook next to the door and put it on. She gave Mary a warm hug, thanked her, and then stood looking at Rose. "Are you ready?"

A feeling of unease stopped Rose from moving. She looked at the brother and sister and wondered why she should feel nervous about leaving the Larson home. Yes, there had been a robbery and a shooting, but the bandits were probably long gone by now. Plus, the girls would have Zach to protect them.

"Come on. The bank robbers took off the opposite direction of our homes and have been gone for over two hours now," Zach said. "It is snowing, but not too hard. We'll be fine."

"I really think we should stay."

"We'll let Daniel know where you are. Come on, Katie." Zach took his sister by the elbow and steered her toward the door."

As Katie stepped into the stormy night, Rose couldn't get rid of the dark feeling. "Zach, please let us stay the night here. Daniel won't worry too much."

"Don't be a ninny. We'll be fine." Zach glared at her.

Though she wasn't entirely convinced, Rose put on her coat, wrapped her shawl around her head, and gave Mary a hug. "I hope Luke is all right."

Zach put an arm behind Rose and ushered her out of the house. Katie chattered on to Zach about all that had happened since he rode off with the posse. She seemed to think it had all been a grand adventure.

"When did the posse get back?" Rose asked suddenly. "We didn't hear anything."

"It was kind of funny." Zach pulled his hat lower over his face as the wind picked up. "We were out riding and were pretty close on the trail. Then the sheriff reined everyone in, handpicked some men to continue on, and sent the rest of us home. I offered to stay, but he insisted that, as his deputy, I ride with everyone else to make sure nobody tried to go out on his own."

"Why would the sheriff do that?" Katie snuggled up next to her brother to try to stay warm.

"The storm made it dangerous to keep riding. They could barely follow the trail, and if the snow keeps falling, any tracks will disappear. Gibb said fewer men mean it's less likely the tracks will be disturbed by some rider who doesn't do what he is told."

Rose felt her toes turning into ice, so she tucked them under her skirt a little further and wrapped the lap blanket closer around her and Katie. The road ahead of them disappeared in the darkness, and the two lanterns on the front of the sleigh provided little light to the trio huddled on the sleigh bench.

"Actually, that's why I came to get you. I overheard some of the guys talking. They think the bank robbery is connected to all the beatings, but Luke Larson wasn't supposed to get in the way."

"What have they got to gain from causing so much trouble?" Katie asked.

"This is good ranch land. If a select group of people run the town and control the area, so much the better for them. It's all about greed and power."

Rose shook her head. "It's hard to believe." She pulled her shawl forward to hide more of her face from the bitter wind as the sleigh continued into the night. The crisp sound of the bells attached to the horses echoed through the frigid air. She felt colder still from her new knowledge about the affairs of Spring Creek. What had seemed such a pleasant town now seemed anything but. Miles was treating a young man shot in a bank robbery, and Zach worked with a sheriff none of them trusted. "Where's Ian?" Rose sat bolt upright and felt a moment of panic.

Zach pulled the lap blankets closer around them. "I don't know. I guess I didn't worry about him. He rode off with Mr. Larson. I'm sure they are going to check in on Luke and then go back to the house for something warm to drink. A bunch of the men from the posse were returning to the hotel to discuss what they should do next. They weren't very happy about being sent home."

As she relaxed back into the blankets, Rose felt her eyelids grow heavy and start to droop. Katie slept next to her, and Rose half suspected Zach would catch a few winks as well. The horses knew the road home and needed no encouragement to be on their way to a warm barn.

They rode in silence for a time. Rose could hear the occasional snorts of the horses, but then another sound caught her attention. She opened her eyes and noticed Zach sitting alert and still, listening. He urged the horses on a little faster. "What is, it Zach?" she whispered.

"Someone's behind us."

"Maybe it's Ian."

"Nope," Zach said. "More than one horse."

Rose turned to look behind her. In the darkness she could see nothing, but the sound was becoming more distinct and she knew something was getting closer. Zach whipped the horses into a run.

Katie sat up with a start. "What's happening?"

"Hang on, girls," he said.

Rose could see dark shapes taking form behind the sleigh. The snow flew beneath the horses' hooves, and Rose could hear riders calling to each other. Finally, two men pulled up alongside the sleigh.

"Zach, you have to turn around. The sheriff needs you," said one man with a large handlebar moustache. Rose thought he was the same man Sam referred to as his uncle.

"I need to get my sister and her friend home first, then I can return to town." Zach didn't slow the sleigh, and the men easily kept up on their mounts.

"Well, now," the second man said, "why don't you just take my horse and I can get these young ladies home? Haven't seen your pa in a while. It might be nice to say hello."

"I'm awfully close to home now, gentleman," Zach said. "I don't really see any need to stop here. I can turn around and head back to town on a fresh horse and be there much quicker than if I turn a sleigh around and try to make it with two tired horses."

Katie gasped as the first man pulled a gun from his coat. "I think you need to stop the sleigh now," he shouted.

Zach turned to Katie and Rose. "Get under the seat!" He pushed his sister down with one hand and handed her the reins with the other. "Hold tight to these, Katie." The sleigh continued smoothly over the snow as Katie encouraged the team to hurry for home.

Zach was quiet for a time, and Rose assumed the men had pulled back to consult with each other. She prayed they would just ride away. Then a gunshot rang out and she looked up to see Zach pull a firearm from under the seat. Another shot whizzed past them and Rose felt real fear.

Zach turned in his seat and fired back, but the men were gaining on them again. Another shot and Rose heard Zach grunt in pain. His gun clattered to the floor and Rose picked it up. "Put it down, Rose." Zach's eyes were pleading. "I don't know what they want, but it isn't worth you girls getting hurt."

"But Zach, they shot you," Katie exclaimed.

"It's just my arm," he said, the pain evident in his voice.

Katie crawled up on the seat and pulled the steaming horses to a stop. "What do you want?" she asked the men.

"What we really want is Dr. Crandall, but he's holed up in that clinic of his with the Larsons and there's no way to get him to come with us." The man with the handlebar moustache put his hand on the sleigh next to Rose. She tried to inch away from him.

"Besides that, he won't come to treat a bank robber without a little encouragement." Handlebar leered at Rose and Katie. "We figured we'd give him a little motivation."

The man on the other side of the sleigh pulled Zach from his seat onto the snow-packed ground.

"What do you want me to do?" Zach asked as he sat bleeding into the snow, his face twisted in agony.

Handlebar dismounted and climbed up into the sleigh. "Take my horse into town. Tell your brother that someone will be waiting a mile from his clinic on this road."

Zach stood and mounted the man's horse. "What about the girls? Will you take them home like you said?"

The men laughed.

"You are gullible, boy," Handlebar said. "Isn't he gullible, Jed?"

"I think we will be keeping them as a little insurance that the good doctor will actually come." The man called Jed reached up and put a hand on Katie's knee. She shied away from his touch and grasped Rose's arm. "He might not care about a bank robber, but he'll be worried sick about these two beauties."

Zach hesitated a moment, then urged the horse on and headed back the way he had come, the snow flying behind him. A new terror struck Rose's heart, and she stuck her arm through Katie's and pulled her close.

30

Miles jerked awake at the sound of the front door crashing open. He had been resting in the waiting room but jumped to his feet as Zach staggered in. His hat and shoulders held only a light dusting of snow and Miles could tell he had ridden hard. He tried to reach his brother in time, but Zach stumbled and fell to the floor.

"You have to go." Zach gasped. "They have the girls."

The frozen blood on Zach's sleeve cracked under Miles's touch. "What happened, Zach?"

"They shot me," Zach said just before he passed out on the floor.

Moving quickly, Miles knelt and took off his brother's coat. He heard Mrs. Larson come into the room behind him. "We need to get him off the floor and get him warm." He stood and grasped his brother under the arms. Mrs. Larson took the unconscious man's feet and they carried him to Miles's bedroom, where they put him on the bed. The older woman took the afghan Rose had crocheted for Miles and tucked it around Zach's torso and legs.

Miles examined the bullet wound on Zach's shoulder. "This isn't bad. He's in shock and has lost a little blood, but it looks like the bullet passed right through."

With Mrs. Larson's assistance, Miles cleaned and dressed the injury. Then he sent Mrs. Larson back to sit with her son in the examination room. As soon as she left, he tried to rouse his brother.

"Hey, Zach, you need to wake up." When his brother didn't respond, Miles continued to shake his good shoulder. "Zach, what about the girls? What happened? You need to wake up and tell me what's going on!"

Desperation filled Miles's heart. He thought Rose and Katie were at Mary Larson's, but what other girls could Zach be talking about? Just as Miles had convinced himself to run over to the Larsons' and check on them, Zach stirred.

"Miles, are you there?"

Miles sat back down beside the bed. "What happened?"

"We were in the sleigh on the way home when they made us stop." Zach's voice came out in a hoarse whisper. "They kept the girls and said I should send you to them. They have an injured man and figured you wouldn't venture out to treat a bank robber in this weather without some motivation."

"What do they want me to do?" Miles asked as he grabbed some warm clothing and his bag of supplies.

"Start riding toward our place. Someone will be waiting about a mile out of town for you." Zach closed his eyes. "Give me a minute and I'll come with you."

"No. You're no good like this. Just stay and rest. I'll have Mrs. Larson look in on you and make sure you're all right."

Miles left the clinic. He tied his medical supplies to the saddle and mounted the already tired horse. As he rode, he wondered where the outlaws were hiding out in this cold winter weather.

He pulled his hat farther down over his ears and tucked his scarf around his neck, hoping the girls were warm enough.

Almost exactly a mile from town, Miles came upon a lone rider along the side of the road. Without a word, the man nodded and beckoned him on. Miles followed the other man down the road in silence. After some time, they came to the Crandall sleigh, pulled to the side of the road and abandoned in the deep, powdery snow. The horses and the girls were nowhere in sight. The man in front of him said nothing, and though Miles seethed in anger at the sight of the carriage, he didn't want to put the girls in danger, so he continued to follow silently. They veered off the road and followed the river. As they rode on, Miles was fairly certain he knew their destination. He pictured the picnic spot and the deep cliffs and dark caves across the river from the family's favorite swimming hole.

Sure enough, they crossed the frozen water and stopped in front of a gaping hole in the bluff. Several horses stood tethered there, including Flossy and Big Red. Miles could smell smoke coming from the cave and hurried toward it, dreading what he might find inside.

His guide stepped into the opening and removed his hat, then smiled menacingly at Miles and ushered him into the cave.

"Sheriff!" the man called.

Despite all the rumors about the man, Miles had hoped Arthur Gibb was still honest. Miles looked around the cave and, with disappointment, recognized Gibb's brother and his hired hand. If Sheriff Gibb had tried to get a doctor without shooting Zach and assaulting innocent women, Miles might have believed the men had just tried to find shelter after becoming separated from the posse. But innocent men didn't resort to kidnapping.

Suddenly, the sheriff emerged from the far side of the cave. "Welcome, Doctor. Now if you will come this way, I'll show you your patient." Arthur started to lead the way to the rear of the cave.

Miles didn't move. "My brother is lying in the clinic recovering from a gunshot wound, and he tells me you have my sister and Rose Sterling. I won't treat your injured man until you tell me where they are."

"The girls are fine. They are helping him as well as they can in your absence, but I am sure they'll appreciate your presence." Again the sheriff turned and started walking toward the rear of the cave.

After hesitating for a moment, Miles followed the lawman. He could hear moaning and Rose's quiet, soothing voice. Soon, he saw Katie sitting on the floor leaning against the cave wall, her head nodding as she slept. She looked so young and vulnerable.

Then there was Rose. She looked bedraggled, her beautiful silk dress wet at the hem and torn in a few places. But what caught Miles's attention was that she cared for the injured man as if she were a trained nurse.

The sheriff left them under the watchful eye of one of the men, telling Miles to do what he needed to in order to help the injured man.

Miles went to Rose and knelt at her side. "Are you all right?"

She turned and gave him a tired smile. "Katie and I are fine. I'm just a little tired. Where is Zach?"

"He barely made it to the clinic. I would have come sooner, but he passed out and it was a while before he could tell me anything. He is resting at the clinic, and Mrs. Larson is there to check on him. He'll be fine, but what about this fellow?"

Tears filled Rose's eyes. "He fell from his horse and I think his leg is broken. He also sounds pretty bad, like he's having difficulty breathing."

Miles looked down and realized he was nothing more than a boy, barely old enough to shave. His leg was bent at an odd angle and, sure enough, raspy sounds came from his chest. Miles looked closely at the boy and thought there was something familiar about him. He turned to Rose, questioning her with his eyes.

"It's Sam, the sheriff's son. The others keep telling Sheriff Gibb that when an injured man goes down, he gets left behind. But the sheriff won't hear of it." Rose brushed the damp hair off Sam's forehead. "He's so young."

Miles reached into his bag and found some bandages. "Can you go tell the sheriff we need some hot water and something to use as splints?"

Rose found the sheriff and requested the needed items, ignoring the other men. As she walked away from him, Miles watched her, amazed at her confidence in such a difficult situation.

He turned back to the moaning boy. "Are you awake?"

The boy nodded as he continued to struggle to breathe.

Miles examined the twisted leg. "How did you hurt your leg, Sam?"

"I fell off my horse after the posse started chasing us, and my foot caught in the stirrup." Sam coughed again and held his hand to his mouth.

Miles saw blood on the boy's hand. He reached up and felt Sam's ribcage, then sat back and wiped a hand across his own brow. Several ribs were broken and he suspected there was some internal bleeding. He saw Rose returning with a pot of hot water, followed by a man carrying some pieces of wood.

"Do you need help straightening the leg, Doc?" The man dropped the wood and knelt next to the injured boy.

"Rose, come hold on to Sam and try to comfort him a little." Miles looked at the other man. "Hold him still and don't let him move."

Getting a good grip on the leg, Miles proceeded to pull the bones into place. Sam screamed in pain and then, mercifully, passed out. Miles splinted the broken limb and bound it with some bandages from his medical bag. He noticed that even though the sheriff didn't come near the boy, he kept a close watch on his son. As soon as Miles finished wrapping the leg, the other man walked away to join the others.

Miles whispered to Rose, "He's not going to make it. I think he is bleeding internally, and I can't do anything for him here."

"Tell the sheriff," she whispered back to him. "I'm sure he will let us take him back to the clinic."

"Rose," Miles said softly, "he's not going to let us leave."

31

The next day, Rose, Miles, and Katie took turns watching Sam. He seemed more comfortable, but Miles told Rose he didn't think the boy would last long. His fever wouldn't break and he was getting weaker.

As she carried the pot back to the fire, Rose listened to the talk between the men. They were used to her coming to get more hot water, so she slipped in and out of their conversations without them seeming to notice.

"If we leave now, we can get to Hole in the Wall before the month is out." Handlebar tossed another log onto the fire.

"What makes you think they will even let us near their hideout?" The sheriff glared at his brother. "We'd be better off to try and fix things here. Once we get people scared enough, they'll abandon their land and we can pick it up for next to nothing."

"With the botched bank job, how do you think you can ever go back to town?" Jed said, sneering in the sheriff's direction. "We've always let you plan jobs since you're the older brother, but I'm tired of things not working out."

Sheriff Gibb kicked the sitting man in the leg. "Stop griping. I'll smooth things over in town. You two will have to leave for a while, but I'll convince them you were pulling the wool over my eyes and I didn't know a thing."

"We'll have to get rid of our guests soon." Handlebar stood and put his hand on the gun slung at his hip. "And that Zach Crandall will unfortunately not recover from his wound. Someone will have to see to that."

"You won't bother any of them until my son is better." Sheriff Gibb's words left no room for argument.

Handlebar shrugged and sat back down. "I guess we can wait a bit longer." He leaned against the rough cave wall and closed his eyes.

Jed and Sheriff Gibb continued talking in quiet tones. Rose couldn't stall any longer at the fire, but she'd heard enough. The outlaws were starting to get restless. She hurried back to Miles and Katie.

"Handlebar is getting frustrated over having to wait for an injured boy. They keep reminding the sheriff that if Sam weren't his son, they would've left him in the snow to die."

"Nice family," mumbled Katie. "He's their nephew and they don't even seem to care." She went back to keep Sam occupied and quiet, telling him some of the tall tales her father told her as a young girl.

"They want to join up with Butch Cassidy and his gang, and they want to head south as soon as the storm clears." Rose brushed a loose curl away from her face.

Miles motioned for his sister to sit by him. Rose sat next to Sam and watched as the brother and sister conversed. She knew Miles was trying to find a way to get them out of the situation. Zach wouldn't be coming anytime soon, and he wouldn't know where they were anyway. They were on their own.

"Miss Sterling, I hurt so much."

Sam looked at her but she couldn't meet his gaze.

"Will you pray for me like Mama used to?" he begged.

Rose nodded. Holding his hand, she closed her eyes and offered a brief prayer. The words calmed him and he smiled his thanks to her. While she realized she couldn't have changed what happened, she desperately wished there was some way to save Sam. Tears streamed down her face as she started to sing. Keeping her voice quiet, she sang of God and His love for His children. The boy's face relaxed, and soon his breathing deepened and he slept. She looked down at her student and let the last note die away. *He's so young and had so much promise!* She wondered what his side of the story would be and knew he would never get the chance to tell her. She closed her eyes and said a silent prayer for her young friend, then stood and made her way over to Miles.

Rose sat and laid her head on his shoulder. On the other side, Katie did the same. They always pretended to be sleeping whenever they talked. Miles didn't want the sheriff to think they were planning anything.

"That was beautiful," Miles whispered. "Music is probably the best medicine for him now."

"Sam acts like he is feeling better, and the sheriff said he would let us go when that happened," Katie said.

Miles leaned his head back and pulled his hat lower over his face. "The boy's leg will take weeks to heal enough that he can ride. But I don't think he will last long enough for that to happen. The men here are getting antsy already and they aren't going to wait much longer."

"Katie, you don't think they will really let us go, do you? We have seen all of them and know their names." Rose looked at her friend and shrugged. "It would just be easier to make us disappear."

The trio watched the knot of men on the other side of the cave, milling around with no real purpose. Rose had overheard enough to know the original plan had been to meet in this cave and then gradually trickle south to join Butch Cassidy at the Hole-in-the-Wall hideout. The Spring Creek thieves had hoped the money from the bank would be enough to show their value and buy their way into the gang.

The sheriff would return to town and tell everyone the trail had been lost in the storm. But Sheriff Gibb hadn't counted on his own son showing up and getting injured in the process, and he didn't trust his brothers and wanted them to stay where he could keep track of them. And so they waited.

"The men say it's turned into a blizzard out there and the temperature keeps dropping," Rose said. "They figure if the sheriff turns up in town now with three bodies, no one is going to argue when he says he stumbled across them, frozen in the snow, while he searched for the robbers. They brought your father's sleigh up to the caves and are figuring to take it, with our frozen bodies, back to town in the morning."

For a time, the three prisoners sat in silence.

"There is another way out of this cave. We used to play here when we were kids." Miles picked at the skirt of Katie's ball gown as it lay across his lap. "Katie has never seen it because she doesn't like the dark."

"These men aren't any improvement," Katie said.

Miles grinned. "I guess you're right. I don't know how we can all leave without being noticed, but if one of us goes for help . . ."

Rose felt the weight of his arm across her shoulder and wished he would pull her closer. She had never been so afraid. Earlier, Miles had told her how proud he was of her strength in the situation and she hadn't dared contradict him. She didn't want him to know how much she feared they would never get out of the cave. Now, she forced herself to listen to the plan.

"If we take our petticoats off, maybe we can arrange it to look like we are still here and are sleeping. The path home isn't that far from the opening to the cave, so it shouldn't take us too long to get help." The fear in Katie's voice matched the fear Rose felt, but she knew this might be their best chance.

"Your dresses and coats should keep you warm enough to get home," Miles said.

"Aren't you coming with us?" Rose touched his arm.

"The boys and I grew too big for the tunnel years ago. There's a real narrow spot in the middle, but you girls should be able to get through." Miles looked at Sam. "And I can't leave my patient. Even though I can't do any more for him, I won't let him die alone.

"After we have our supper, I'll draw attention away from you. I'll tend to Sam and then approach the sheriff at their fire, making a real fuss about how hard it is to treat his son in these conditions."

"Don't make them mad," Rose said in alarm.

"From what you say, they plan on killing us tonight anyway." Miles looked into her eyes. "Just get home and find help."

They had been in the cave for two days. As the second day drew to a close, the girls stayed near Sam. They managed to get a few blankets from the men, saying they needed them for the boy. They picked a spot away from the main group and built it up to look like two sleeping bodies.

After Jed brought them each a bowl of thin soup and a biscuit, he returned to the main part of the cave to eat with the other men.

The girls ate the hot supper and then removed their voluminous petticoats and handed them to Miles. He arranged them carefully over the blankets, and soon the pile did look a little like two sleeping girls.

"Good luck, Katie. Hurry and get Pa." Miles gave his sister's hand a squeeze and looked at Rose. "Stay together. Katie can find her way home in the storm. Be careful."

He brushed Rose's cheek with the back of his hand. "Good luck, my Rose." The endearment made her heart leap. She realized there was so much she wanted to say to him, but the words stuck in her throat. *If only we could have a minute alone.* Instead she acknowledged him with a nod, and then impulsively kissed him on the cheek.

He took her hand and held it for a moment. "No one is watching right now. Go and I'll distract them as soon as it is necessary."

Rose knew the dark tunnel scared Katie, just as the storm frightened her. Rose was terrified to think of what might happen to Miles after they left, and she knew Katie felt the same. But they must go; it was their only chance.

Katie turned and went toward the small opening in the cave wall. Well hidden behind a pile of boulders, it didn't look like much. Rose followed Katie and paused behind her as she hesitated at the opening.

"I'm scared of the dark."

"Do you want me to go first?" Rose didn't wait for an answer and moved past her friend to enter the tunnel. She crouched down and put her head and shoulders into the hole. Miles had told her how dark it would be, but promised them that once they rounded the corner, they should be able to see the light at the other end. He figured snow would block the entrance, but they should be able to dig their way out.

Checking to make sure the piece of wood she had tied to her waist for breaking away the snow was still there, Rose started to crawl forward. She fit into the tunnel but there wasn't much room to spare. Katie followed right behind her. As they started moving, she could hear the muffled sound of Miles talking to Sam and knew they had to move fast.

To Rose, the tunnel seemed to go on forever, but Miles had said Zach and Ian could crawl the distance in ten minutes. *Clearly, they weren't doing it in skirts*, she thought as she struggled not to get tangled up in the masses of fabric that made up her ballgown. She could hear Katie moving behind her and the soft hiccup of a sob.

"Are you all right, Katie?"

"Do you think we're almost there?" came the reply.

"It does seem lighter up ahead. I think it will be hard to tell for sure, because it's probably starting to get dark outside."

As she said it, Rose felt ahead and found the space widening. Soon she pulled herself into a small hollow and Katie crawled up behind her. They reached forward and found a wall of snow in front of them. Each girl pulled the piece of wood from her waistband and started digging at the snow. After a short time, the wall gave way and they looked across the valley at a world swirling in white.

Rose hugged her coat around her and pulled her scarf tighter around her head. "This is your part, Katie. I don't even know where I am."

Katie hesitated. "Do you think we could pray?"

The girls bowed their heads and Rose offered a short but heartfelt prayer. A warm, reassuring feeling washed through her and she smiled at Katie. "Let's go."

Taking the first step into the snow, Katie held her other hand out to Rose. She grasped it and they hurried across the field towards the river. "If we follow the river here until we see the grove, we can cross on the bridge and get to the house in no time," Katie said.

She hurried forward, practically dragging Rose along. The girls often stumbled in the snow, and they found themselves on their knees more than once. Soon they could see the dark shadow of the trees as Katie led the way to the river. Rose followed carefully across the small footbridge, not wanting to fall onto the thin ice below. She was surprised at how far she had run, her breath still coming even and sure. *I have to tell Miles,* she thought. She bit back a sob. *I hope I'll see Miles again so I can tell him.*

"Mama! Papa!" Katie started calling as soon as they entered the grove. The lamps were lit in the Crandall house and the front door swung open as the girls drew near. Before Rose took many more steps, she felt strong arms scoop her up out of the snow.

"Oh, girls!" Elizabeth started fussing over them as soon as they were carried through the kitchen. John deposited Katie in front of the fire in the sitting room, Ian following right behind him with Rose.

They sat shivering as Elizabeth ushered the men out of the room. "Let me get their wet things off. John, go make some tea."

Elizabeth soon had Rose and Katie out of their sodden dresses and into warm nightgowns. Each girl wrapped herself in a quilt while Elizabeth called the men back in.

John knelt in front of Katie and embraced his daughter. "Oh, my girl, what a blessed sight you are."

"Where's Miles?" Ian asked, his voice breaking as if he feared the answer.

Everyone waited in anticipation of Katie's reply, but she started to cry and couldn't speak. Elizabeth pulled her daughter close. "There, there." She patted Katie's back and looked at Rose.

Rose saw the question in Elizabeth's eyes and wished she had a better answer. She quickly told the family what had happened the night of the dance. She told about the sheriff's involvement and his threat to put the prisoners out tonight to freeze in the storm. As she related the last part of her tale, the men started to bundle up.

"What are you going to do?" she asked.

"We need to go get Miles. I don't know how, but we'll bring him home." John tied a woolen scarf tight around his face and took an extra coat off the hook. "Abe, go tell the Weavers that Rose is here, then get to town and tell Zach the girls are safe. Ian, you come with me." The snow blew through the open door. "Elizabeth, I'm going to get my boy."

32

The three women sat quietly in the house. When Katie started to drift off, Elizabeth led her to bed and tucked her in.

"You should get some sleep too," the older woman said to Rose when she returned to the sitting room.

Rose couldn't be swayed. For a long while she sat by the window looking out on the snow-covered yard, hoping and praying John would return soon with Miles. Just as she thought her eyelids were too heavy to hold open anymore, she thought she saw movement in the yard.

"Elizabeth, someone is coming," she said when she knew it wasn't her imagination.

They continued to watch until they were sure it was the men they waited for and not someone else. Elizabeth bustled into action, refreshing the kettle and adding more quilts to the pile by the fire. Soon the men burst into the house in a flurry of cold air.

John and Ian supported a stiff figure wrapped in the extra coat, with Daniel following close behind. Rose put her hand to her mouth and stifled a sob as she watched them lay Miles's body on the warm blankets near the fire. His skin looked blue with cold and he kept muttering under his breath. As the warmth of the room started to reach him, he shivered violently.

"Don't just stand there, Elizabeth. He's still with us but near froze to death. We need to warm him up. Rose, say something to him. Since we found him he's been mumbling about saving you and Katie. Maybe if he hears your voice he will calm down."

Elizabeth jumped to action and rushed to help her son. Underneath the coat his father had taken to put around him, he wore only a white shirt and black woolen pants. His bare feet were white with cold. With the help of her husband, Elizabeth began to remove Miles's frozen clothing.

"You're home, Miles. Katie and I made it." Rose said the words several times to him until he quieted. She stood and moved out of the way as Elizabeth brought another quilt.

Daniel put his arm around Rose's shaking shoulders and led her out of the room. "Go in and rest for a while. This is no place for you right now."

Rose let him lead her to Katie's room. She peered one last time into the sitting room, and then gently shut the door. Katie slept peacefully, so Rose slipped under the covers on the bed and lay listening to the murmuring voices in the other room. Every so often she could hear Miles cry out, and she thought her heart would break.

She awoke with a start and realized the sun shone high in the sky. Katie was gone and Rose knew it had to be almost noon. She got out of bed and wrapped the quilt around her. No sound came from the main part of the house and Rose wondered where everyone had gone.

The sitting room was empty and the spot where Miles had lain the night before was clear of blankets. Rose made her way into the kitchen to find Katie sharing a steaming cup of peppermint tea with Abe and Daniel.

"So you're finally up," Daniel teased.

"What time is it?" Rose accepted a cup of tea from Katie and sat at the table. "Where is everyone else?"

"Mama is sleeping in the rocking chair next to Miles's bed, and Papa has gone to bed for a little rest before he goes out to look for those outlaws." Katie handed Rose a plate with a slice of bread and butter.

"Ian went into town to talk to Zach and rouse a group of men. They're aiming to go after those criminals and bring them in for justice. 'Course, now they will be looking for a new sheriff." Daniel reached for another slice of bread. "I need to get you back home. Abigail is just sick with worry about you, and the children miss you fiercely."

Rose pulled the quilt closer around her shoulders. "How is Miles?"

Daniel frowned.

"He got right cold, miss," Abe finally said. "It took us a while to warm him up, but he hasn't woke up none since we brought him in."

"Mama says he will recover in time, but I'm not sure she isn't just trying to convince herself." Katie stood. "I should go and spell her off for a while." She started to walk out of the kitchen and then turned. "Borrow one of my dresses, Rose, and go home with Daniel. Abbie needs to see you and know for herself that you are fine."

Wanting to argue but knowing she had no place caring for Miles, Rose held her peace. Daniel looked at her expectantly.

"Thank you, Katie. It will be good to see Abbie and the kids.

You will let me know how Miles and Zach are doing, won't you? I won't stop worrying until I know."

"Of course."

The threat of tears made Rose's eyes tingle and she turned her back to her uncle and tried to smile. Then she left the kitchen and hurried to Katie's room. She found a dress lying on the bed and changed out of the borrowed nightgown into the dress. Her green silk gown lay in a heap on the floor, muddy and torn, her petticoats left behind in the cave with a bunch of outlaws. She sighed and wondered how the evening that had started so wonderfully could end like this three days later.

Daniel was waiting for her. They said good-bye to Abe and headed out into the snow. The storm had stopped and Rose felt a warm wind blowing. She looked at Daniel in amazement. "Last night was so cold!"

He laughed. "They call it a Chinook. The weather here can change so fast, you can dig out to your barn to do chores in a foot of snow and come out an hour later to find you have to wade back to the house in mud puddles."

Rose lifted her face to the breeze and felt the freshness of the air. "Is winter over this early?"

"Oh, no. Another snowstorm could hit at any time, but the Chinook does break up the winter and keep it from being too cold too long." He mounted his horse and pulled Rose up behind him. "Hang on."

Rose held tight to her uncle's waist as the horse negotiated the drifts on the road. Soon they came to the Weaver farm and stopped in front of the house.

The humble home looked so welcoming. She slid off the horse, ran to the door, and flung it open. "Abbie!"

Her aunt came from the kitchen, drying her hands on a tea towel. "Rose! Are you all right? I was so worried about you." She hugged her niece but not before Rose noticed the sheen of tears in her aunt's eyes.

Rose hugged Abbie back and started to cry. "I'm happy to be back. I was so scared I wouldn't get to see you or the rest of my family again."

"Did they hurt you?"

At Abbie's concern, Rose cried all the harder.

"No. Katie and I got out before they could harm us." She started to take off her coat. "Miles wasn't so lucky."

Daniel came in and told Abbie the story of finding Miles tied to a tree outside the cave, wearing only a shirt and pants. John and Ian overpowered Miles's guard and tied him to the tree in Miles's place. Before they tied him up, the man told them the sheriff assumed Katie and Rose were lost in the storm.

"They didn't have any idea what a great sense of direction Katie has. She can find her way better than a lot of men I know, and she spent enough time playing near the cave as a child that she knew her way home with her eyes closed." Daniel chuckled. "I wonder what they thought when they came out in the morning to find the wrong man tied to the tree."

"Daniel, it isn't funny. He's a human being too," Abbie scolded as she picked up the fussing Tempest from her cradle and sat to nurse her.

"I know, Abbie, but when I think what could have happened to Miles . . ."

Rose absently picked up the sewing she had left next to the rocking chair several days earlier. She found comfort in the repetitive motion of the needle, and her frazzled nerves started to relax. *Miles will be fine,* she recited over and over in her head.

The baby finished eating, and Abbie handed her to Daniel. As he made silly faces at the cooing infant, Rose couldn't help but smile. Abbie went to the kitchen to put together some food for Daniel to take with him when he rode out with the posse.

Rose heard a commotion in the yard, and Daniel jumped to the window.

"It's the Crandalls," he said. "I guess they're ready to go." He gave Abbie a kiss and patted the baby gently on the head.

As Daniel entered the yard, Rose could hear him calling Tommy. The boy came running from the barn and stopped at his father's side. Daniel put his hands on Tommy's shoulders and said something to him. Tommy straightened and looked more determined than Rose had ever seen him. He stood and watched Daniel ride off with the other men and then turned and ran to the house.

He didn't say anything when he came in, but he eyed the rifle hanging over the door. Rose knew Daniel had asked him to be the man of the house in his absence. She felt a quiver of fear deep inside but tried to ignore it. Abbie caught her eye, and the women worried together.

33

Two days passed. Daniel hadn't returned, and they had no word from town or from the Crandalls. Abbie and Rose tried to keep each other busy so they wouldn`t think about the lack of news. Rose continued to teach Diana new stitches for her sampler, and she and Abbie finished a quilt for Tommy's bed. Tommy watched the roads and took care of all the outside chores, but Rose could tell the novelty of being the man had worn off.

Finally, Rose decided she'd had enough of being cooped up in the house. She urged Tommy to let her go out and help with the chores. As the cousins made their way to the barn, Rose reveled in the fresh air and stopped to just stand in the sunshine, breathing it all in. Daniel had been right. The Chinook lasted for a day and then the snow had started again. This time, just a light sifting of flakes fell, and Rose loved the feel of them on her face.

"Now that's a sight I'm glad to see."

The voice startled Rose, and she chided herself for not paying more attention to her surroundings. She turned and found Zach looking down at her from his horse.

He dismounted, favoring his injured shoulder. "I'm glad to see you looking so good."

She held out her hand to him and he gave it a quick squeeze. "I thought you went with the rest of the men," she said.

"Boy, I sure wanted to, but they had good reason not to let me. I'm not much use until I can ride and shoot again, and that will be a while."

"Have you heard anything yet?"

"Everything in town is quiet. Some of the men have trickled back. I suppose the thrill of chasing outlaws in the cold grows tiresome real fast."

"Where are my manners?" Rose turned to lead the way to the house. "Come in and say hi to Abbie. She will be glad to see you doing well."

"I'll let you give her my regards, but I am on my way to check in on Miles, Mama, and Katie. I just wanted to see you for myself." He mounted the horse and rode off.

"Please stop on the way back down, Zach," she called after him.

He waved in reply. Rose watched him ride away and then ran into the house to tell Abbie about the visit. She hoped the evening would bring good news.

It didn't seem like Zach had been gone for very long when he came riding back into the yard at full speed. He jumped from his horse and started talking as soon as Rose opened the door. "Rose, I need you. Katie took ill and Mama has been trying to nurse both her and Miles back to health. I think she is feeling poorly as well, but won't admit it."

Rose grabbed her warm coat before Zach finished speaking. Abbie rushed to gather some food and wrapped it for Rose to take with her.

"Will you be all right?" she asked Rose.

"I tended to my father many times before he died. I'm used to the sickroom." Rose wrapped her shawl around her head and followed Zach out of the house.

"You'll be in my prayers," Abbie called to her.

Rose slid from the horse and rushed into the Crandalls' house. Elizabeth sat in her rocking chair, barely moving back and forth. Her face was flushed and her hair hung in damp, blond tendrils around her face. Rose knelt at the older woman's side and felt her forehead.

"Elizabeth, you need to go to bed. I've come to help." She motioned to Zach, who stepped forward and took his mother's hand.

"Come, Mama," he said. "You're tired and sick. You need your rest."

She responded slowly, but finally stood up and let the two young people guide her to her bed. Zach went to put some hot water on the stove while Rose helped the older woman change into her nightclothes. Then she tucked Elizabeth in under the quilts and sat with her until she fell into a fevered sleep.

Zach paced in the kitchen, waiting for Rose. "I've looked in on Miles and Katie and they are both sleeping soundly. I'm sorry to leave you here, but I'm expected back in town. We're still waiting word on the search, and I have been acting as sheriff in the absence of any real authority."

"I'll be fine. You go on and do your job." She smiled and gave him a gentle shove out the house. She waited for him to ride out of the yard, then latched the door.

Realizing how much Miles, Katie, and Elizabeth needed her help, Rose suddenly felt nervous. She knew she could nurse them back to health if no complications set in, but the lonely hours stretched ahead with no one to talk to.

To take her mind off the isolation, Rose busied herself in the kitchen, putting away the bread and cookies Abbie had sent, and then doing some cleaning. Elizabeth always kept such an immaculate house, but dirty dishes on the table and the half-full wood box reminded Rose there were chores to be done.

They would need wood before the evening came, so Rose put on her wraps and ventured back outside. The afternoon was still pleasant and she made several trips with full arms to stock the bins in the house. After she built up the fire, she heated some water to clean the dishes and decided to make soup for dinner. She didn't know if any of her patients would be hungry, but at least she would have something to offer them.

Soon the broth bubbled in the pot and the dishes were done. The house felt homier with the smell of dinner and a crackling fire in the fireplace. Rose stirred the soup and then went to check on Elizabeth.

She was sleeping, so Rose didn't enter the room. Katie was in the next room, and when she saw Rose she tried to sit up. At the disoriented expression on her face and the feel of her hot skin, Rose pushed Katie back onto the pillows.

"Lie still, Katie. You're not well and you need your rest." She lifted the glass of water from the table next to the bed and held it to Katie's lips.

The ill girl took a few sips, then lay back down and fell asleep again. Rose stayed with her for several minutes. As she sat there, she heard Miles calling from the other room.

She left Katie and went into the boys' room to find Miles propping himself up in the bed with a pillow. Noticing the bandages on his hands, Rose rushed to his side and helped him find a comfortable position. Only then did he seem to see her.

He tried to look past her out the door. "Where's Mama?"

"Elizabeth and Katie are both ill. Zach came to the Weavers' and said you needed help."

Miles tried to get out of bed. Rose wasn't sure if she should let him or not until he tried to put his feet on the floor. Then she noticed the toes on his right foot, red and blistered from his ordeal in the cold. As he tried to put weight on them, he winced in pain and sat back on the bed.

"I guess I won't go anywhere right now," he said.

Tears sprang to Rose's eyes and she fought to hold them back. "Are you hungry? You need to eat." Without waiting for an answer, she left the room and hurried away, her hand over her mouth to stifle the sound of her sobs.

Miles knew it upset Rose when she saw his feet. He hadn't thought about what her reaction would be; he had only wanted to check on his mother.

"Rose," he whispered, knowing she couldn't hear him. He loved her, but how could he interfere with his brother's wish to court her?

He heard Rose coming toward the room again and sat up straighter. When she approached the bed, he noticed her red-rimmed eyes and a single tear balanced on an eyelash. She brought him a steaming bowl of soup and a thick slice of bread. At the smell of the food, his mouth began to water.

Rose put the tray on the bedside table and pulled up a chair. "Dr. Crandall, it seems to me you might use a little help eating this evening."

Miles's face went red. "I tried to get Mama to send for someone earlier, but she insisted that she has always taken care of her children and wasn't about to stop now. She doesn't see me as a doctor yet, just a bossy son."

"Give her a chance. I only thought of you as my brother's annoying friend until you doctored me when I fell ill." Rose continued to spoon the soup into Miles's mouth.

"Annoying?" Miles pointed at the bread with a bandaged hand. Rose broke off a piece and gave it to him. "And here I always tried to be so pleasant."

She appeared lost in thought. "I guess it bothered me when my family liked you instantly, but they didn't seem to like my friends."

"Even you have to admit Karl wasn't the best choice."

Rose glared at him. "Maybe not, but they didn't have to be so obvious about their dislike for him. Just before he died, Father came right out and told me I should give you a chance because you would be a good catch."

The revelation caught Miles off guard. No wonder she had been so cool to him! Being sent to live near his family, far away from Karl, must have seemed like a setup to her. She probably thought Miles had helped plan it.

"So I get sent here," she continued, "and have the adventure of a lifetime. I was upset at being sent away from my home, but I can't imagine how dull my life would have been if I had stayed in Utah." She smiled as she gave him the last of the bread. "You were right, Miles. This land does grow on a person." She took the empty soup bowl and placed it back on the tray.

Rose stood and turned to leave the room. "Did Zach tell you that he asked me to marry him?" She opened her mouth to say more, but Miles held his hand up and turned to face the window.

His heart sank. Of course she would say yes to his brother. All the women loved Zach, and Rose always seemed happy in his company. They would make a good couple.

"Congratulations," he said as she walked out of the room. She kept going and didn't look back.

34

With a sigh, Rose put the tray down on the kitchen table. Miles had seemed shocked to learn that Zach had proposed to her, and now she was certain Zach hadn't said anything to his brothers. She wondered why, even as she reminded herself that she had turned him down anyway. If only Miles would protest and declare his undying love for her!

As night fell, Rose cleaned the kitchen. Then she checked the latch on the door and pulled the gingham curtains closed against the growing darkness. Looking in on Elizabeth, she was relieved to hear the woman's deep, peaceful breathing. Several hours of solid sleep would do her good.

When Rose looked in on her, Katie lay in her bed fiddling with the quilt. Rose convinced her to eat a small bowl of soup, and then they talked of their terrifying experience with the bandits.

"Your fever has broken," Rose finally said. "Get some more rest and maybe you will feel like getting up in the morning."

"Thank you." Katie lay back down on her pillow. "How did you manage to stay well this time, when the rest of us are sick?"

"I guess I'm just tired of being the invalid. It's your turn now." She blew out the lamp. "Good night, Katie."

Rose looked in on Miles and was pleased to see him sleeping soundly. Then she went to the sitting room and sat in the rocking chair. Since the evening was still early, she pulled Elizabeth's mending box close to her and got to work. Soon Rose had patched two pairs of trousers and darned several socks.

After she finished the mending, Rose sat looking at the fire and thinking about her time in Montana. The Weavers and the Crandalls were wonderful people. She knew Abbie and Daniel would never tell her to leave, but Abbie could take care of her own home now. Rose would miss the children and her aunt and uncle, but she knew her welcome had almost run out.

Since she had told Zach she couldn't marry him, there was nothing at the Crandalls' to hold her in Montana. They had been good to her and treated her like a daughter and a sister, but she had no real ties to them. She admitted to herself that one person could convince her to stay, but she knew he would never say a thing.

A small lap desk rested on the mantle. Rose took the desk from its place and sat in the rocking chair again. Opening the desk, she pulled out paper and a fountain pen, then started a letter to her mother. After explaining everything that had happened, Rose pleaded with her mother to move up the family's plans and come for her soon. *I want to get to Canada as soon as possible,* she told herself.

Soon the fire died and the pen slipped from Rose's fingers. Her head tipped back against the chair and she fell into an uneasy dream.

Katie found her sleeping in the rocking chair the next morning. She took the letterbox from Rose's lap and set it on the nearby table. "Wake up, Rose."

She sat up with a start. "Oh, Katie, some nurse I make, falling asleep on the job."

"You helped us through the night, and I am feeling much better this morning."

Rose stood and shook out her wrinkled skirt. "Are you sure you should be up and about so soon?"

Katie did a little twirl around the room. "I feel much more like my normal self."

"That makes two of us," Elizabeth called from the kitchen.

Only then did Rose notice the smell of breakfast cooking.

"Thank you for your help yesterday." Elizabeth walked over and gave Rose a motherly hug.

The letter forgotten, Rose went to Katie's room and washed her face. Then, she borrowed a hairbrush and fixed her hair. The girl in the mirror looked back at her with a wisdom that hadn't been there a year before, and Rose thought about how much she had learned since her father's death. She squared her shoulders and joined the other two women to help with the morning meal. Elizabeth looked much better, while Katie fairly bounced around the kitchen. Katie hadn't seen Miles since they brought him home from the cave, so she offered to take him breakfast and visit with him.

Rose looked outside and noticed the snow had stopped. "I don't want to be in your way, Elizabeth. I think I would like to walk home across the meadow."

"Are you sure? The path will be covered in snow. Zach will stop by later and give you a ride if you want to wait."

"I'll be fine and I could use the exercise and the fresh air. Are you sure you got enough rest?" Rose studied the older woman's face and decided she looked much better.

"Oh, yes, I'm fine. Would you like to say goodbye to Miles and Katie?"

"I don't want to interrupt their visit. I'll come again soon. Please tell Katie I would love her to drop in when she is feeling up to it." Rose gathered her shawl and coat. "If you need anything, send someone down." She waved at Elizabeth and let herself out the door.

The fresh air brushed her face and Rose set her steps towards the meadow. She walked briskly so as not to spend too much time in the cold. A few minutes after leaving the Crandalls' home, she remembered the letter she had left in the lap desk. She stopped in the middle of the path, deciding whether or not to go back for it. Then she decided none of the Crandalls would be writing any letters soon, so she would just get the letter the next time she visited.

Miles lay back in the bed. Time had passed slowly and he felt much better. He had removed the bandages from his fingers the previous week, and his feet were starting to feel more like normal. He couldn't stop thinking about how blessed he was not to have lost a hand or a foot.

John had returned two days after Rose spent the night nursing the family. Jed and Handlebar had been captured and delivered to Helena for trial, but no one had seen Sheriff Gibb or Sam. He tried to pity them for their fate, but memories of almost freezing to death made it hard to feel anything but relief that they wouldn't harm anyone else.

He remembered sitting on the ground outside the cave, tucking his head into his arms. His feet had received the worst of it, and it still hurt to put weight on them for any length of time. The doctor in him knew they would heal and he would walk soon, but he also knew they would always trouble him.

If only he could be as sure about Rose. Every time she entered the room, he lost his senses. He knew how to deal with a medical situation, but not with a situation of the heart.

"Katie," he hollered. "Bring me the lap desk, please."

It didn't take her long to bring the desk in. "I can't wait until you are up and moving around, Brother."

"You aren't the only one."

After Katie left the room, Miles positioned the desk on his lap and opened the lid. He knew Rose thought of him as a friend and felt some connection with him after their discussion about Lena on Christmas night. He hoped her marriage to Zach would be a happy one for both of them. It worried him that Zach had been so reluctant to hear more about the Church, but given time, he might still come around. Miles decided to write a letter to Rose's family, telling them about Zach and giving his approval of the match. Miles would simply have to keep his emotions out of his words.

When he opened the box he found a sheet of paper covered in handwriting, lying on top of the rest of the stationery. He didn't recognize the feminine writing and started reading to find out who it belonged to. It didn't take him long to realize Rose had left behind a letter to her family. The words tore at his heart.

> *. . . I need to be with my family, Mother. This is a stunning and a beautiful land, but I miss you all so much and can't wait to see you again. Miles's brother Zach proposed to me, but I told him I couldn't marry someone I didn't love and who doesn't share my beliefs. I would rather end up an old maid than marry without love in my heart.*

Stunned, Miles thought back to the night Rose had told him about Zach's proposal. He had assumed she said yes, and though Zach still hadn't said a word, he just thought they were waiting for the right time to make their announcement.

The letter continued:

> *There is nothing for me here. Please hurry. I can't wait to see you all again and be on our way to Canada as a family.*
>
> *Love, Rose*

Miles quickly put the lap desk away. He couldn't summon Rose to his bedside; he needed to approach her as a man, on two good feet. He swung his legs over the side of the bed, then gingerly put them on the floor. "Mama!"

Elizabeth rushed into the room. "Miles, what are you doing?"

"I've been laid up long enough. Could you please get that ointment out of my bag and help me rub some into my feet? It's time I stop being an invalid."

35

Every time she went outside to help with the chores, Rose noticed the advancing of spring. Buds covered the trees and the April air felt warm with promise. Daniel talked about planting almost constantly, and they all anxiously awaited the birth of a new calf. Tempest entertained them all with her happy, giggly personality, and Diana loved to spend her days playing with her little sister.

The letter in the Crandalls' lap desk had been forgotten, but Rose's desire to leave still nagged at her daily. Daniel and Abbie convinced her to be patient, that her family would come through Montana soon enough. "Don't add to their worries," her aunt advised her. Both Daniel and Abbie asked her to stay on with them, but Rose knew Abbie looked forward to having her home to herself again. Plus, they needed the space in Diana's bedroom for Tempest, who still slept in her parents' bedroom.

Rose expected her brother to arrive at the Weaver farm any day. Her mother and Carrie would take the train to Great Falls, where Sean planned to meet them. Then Maggie, Carrie, and Sean would visit Miles and get Rose before going on to Canada.

"I'm meeting Katie at the picnic spot," Rose said to Abbie one Tuesday, then grabbed her shawl and headed out the door. She hurried along the path, jumping over the mud puddles left by the melting snow. The two girls had taken to meeting every Tuesday to visit.

As Rose rounded the bend in the path, she saw Katie sitting with her brothers on the fallen log. She hadn't expected to see the men, and she stopped to watch for several moments. They talked with each other in an easy manner, and she could tell Zach was teasing Ian about something. Ian gave him a playful punch in the arm and they all laughed.

Rose walked up to the group, waving as she approached them. She looked at the brothers. Even though she still wished Miles would return her interest, she knew it was too late. Sean would come soon, she would leave, and someday she would marry someone else. Miles would become a faded dream. This day was about creating a last memory with her friends—something to take to her new home and think about when she missed this place.

"You look like you've been here a while." She sat on the log next to Katie.

Reaching forward to put some potatoes on the coals, Katie pointed at Zach. "He couldn't wait to get up here and do some fishing."

"Well, you better hope they are biting," Zach replied, "or you'll get just a potato for your lunch." He picked up his fishing supplies and headed toward the river. "Who's coming?" Ian jumped up and ran after his brother.

Miles didn't move from the log. He had moved back to the clinic to resume his practice. He still came to the Weavers' home every Sunday for church, but he and Rose didn't take their walks anymore. In fact, they hadn't had a real chance to talk in weeks.

Rose wanted to sit on the log next to him and chat, but Katie slid closer to her brother.

"You better go keep an eye on those boys, Rose," Katie said. "They're bound to start playing around and forget about our lunch."

Unsure why she had been dismissed, Rose stood to follow Zach and Ian to the fishing hole. Now she would never get a chance to sort things out with Miles before Sean arrived. Maybe it didn't matter; after all, he had never said he loved her. In the last few months, he had even stopped being so protective of her. She stole a look back at him and wondered if she would ever be able to forget him.

Following the twins, Katie decided to ask Zach if she could try her hand at the river. She hadn't done any fishing since the last time she went with Sean, but she needed something to take her mind off Miles. She reached the river and found the water high with spring runoff.

"Over here, Rose," Zach called. He showed her a relatively quiet pool and motioned to a tree stump. "You can sit there if you want."

"If you have an extra line, I'd like to try catching something."

Zach laughed. "Are you afraid I won't? Do you think you'll go hungry for lunch?"

"No, because I brought apple fritters for dessert. I just like to fish."

She took the line and cast it into the water. Zach raised his eyebrows in surprise, and Ian yelled his encouragement from down the river. They sat in silence for a while until Rose couldn't hold her tongue any longer.

"Zach, about New Year's Eve, we never did finish our conversation." She turned to look at him.

He shrugged. "I won't mention it to anyone if you won't."

"Just like that?"

"You were right. We don't love each other more than a brother and sister might. You are awfully pretty, though, and I let myself get carried away. Anyhow, I can't convince myself to join your religion, no matter how hard I try." Zach tugged at his line and then relaxed again. "Would you mind just considering me another brother?"

"Of course, Zach. I would be honored to call you brother."

"Anyway, I've been thinking a lot about Emma Watt. She came and helped Mrs. Larson and Mary at the clinic quite a bit when my arm was shot up, and we had lots of time to talk."

Rose laughed and pushed him over. "You've been holding out on me!" She stood and pulled on her line. It went taut and she knew she had something. "Here I thought you would regret losing me till your dying day."

Zach blushed at her teasing and then jumped to his feet. He watched in admiration as she hauled in a good-sized trout. "We'll have to have a fish-off between you and Katie. I think you could give her a run for her money." He called across to Ian, "Looks like we have lunch."

Just then Katie came down the path. "I want a go at it. We could take some home to Ma for dinner." Ian started walking down the path and Katie motioned him back. "Rose, why don't you take the fish back to the fire? Miles will clean it."

Rose walked down the path with the fish held in front of her. When she came to the fire, she handed the fish to Miles. "Dinner, sir."

He took the fish from her and proceeded to clean it, and soon it was roasting over the fire. Rose watched the fish closely so it wouldn't overcook, and before long she looked up to find Miles observing her.

"Are you excited to leave?" he asked.

"I can't say I'm looking forward to another journey on bumpy roads. The last one didn't go so well." Rose focused her eyes on the coals near her feet.

"Rose, I found the letter you wrote the night you stayed at the house."

"Oh, my." Rose blushed. "I was so tired that night, I forgot all about it."

"Why didn't you tell me you turned Zach down when he proposed to you?"

"I don't know. I wanted to know how you felt, but when you didn't react either way, I didn't know what to think." She turned the fish and rolled one of the potatoes over with a stick.

"Did you mean it when you told your mother there is nothing for you here?" Miles took her arm and turned her to face him. "Am I nothing?"

She could see the hurt in his eyes and realized his feelings for her went deep and sure. "If you cared, Miles, why didn't you say anything? You pulled me close and I thought there might be the beginnings of something, but then you pushed me away."

"I'm sorry. I was so busy being the good doctor when I first brought you here, I didn't make my feelings clear to Zach. Pa always taught us to respect each other. One time Zach and Ian fought over the same girl, and Pa made it clear he would never tolerate his family being torn apart by a woman. The first few weeks you were here, Zach made it very clear that he wanted to court you. Out of respect for his feelings and for my family, I had to let him have a chance to win you over."

"Didn't anyone think to ask me how I felt?"

"You let him court you. It was pretty obvious how you felt."

Rose blushed. She had led Zach on, not through any malice, but through her own indecision. She stood and walked away from

Miles, pacing around the fire. "Why didn't he tell you he asked me to marry him?"

Miles stood and started following her around the fire. "I don't know. Zach always does things his own way. And then all that stuff with the sheriff happened, and we all became a little distracted."

Rose stopped and turned. Miles nearly bumped into her but steadied himself by grabbing her shoulders. "You should sit," she said. "Your feet."

Shaking his head, he pulled her closer. "I'm right where I want to be, my Rose."

He leaned his head forward and gently kissed her. The touch of his lips melted away all the frustration and anger. She closed her eyes and wrapped her arms around him, then lay her head on his shoulder as he buried his face in her hair. They stood just holding each other for some time, not moving.

A noise startled her and Rose pulled away. "I hear the others coming." They sat back on the log and began tending to the fish, but when Katie came up the trail she looked at Miles and winked. Rose saw the signal and realized Katie had conspired with Miles to get her away from the river. She smiled and mouthed a thank you to her friend.

The picnic continued with laughter and friendly bantering as the five young people ate the soft potatoes and flaky trout. Everyone raved over Rose's apple fritters, and soon the afternoon was almost gone.

"We ought to be getting home," Ian said.

They put the fire out and packed up the picnic. Katie gave Rose a hug. "I'll come down and visit you tomorrow if Mama can spare me."

She turned and linked one arm through Zach's elbow and the other through Ian's. "Come on, boys, the chores await."

Miles turned to Rose. "I'd like to walk you home, but I don't think my feet will get me there and back again." He brushed one finger down her cheek and let it linger on her chin.

"I'll be fine. There's plenty of daylight left." The longing in his eyes took her breath away, but she managed to mumble, "I'll see you soon."

"Goodbye for now, my Rose." He turned and started slowly toward home.

As she watched him leave, Rose's heart felt light. He didn't ask her to stay in Montana, she reminded herself, but knowing he cared for her was enough for now.

She sat back down on the log and sang softly to herself, letting her voice carry with the spring breeze. Several minutes passed before she realized she had an audience.

"I ain't ever heard anything so pretty." The familiar voice almost stopped her heart.

Rose looked up to see Arthur Gibb standing near the end of the log. "Sheriff! We all thought you perished in the storm."

"I don't believe 'thought' is the right word. I think you rather *hoped* I perished in the storm." He took a step toward her. "My son, on the other hand, didn't make it."

"I'm so sorry. I really liked Sam."

The bedraggled man kept glancing around like a hunted animal. "Well, that leaves me in a hard spot. You see, my brothers are in prison, I'm a wanted man, and my wife and boy are dead. All I have is the cave." He sat on the log next to Rose.

She forced herself not to cringe at the stench emanating from him. "You've been there the entire time? But they searched and it was empty."

"Well, now, the same tunnel that provided your escape made a good hiding spot for a wanted man. After they checked the cave, I crawled out of the tunnel and I've been living in the cave ever since." He took the worn hat off his head and started scratching behind his ears. "I didn't want to leave my boy, so I've been watching out for him."

Rose looked around for a way to distract Authur so she could run. "Is Sam still in the cave?"

"I dug him a shallow grave near the back and moved some of them boulders to cover it up." Arthur turned and leered at her. "Now, I've just got to find a way to make the good doctor pay for not saving my son."

"He did his best, Sheriff. Your son's injuries were so severe, there was nothing anyone could do for him." Rose stood and started to back away.

Arthur stood and grabbed her roughly by the arm. "So now you think you know as much as the doctor?"

She jerked her arm away.

"Come sit with me, Rose." He pulled her back toward the log and she sat meekly, hoping her cooperation would calm him. "Anyway, I thought of something good. See, the doctor should've fixed my son, and he didn't." Tears now streamed down Arthur's face.

Rose could almost feel sorry for him, but she kept reminding herself that he had created his own tragedy. He could have had the respect of the community if he had honestly fulfilled his duties as sheriff. Instead, he stood before her, tortured by what could have been.

"I'm truly sorry about Sam." She tried to stand but Arthur grabbed her arm again.

"You don't understand. You, Rose, are the answer to my problems. I watched your cozy little picnic today. Seems like you and Doctor Crandall are much closer than I remembered. So it occurred to me, by taking you away from the good doctor, I can hurt him in a way he won't forget." The tears in the man's eyes had dried up and he looked her up and down as if examining merchandise. "I benefit in two ways, because not only will the doctor lose you, but I think maybe you might be a fine wife. You might even be able to give me another son."

At that, Rose tried to run, but Arthur tightened his grip on her arms and began hauling her towards the river. She fought and kicked, but he simply picked her up off the ground and threw her over his shoulder. All her kicking and pounding didn't slow him at all. She saw the river coming closer and screamed.

36

Miles slowly walked home. His siblings were far ahead of him, laughing and singing. His feet didn't hurt as much as he thought they might after the day's outing, but he didn't tell the others so they wouldn't push him to keep up. He wanted time to himself, time to think.

The conversation with Rose kept repeating itself in his mind. He could still feel the softness of her skin as he traced the outline of her face. He didn't know if her feelings for him were deep enough for her to stay when her family went on to Canada, but he knew if he didn't ask her tonight, he would never sleep.

"Katie," he called ahead to his sister, "tell Ma I've gone down to the Weavers'."

The trio ahead of him waved and continued on. Miles turned and walked back the way he had come. He hadn't gone far when he heard the scream. He listened and had almost convinced himself Rose had seen a garter snake when the screaming began again.

Ignoring the pain in his feet, he ran back up the trail. From her screams, he could tell Rose was moving towards the river. Miles cut through the trees, following an old trail he and his brothers had made as children. He ran until his lungs felt like bursting. The river was suddenly in front of him and he stopped to catch his breath and listen.

The screaming had ceased, but he could hear Rose pleading with someone to let her go. He slipped behind the trees and moved closer.

When Arthur dropped Rose onto the ground, she tried to get her feet under her and crawl away, but he grabbed her skirt and pulled her back towards him. "We're crossing the river right here."

"It's too high. We need to find somewhere safer to cross."

Arthur jerked on Rose's skirt, ripping the fabric. She cried out in protest and tried once again to stand so she could run. He was on her in an instant, pushing her to the ground. "Don't ever run from me, Rose," he said menacingly, only inches from her face. "My first wife ran away with those Mormons but I won't let you do the same."

She turned to avoid the rotting smell of his breath and saw Miles approaching in the underbrush. He motioned for her to keep quiet as he came toward the river. She turned her face back to her captor. "Let me up, Arthur. I'll cross the river with you."

Suspicion showed in his face, but he jerked her to her feet and started dragging her once more. Rose looked at the churning water in front of them and knew it would be a miracle if they made it across in one piece. She felt panic coming on and looked to where she had seen Miles, but he was gone.

Then she heard him call, "Arthur, stop!"

The former sheriff acted as if he had heard nothing. Rose

could see Miles racing toward them, but knew they would be in the water before he could get there.

They reached the bank of the river and Arthur pushed Rose. She fell and found herself buried in the cold mountain water. When she came up seconds later, choking and coughing, she focused on keeping her balance in the raging current. Arthur stepped in behind her and started pushing her toward the opposite bank.

Rose's feet went numb almost immediately, and her skirts tangled around her legs and hampered her movements. Arthur now forged ahead of her, pulling at her hand. The water rushed past her chest and she had a hard time staying upright. He gave her hand a yank and she went under again.

Miles watched from the bank, his mind racing back to the time he had watched someone he loved die in this very spot. Rose went under the water, and Miles rushed into the frigid river. His feet started burning the moment the water touched them, but it didn't matter.

Rose came back up out of the water and Arthur Gibb dragged her on. Miles could see that Arthur was slowing as well, and he tried to gain on him. Then, a strong current caught the former sheriff off guard and pulled him under. Rose broke Arthur's grip and started back toward Miles.

"Go to the other bank. You're closer to it," he yelled. "You need to get out of the water." She turned and made her way to the opposite bank.

Arthur came up sputtering a few feet from where he'd submerged. When he saw Miles, his face filled with rage and he charged at the doctor. They met with a splash and went under the water.

Miles grappled with the other man, trying to get a good hold on him. Arthur fought back with fury and the two men started slipping down the river with the current, though Miles somehow kept his feet on the riverbottom. Having played in this river all his life, Miles knew he had to gain control of the situation before the water deepened around the bend and he lost his footing completely.

Just as Arthur started to get the upper hand, Miles felt another pair of hands enter the fray. He focused for a minute and saw Rose aiming for the back of Arthur's head, a large stone in her hand.

Everything seemed to move in slow motion as Rose brought the rock down on Arthur's head. A stunned expression crossed the sheriff's face and he turned to see what had hit him, giving Miles the chance to grab his hair. Arthur continued to fight, and Miles motioned Rose away from the man's flailing arms and feet.

Miles pushed Arthur under the water, holding him there until his struggling weakened. He didn't want to kill the man, only gain control of him. He pulled Arthur up just long enough for him to get a breath of air, then pushed him under the water again.

Just as he began to wonder how to get Arthur to the shore, Miles heard the welcome voices of his brothers. Soon, Zach and Ian were next to him in the water, each of them taking one arm of the wanted man. They dragged the former sheriff to the shore, then pulled him out of the water and held him on the bank.

Miles saw Rose on the opposite bank, still in the water. "Get out!" he yelled.

She grimaced and he could see the panic in her eyes. "I can't. My skirts are caught on something!"

It was then Miles realized her hands gripped the roots of the tree that had pinned his sister so many years before. He swallowed the memory and worked his way toward her. When he reached her, he struggled to tear away the portion of her skirt that was tangled around the tree root. They finally climbed out of the rushing water and clung to each other. What had felt like a warm breeze during their picnic now chilled them both. They waved at the brothers across the river.

"Can you make it down to the footbridge?" Rose asked Miles.

"The bridge was washed out last night." He sat on the bank and held his feet out in front of him as he watched Zach and Ian lead away Arthur Gibb. "Anyway, I don't think I'm going very far right now."

"Help is coming." She pointed across the riverbank to where Katie ran alongside her father and Abe. The men fashioned a loop out of the rope they were carrying and swung it across the shallowest part of the river. The loop landed in the water without making it across, so Abe pulled the loop back and threw again. Again it landed just short of the bank.

Miles started to stand. "I'll have to go get it." Rose watched him try to balance on his aching feet. She gently pushed him down and made her way back into the river. She waded out into the water until it reached her waist.

"Stop there, Rose," John yelled.

Abe threw the rope again and landed it around Rose's shoulders. She settled it under her arms and worked her way back to the bank. Soon she had the rope secured to a tree, and she and Miles made their way, hand over hand, back across the river to the waiting arms of their rescuers.

As Abe carried her home, Rose learned the significance of where she had been caught in the river. "I'm sure glad you got out of there, Miss Rose," Abe said. "Don't think Miles could have taken it if he lost someone else to the same river." Abe jostled her a bit, adjusting his hold. "I remember takin' the body of that poor little girl out of the water that day, right where you were today, and Miles just standin' there cryin'. Near about broke my heart."

"Abe, please . . ."

"Sorry, Miss Rose." The old farmhand blushed under his whiskers. "Guess I'm just so relieved to see you out of that water, I ain't thinkin' much about what I'm sayin'."

They came over the hill and Rose saw Daniel walking toward them. As soon as he saw Rose being carried by the hired hand, he broke into a run. "What happened this time?"

Abe and Rose started talking at the same time until Daniel held up his hands in protest. "Let's get you inside where it's warm, Rose. I want to hear everything."

37

Rose spent the rest of the week at home with a chest cold, halfheartedly packing her trunks. She wanted to go to the Crandalls' and check on Miles, but Abbie insisted she stay near the house until she recovered from her cold. Every day, she hoped to hear from Miles, but the only news she had came from Katie's visit earlier in the week. She said Miles was confined to his bed again, as the river ordeal had weakened his already damaged feet.

Even though Rose dropped several hints, Katie had said nothing else about Miles and instead busied herself talking about Ian and Mary's upcoming wedding. Rose had let herself get caught up in the excitement as the two girls worked together to make Mary a fine tablecloth for her new home.

After shaking her head to clear her thoughts, Rose reached down into the basket for more clothes to hang on the line. The wet laundry snapped in the brisk spring breeze and she put a clothespin on the last diaper. Then she picked up the empty laundry basket and walked to the house. As she reached for the back door, it swung open. Rose dropped the basket in surprise and threw her arms around the man in the doorway.

"Oh, Sean. You made it!" She felt tears slip down her cheeks and brushed them away. "Where's Mama?"

He laughed as she gently pushed him aside to run into the kitchen and her mother's embrace.

Miles looked at his feet in frustration. They hurt more than ever and he knew the river incident had done serious, permanent damage. With his injuries, it would be impossible for him to run around the countryside in all sorts of weather, taking care of everyone's aches and pains.

The paper in his hand solved one of Miles's problems. His friend from medical school had responded to his letter and would arrive within the month to take over the clinic. Miles felt better knowing he wouldn't leave the people of Spring Creek in a lurch, but now he was without a career and without a way to support a family.

How could he ask Rose to marry him now? Every day, Katie told him Rose wanted to see him, but he couldn't face her until he found some answers.

A knock on the door startled him out of his thoughts, and he sat up straighter. "Come in."

The door opened and there stood Sean. "Hey, Miles."

Miles fell back on the pillow with a grin. "Sean." He motioned his friend into the room. "I think you are the answer to my prayers."

"We arrived at Daniel's a little bit ago. Rose sent me up here to see how you're doing." Sean pulled up a chair. "What can I do to help?"

Miles told his side of the story. "I love your sister," he finally said. "But I can't marry her if I have no way to support her."

Sean leaned forward. "So how am I the answer to your prayers? Shall I take her away from here?" He whispered the next words. "She's outside talking to Katie and waiting for me to talk some sense into you. I don't think she'll leave without a fight." He grinned at Miles. "Wish I had a girl talk about me like that."

Miles swung his legs around and placed his feet on the floor. "Sean, would you give me a priesthood blessing?"

Sean stood, all humor gone from his face. "You know I will. Let me get Daniel." He walked toward the door, but stopped before he opened it. "While I'm gone, will you do me a favor?"

"Anything."

"Talk to Rose."

Rose jumped to her feet as soon as the bedroom door opened.

Sean motioned toward the front door. "I'm going to get Daniel so we can administer to Miles."

She nodded and watched her brother leave. Then she heard Miles call to her.

Katie winked. "See if you can make him smile. He's been so grumpy lately." She left the room and went to help Elizabeth in the kitchen.

Rose turned to see Miles standing in the doorway of his bedroom. He looked pale and tired, but he walked toward her carefully and slowly. She tried to act reserved and ladylike, but of their own accord, her arms reached toward him. He met her halfway and grabbed her in a tender embrace.

"I'm so glad you're okay," he said, brushing her hair from her shoulders. He led her to his mother's rocker and then retrieved a straight-back chair and sat next to her. Then he handed her the letter.

Rose took the paper and smoothed it on her lap, then read the careful handwriting. Confusion spread across her face. "You want another doctor to come here?" She looked at Miles for confirmation as she held the letter out to him. "Why are you giving up your practice?"

"My feet are too bad to run around doctoring. Besides, I miss being with the Saints."

Rose sighed. She would be on her way to Canada as Miles headed back to Utah. Twisting her skirt in her hands, she wondered how to tell him she wished they could be together. Then a knock rattled the door, and a few seconds later, Elizabeth ushered in Sean and Daniel. The three men shared handshakes as Rose allowed herself to fade to the background.

"Ma, get Pa, please." Miles pulled a chair to the center of the room and sat. The other two men bantered easily as they waited for John to join them. When the older man entered the room, Daniel explained to him what they were about to do. Miles looked at Rose and smiled, then closed his eyes.

Rose closed her own eyes and listened as the simple but powerful words flowed from Sean as he pronounced a blessing of healing. The Spirit permeated the room, and when Rose looked at Elizabeth after the amen, the older woman's face was streaked with tears.

"Is it true? Will you be completely made whole?" Elizabeth asked her son.

"With enough faith, anything can happen." Miles looked at his father and smiled.

Rose walked along the path with her uncle and her brother. The Weaver farm came into view and Rose realized how much she would miss Spring Creek. They entered the house just as Abbie was serving supper to her younger children.

Maggie embraced her eldest daughter. "How did it go?"

Rose shrugged. "I don't know. We didn't get much chance to talk. But Sean gave him a beautiful blessing." She felt warm at the memory. "I believe his feet will be healed. But he has already promised the clinic to someone else, and he told me he wants to be with the Saints." Her mother wiped a tear from Rose's cheek before Rose even realized she was crying.

"You need to have faith, too. The Lord can heal Miles's feet and He can also make things work out the way they need to." Maggie took Rose by the shoulders. "Now chin up and let's go eat the meal your aunt has prepared."

After supper, the family visited late into the evening, and Rose enjoyed watching them all together. It would only be another day or two before Sean would drive the wagon back out of Spring Creek, and she would be in it. She finally excused herself and went to bed, but she spent a fitful night's sleep knowing the next day might be her last in Montana.

Morning dawned and Rose got to work on her chores. She wanted to help Abbie as much as she could before the wagon pulled out. She was elbow deep in bread dough and laughing with Carrie, who was entertaining Tempest, when she heard a horse in the yard.

Sean poked his head in the kitchen. "Rose, you have a caller."

Rose held up her arms and Sean laughed.

Maggie rushed to the table. "You go on, dear. I'll finish the bread."

Rose cleaned the dough off her hands and arms and went outside. Sean and Miles were throwing bags into the back of the wagon, and Sean kept crawling in and out as he arranged all his goods.

"How many more supplies did you need to get?" Rose teased.

Miles grinned at her. "You can never be too prepared."

"How are the feet today?" she asked him.

"They're much better. Mother is amazed at the change in one night. I know they will only continue to improve." He winked and held his hand out to her. "Come for a ride with me."

Sean nodded his agreement and Rose allowed Miles to help her onto his horse. He mounted behind her and picked up the reins. They rode in silence for a time, and then Miles said, "Everything seems to have fallen into place."

"What do you mean?"

Miles stopped the horse under a large tree and dismounted, then helped Rose down.

"I wanted your family's permission before I asked for your hand. I know you are ready to leave, but I love you." He pulled her close and looked into her eyes. "Will you consider being my wife?"

Rose threw her arms around his neck, buried her head into his shoulder, and started to cry. "Why did you wait so long? You're going to Utah and I'm leaving for Canada in the morning."

Miles gently disengaged himself from her arms. "Think about it a bit, my Rose."

Rose wanted to be angry at him for waiting until the day before she left, but found she just couldn't. She had grown to love this man, not because he was flashy and exciting, but because he was Miles. As long as they had each other, they could build a home anywhere.

She reached up and took Miles's face in her hands. "Yes," she said softly. "I'll go wherever you go. I love you too."

Miles whooped and threw his hat in the air. Rose watched it land and laughed at his excitement. Then he grew serious again and his lips found hers. She let herself be swept away in his kiss, but just before she thought her knees would give way, she pulled back and looked into his eyes. "How will we tell Mama?"

He grabbed her for another kiss and then helped her mount the horse. "We just will." He climbed on the horse behind her and they rode back to the farm at a brisk pace. Then he helped her down, took her hand, and led her to the house. Rose heard too many voices when he opened the door, and she looked at him in confusion.

Miles smiled and stepped ahead of her into the kitchen. Rose could only see the flurry of a skirt as Miles picked up the waiting woman and swung her around.

"She said yes," he announced as he put Rose's mother back on her feet.

"Well, I hope so. It really would be awkward, you coming to Canada with us after she turned you down," Sean said as he shook Miles's hand.

Maggie pulled Rose into her arms. "Oh, Rose, I'm so happy for you. Miles sent us a telegram asking for your hand and telling us he wants to join the Saints in Canada." She laughed. "It's been the hardest thing keeping it a secret."

Rose watched as Sean and Carrie congratulated Miles. Zach, John, and Elizabeth grinned, and Katie clapped her hands. All the people Rose loved had gathered to share this moment. She looked around at her family and saw her world settle into place. Miles caught her eye and she laughed. Canada awaited, and she would arrive holding her husband's hand.

Stephanie Humphreys was born in Utah to an American mother and a Canadian father. The family moved often when she was young, and by the time she celebrated her thirtieth birthday, she had moved thirty times. All those different locations gave her ample opportunity to observe people and discover interesting characters for her stories.

At an early age, Stephanie discovered the joy of the written word. As the oldest of six children, she had many opportunities to practice her storytelling skills on her siblings. She filled notebooks with poetry, and her brothers, sisters, and neighborhood friends all took turns participating in plays she wrote. But her biggest dream was to be a novelist.

Stephanie and her husband Rick have a combined family of six children. She stays involved with the theatre by serving on her community's cultural arts board, and she supports literacy by serving on the public library board. She has always used books to escape the pressures of life, explore faraway places, and learn new things. When she isn't writing, she loves to spend time with her family, sew, embroider, and read. Stephanie and her family reside in Alberta, Canada.

Finding Rose is Stephanie's first novel. She would enjoy hearing from her readers and may be contacted at stephanie@ stephaniehumphreys.net. Please visit Stephanie's website, stephaniehumphreys.net.